D1277725

JOURNALISM

Allen Kirschner
and Linda Kirschner

JOURNALISM

READINGS IN THE MASS MEDIA

The Odyssey Press · New York

A division of
The Bobbs-Merrill Company, Inc.

Copyright © 1971
by The Bobbs-Merrill Co., Inc.
Printed in the United States
Library of Congress Catalog Card Number: 76-158976

ACKNOWLEDGMENTS

Spiro Agnew. For speech delivered November 20, 1969. Reprinted by permission.

American Society of Newspaper Editors. For "Code of Ethics." Reprinted by permission.

The Atlantic Monthly. For "Controlling Crime News," by Robert M. Cipes. Copyright © 1967 The Atlantic Monthly Company, Boston, Mass. Reprinted by permission.

The Bobbs-Merrill Company, Inc. For "News and the Whole Truth," from But We Were Born Free, copyright © 1954 by Elmer Davis, reprinted by permission of the publishers, The Bobbs-Merrill Company, Inc.

James Brown Associates, Inc. For "A Free Press," from The Press by A. J. Liebling. Copyright © 1961 by A. J. Liebling. Reprinted by permission of The Estate of the Author and its agent, James Brown Associates, Inc.

Columbia Journalism Review. For "Media Myths on Violence," by Terry Ann Knopf. Copyright © 1970 by the Columbia Journalism Review. Reprinted by permission.

———. For "The 'New Journalism' We Need" by Gerald Paul Grant. Copyright © 1970 by Columbia Journalism Review. Reprinted by permission.

Commonweal Publishing Co., Inc. For "Presidential Candidates and the Backing of the Press," by John Deedy, Copyright © 1968 by Commonweal Publishing Co., Inc. Reprinted by permission.

Crown Publishers, Inc. For "The Day," taken from Deadlines, by Henry Justin Smith. © 1922 by Covici Friede. Used by permission of Crown Publishers, Inc.

Editor & Publisher. For "A Negro Leader Looks at the Press," by Rick Friedman. Copyright © 1964 by Editor and Publisher. Reprinted by permission.

Fleet Press Corporation. For "The Newspaper that Will Endure—A Summing Up," by Mark F. Ethridge, from The Responsibility of the Press, edited by Gerald Gross. Copyright © 1966 by Fleet Press Corporation, New York City. Reprinted by permission.

———. For "The Responsibility of a Newspaper Syndicate," by S. George Little, from The Responsibility of the Press, edited by Gerald Gross. Copyright © 1966 by Fleet Press Corporation, New York City. Reprinted by permission.

Harper and Row, Publishers, Inc. For "Hitting Them Where They Live," from Madison Avenue, U.S.A., by Martin Mayer, Copyright © 1958 by Martin Prager Mayer. Reprinted by permission of Harper and Row, Publishers, Inc.

Ray E. Hiebert. For "The Role of the Press in a Democratic Government," by Thomas Schroth, from The Press in Washington, edited by Ray E. Hiebert. Copyright © 1966 by Ray E. Hiebert. Reprinted by permission.

J. B. Lippincott Company. For "What's Wrong with Our Press?" from the book But Will It Sell? by Marya Mannes. Copyright, ©, 1964 by Marya Mannes. Reprinted by permission of J. B. Lippincott Company.

Robert J. Manning. For "Foreign Policy and the Press" ("Journalism and Foreign Affairs"), by Robert J. Manning. Reprinted by permission.

McGraw-Hill Book Company. For "Government by News Leak," from Understanding Media: The Extensions of Man, by Marshall McLuhan. Copyright © 1964 by Marshall McLuhan. Used with permission of McGraw-Hill Book Company.

The Nation. For "Underground Press: Growing Rich on the Hippie," by Thomas Pepper. Copyright © 1968 by The Nation. Reprinted by permission.

The New Leader. For "Press Failure in Vietnam," by S. L. A. Marshall; "Reporting Vietnam/Two Views," by Dale Minor and M. W. Browne. Copyright © 1967 The American Labor Conference on International Affairs, Inc. Reprinted with permission from The New Leader.

The New York Times. For responses, November 21, 1969, to Spiro Agnew speech of November 20, 1969. © 1969 by The New York Times Company. Reprinted by permission.

LANSING COMMUNITY COLLEGE LIBRARY

W. W. Norton & Company, Inc. For "What the Press Can Do," by William J. Lederer. Reprinted from *A Nation of Sheep*, by William J. Lederer. By permission of W. W. Norton & Company, Inc. Copyright © 1961 by William J. Lederer.

Joseph Pulitzer, Jr. For "The Press Lives by Disclosures," by Joseph Pulitzer, Jr., from *Nieman Reports*, July, 1961. Reprinted by permission.

G. P. Putnam's Sons. For "The Story Behind the Jewish Klansman," by McCandlish Phillips, from *The Working Press*, edited by Ruth Adler. Copyright © 1966 by The New York Times Company. Reprinted by permission of G. P. Putnam's Sons.

The Reader's Digest. For "Trial by Newspaper," by Irwin Ross. Copyright © 1965 by The Atlantic Monthly Company, Boston, Mass. Reprinted by permission of *The Reader's Digest*.

James Reston. For "The Laggard Press," by James Reston. Reprinted by permission of the author.

———. For "A Letter to Santa," by James Reston. Reprinted by permission of the author.

Saturday Review. For "Global Freedom of the Press," by John Tebbel. Copyright 1968 Saturday Review, Inc. Reprinted by permission.

———. For "Who Writes the Letters to the Editor," by Irving Rosenthal. Copyright 1969 Saturday Review, Inc. Reprinted by permission.

Charles Scribner's Sons. For "There is No Other News," by W. A. Swanberg. Reprinted with the permission of Charles Scribner's Sons from *Citizen Hearst*, pages 137–140, by W. A. Swanberg. Copyright © 1961 W. A. Swanberg.

I. F. Stone. For "When the Government Lies, Must the Press Fib?" Copyright © 1961 by I. F. Stone. Reprinted by permission.

The University of Chicago Press. For "A Free and Responsible Press: Report of the Commission on Freedom of the Press." Copyright 1947 by the University of Chicago Press. Reprinted by permission.

The University of North Carolina Press. For "Social Control in the News Room," by Warren Breed. *Social Forces*, May, 1955. Copyright 1955 by the University of North Carolina Press. Reprinted by permission.

The World Publishing Company. For selection from *The Kingdom and the Power*, by Gay Talese. An NAL book. Copyright © 1969 by Gay Talese. Reprinted by permission of The World Publishing Company.

———. For "The Newspaper Game and the Big Story," from *For 2¢ Plain*, by Harry Golden. Copyright © 1959, 1958, 1957, 1956, 1955, 1952, 1948, 1945, 1943 by Harry Golden. Reprinted by permission of The World Publishing Company and Harry Golden.

For Ernie Strauss and Don Haurie
who believed in Readings in the Mass Media *and in us.*

CONTENTS

Introduction, 3

1 FORM AND TECHNIQUE

2 AUDIENCE AND EFFECT

3 CRITICS
AND
CRITICIS

JOURNALISM

INTRODUCTION

"I read in the paper . . . ," begins a common American refrain. The speaker then proceeds to quote some truth that he has just swallowed whole and digested. What he has read may be the truth; it may be one man's limited version of the truth. The bold front-page headline of an October afternoon: REDS SLAUGHTER YANKS is one kind of truth to a baseball fan and quite another kind of truth to one jittery about the state of the cold war. A silly example? Perhaps. And yet perhaps not so silly. So readily do we accept the news we read and so eagerly do we regurgitate it, we rarely take time to examine our press for what it is.

Newspapers are the oldest of our mass media. They have been with us so long and served us so well that they have become a part of our nation's cultural landscape. Until the twentieth century, with its electronic media, newspapers were virtually our sole source of information about government, the nation, and the world. Like the other media, they appeal to a mass audience, but in a strangely singular way. Groups of people may listen to the radio or watch television or crowd into a theater to share the common experience of a film. But a newspaper, even when read in a public library or on a packed subway, is read alone.

The act of reading is by its very nature an independent act. One man reads the words of another man. Each contributes his biases and his blind spots. Each brings to the words on the printed page his own connotations, his own meanings. As Humpty-Dumpty said in *Alice in Wonderland,* "When I use a word, it means just what I choose it to mean—neither more nor less." Small wonder then that the intentions of the writer frequently become distorted, the meanings derived by the reader, jumbled. Small wonder then that real communication so often fails and that newpapers, as a result, are vulnerable to criticism.

Historically the press has always been criticized. Thomas Jefferson claimed that advertisements were the only thing he believed in the press of his day. A century and a half later another President, Harry Truman, asserted that any American who considered himself well-informed on the basis of newspaper reading went to bed each night a sorely deluded man. In the last decade we have seen another President of the United States cancel his subscription to a famous paper, whose views he found distasteful, and a Vice President attack some of our most respected papers, citing their provincialism. Yet millions of Americans continue to read their daily newspapers believing that the press will fully inform them about world events. After all, they say, if we see it in print it must be true. It would be more accurate, however, to say that what we read in the newspaper is only a part of the truth.

We mistakenly assume that our newspapers print the *whole* truth. We complain when we discover that they don't. Perhaps we are being unfair to the press, for even this introduction, which purports to be the truth, is the truth only as seen through the vision of a single mind. It is a part of the truth as each selection in this book is a part of the truth. For behind every article is a writer with his own vision of the truth just as behind every reader is a human being with his vision of the truth. Print is, in the language of Marshall McLuhan, a "cool medium," a medium which requires a human being to complete it. Words, therefore, fail to exist until they interact with a reader. This interaction does not guarantee, however, that the truth will be the same to every writer or to every reader.

Ask any of the editors of American newspapers what his paper represents. The answer invariably will be the same—the truth. The *New York Times,* perhaps the country's most influential paper, boasts of giving the news "impartially, without fear or favor." And to the best of its ability, perhaps it does. But the *New York Times* is not some computer that collectively and automatically produces "All the news that's fit to print." It is composed of men who write the stories and men who rewrite them and men who place or don't place them in a given position in the paper. Further, the *New York Times* is composed of some 900,000 subscribers who understand or perhaps don't understand the meaning a journalist has intended to convey in a particular article. Perhaps then, in expecting the press to print the *whole* truth, we are asking it to do something that human beings using words alone can never do.

Nevertheless, the intelligent reader should expect certain expectations to be satisfied by a free and responsible press. He has a right, for example, to anticipate as full and unbiased coverage of the news as possible. He must realize that freedom of the press, as guaranteed

by the Bill of Rights, is the fundamental issue. He has a right and an
obligation to call for examination of issues such as the following:

- What role should the press play in a rapidly changing society?

- Should the press merely report on or lead a society?

- What should be the role of the press in foreign and national affairs?

- What should be the responsibility of the press when the government lies?

- What responsibility does the press bear in an election campaign?

- How should the press be held accountable?

- What effect should advertising have on newspaper policy?

- When does an individual's right to privacy end?

- What are the rights of an accused person in newspaper coverage?

- What *is* the role of the press in a democratic society?

FORM AND TECHNIQUE

Marshall McLuhan
PRESS: GOVERNMENT BY NEWS LEAK

Marshall McLuhan, Director of the Center for Culture and Technology at the University of Toronto and often called the High Priest of the New Media, looks at the press, an old medium, in an original way. In his vision, "the press is a mosaic, participant kind of organization and a do-it-yourself kind of world. . . ." The implications of his concept both for the press and the society it serves are manifest.

THE headline for an Associated Press release (February 25, 1963) read:

PRESS BLAMED FOR SUCCESS

KENNEDY MANAGES NEWS BOLDLY,

CYNICALLY, SUBTLY, KROCK CLAIMS

Arthur Krock is quoted as saying that "the principal onus rests on the printed and electronic process itself." That may seem like another way of saying that "history is to blame." But it is the instant conse- quences of electrically moved information that makes necessary a deliberate artistic aim in the placing and management of news. In diplomacy the same electric speed causes the decisions to be an- nounced before they are made in order to ascertain the varying re- sponses that might occur when such decisions actually are made. Such procedure, quite inevitable at the electric speed that involves the entire society in the decision-making process, shocks the old press men because it abdicates any definite point of view. As the speed of information increases, the tendency is for politics to move away from representation and delegation of constituents toward immediate involvement of the entire community in the central acts of decision. Slower speeds of information make delegation and representation mandatory. Associated with such delegation are the points of view of the different sectors of public interest that are expected to be put forward for processing and consideration by the rest of the community. When the electric speed is introduced into such a delegated and representational organization, this obsolescent organization can only be made to function by a series of subterfuges and makeshifts. These strike some observers as base betrayals of the original aims and purposes of the established forms.

The massive theme of the press can be managed only by direct contact with the formal patterns of the medium in question. It is thus necessary to state at once that "human interest" is a technical term meaning that which happens when multiple book pages or multiple information items are arranged in a mosaic on one sheet. The book is a private confessional form that provides a "point of view." The press is a group confessional form that provides communal participation. It can "color" events by using them or by not using them at all. But it is the daily communal exposure of multiple items in juxtaposition that gives the press its complex dimension of human interest.

The book form is not a communal mosaic or corporate image but a private voice. One of the unexpected effects of TV on the press has been a great increase in the popularity of *Time* and *Newsweek*. Quite inexplicably to themselves and without any new effort at subscription, their circulations have more than doubled since TV. These news magazines are preeminently mosaic in form, offering not windows on the world like the old picture magazines, but presenting corporate images of society in action. Whereas the spectator of a picture magazine is passive, the reader of a news magazine becomes much involved in the making of meanings for the corporate image. Thus the TV habit of involvement in mosaic image has greatly strengthened the appeal of these news magazines, but at the same time has diminished the appeal of the older pictorial feature magazines.

Both book and newspaper are confessional in character, creating the effect of *inside story* by their mere form, regardless of content. As the book page yields the inside story of the author's mental adventures, so the press page yields the inside story of the community in action and interaction. It is for this reason that the press seems to be performing its function most when revealing the seamy side. Real news is bad news—bad news *about* somebody, or bad news *for* somebody. In 1962, when Minneapolis had been for months without a newspaper, the chief of police said: "Sure, I miss the news, but so far as my job goes I hope the papers never come back. There is less crime around without a newspaper to pass around the ideas."

Even before the telegraph speed-up, the newspaper of the nineteenth century had moved a long way toward a mosaic form. Rotary steam presses came into use decades before electricity, but typesetting by hand remained more satisfactory than any mechanical means until the development of linotype about 1890. With linotype, the press could adjust its form more fully to the news-gathering of the telegraph and the news-printing of the rotary presses. It is typical and significant that the linotype answer to the long-standing slowness of typesetting did not come from those directly engaged with the problem. Fortunes had been vainly spent on typesetting machines before James Clephane, seeking a fast way of writing out and duplicating shorthand notes, found a way to combine the typewriter and the typesetter. It was the *typewriter* that solved the utterly different *typesetting* problem. Today the publishing of book and newspaper both depends on the typewriter.

The speed-up of information gathering and publishing naturally created new forms of arranging material for readers. As early as 1830 the French poet Lamartine had said, "The book arrives too late," drawing attention to the fact that the book and the newspaper are quite different forms. Slow down typesetting and news-gathering, and there occurs a change, not only in the physical appearance of the press, but also in the prose style of those writing for it. The first great change in style came early in the eighteenth century, when the famous *Tatler* and *Spectator* of Addison and Steele discovered a new prose technique to match the form of the printed word. It was the technique of equitone. It consisted in maintaining a single level of tone and attitude to the reader throughout the entire composition. By this discovery, Addison and Steele brought written discourse into line with the printed word and away from the variety of pitch and tone of the spoken, and of even the hand-written, word. This way of bringing language into line with print must be clearly understood. The telegraph broke language away again from the printed word, and began to make erratic noises called headlines, journalese, and telegraphese—phenomena that still dismay the literary community with its mannerisms of supercilious equitone that mime typographic uniformity. Headlines produce such effects as

BARBER HONES TONSILS

FOR OLD-TIMER'S EVENT

referring to Sal (the Barber) Maglie, the swarthy curve-ball artist with the old Brooklyn Dodgers, when he was to be guest speaker at a Ball Club dinner. The same community admires the varied tonality and vigor of Aretino, Rabelais, and Nashe, all of whom wrote prose before the print pressure was strong enough to reduce the language gestures to uniform lineality. Talking with an economist who was serving on an unemployment commission, I asked him whether he had considered newspaper reading as a form of paid employment. I was not wrong in supposing that he would be incredulous. Nevertheless, all media that mix ads with other programming are a form of "paid learning." In years to come, when the child will be paid to learn, educators will recognize the sensational press as the forerunner of paid learning. One reason that it was difficult to see this fact earlier is that the processing and moving of information had not been the main business of a mechanical and industrial world. It is, however, easily the dominant business and means of wealth in the electric world. At the end of the mechanical age people still imagined that press and radio and even TV were merely forms of information paid for by the makers and users of "hardware" like cars and soap and gasoline. As automation takes hold, it becomes obvious that *information* is the crucial commodity, and that solid products are merely incidental to information movement. The early stages by which information itself became the basic economic commodity of the electric age were obscured by the ways in which advertising and entertainment put people off the track. Advertisers pay for space and time in paper and magazine, on radio and TV; that is, they buy a piece of the reader, listener, or viewer as definitely as if they hired our homes for a public meeting. They would gladly pay the reader, listener, or viewer directly for his time and attention if they knew how to do so. The only way so far devised is to put on a free show. Movies in America have not developed advertising intervals simply because the movie itself is the greatest of all forms of advertisement for consumer goods.

Those who deplore the frivolity of the press and its natural form of group exposure and communal cleansing simply ignore the nature of the medium and demand that it be a book, as it tends to be in Europe. The book arrived in western Europe long before the newspaper; but Russia and middle Europe developed the book and newspaper almost together, with the result that they have never unscrambled the two forms. Their journalism exudes the private point of view of the literary mandarin. British and American journalism, however, have always tended to exploit the mosaic form of the newspaper format in order to present the discontinuous variety and incongruity of ordinary life. The monotonous demands of the literary community—that the newspaper use its mosaic form to present a fixed point of view on a single plane of perspective—represent a failure to see the form of the press at all. It is as if the public were suddenly to demand that department stores have only one department.

The classified ads (and stock-market quotations) are the bedrock of the press. Should an alternative source of easy access to such diverse daily information be found, the press will fold. Radio and TV can handle the sports, news, comics, and pictures. The editorial, which is the one book-feature of the newspaper, has been ignored for many years, unless put in the form of news or paid advertisement.

If our press is in the main a free entertainment service paid for by advertisers who want to buy readers, the Russian press is *in toto* the basic mode of industrial promotion. If we use news, political and personal, as entertainment to capture ad readers, the Russians use it as a means of promotion for their economy. Their political news has the same aggressive earnestness and posture as the voice of the sponsor in an American ad. A culture that gets the newspaper late (for the same reasons that industrialization is delayed) and one that accepts the press as a form of the book and regards industry as group political action, is not likely to seek entertainment in the news. Even in America, literate people have small skill in understanding the iconographic varieties of the ad world. Ads are ignored or deplored, but seldom studied and enjoyed.

Anybody who could think that the press has the same function in America and Russia, or in France and China, is not really in touch with the medium. Are we to suppose that this kind of media illiteracy is characteristic only of Westerners, and that Russians know how to correct the bias of the medium in order to read it right? Or do people vaguely suppose that the heads of state in the various countries of the world know that the newspaper has totally diverse effects in different cultures? There is no basis for such assumptions. Unawareness of the nature of the press in its subliminal or latent action is as common among politicians as among political scientists. For example, in oral Russia both *Pravda* and *Izvestia* handle domestic news, but the big international themes come to the West over Radio Moscow. In visual America, radio and television handle the domestic stories, and international affairs get their formal treatment in *Time* magazine and *The New York Times*. As a foreign service, the bluntness of *Voice of America* in no way compares to the sophistication of the BBC and Radio Moscow, but what it lacks in verbal content it makes up in the entertainment value of its American jazz. The implications of this difference of stress are important for an understanding of the kinds of opinions and decisions natural to an oral, as opposed to a visual, culture.

A friend of mine who tried to teach something about the forms of media in secondary school was struck by one unanimous response. The students could not for a moment accept the suggestion that the press or any other public means of communication could be used with base intent. They felt that this would be akin to polluting the air or the water supply, and they didn't feel that their friends and relatives employed in these media would sink to such corruption. Failure in perception occurs precisely in giving attention to the program "content" of our media while ignoring the form, whether it be radio or print or the English language itself. There have been countless Newton Minows (formerly head of the Federal Communications Commission) to talk about the Wasteland of the Media, men who know nothing about the form of any medium whatever. They imagine that a more earnest tone and a more austere theme would pull up the level of the book, the press, the movie, and TV. They are wrong to a farcical degree. They have only to try out their theory for fifty consecutive words in the mass medium of the English language. What would Mr. Minow do, what would any advertiser do, without the well-worn and corny clichés of popular speech? Suppose that we were to try for a few sentences to raise the level of our daily English conversation by a series of sober and serious sentiments? Would this be a way of getting at the problems of improving the medium? If all English were enunciated at a Mandarin level of uniform elegance and sententious-ness, would the language and its users be better served? There comes to mind the remark of Artemus Ward that "Shakespeare wrote good plays but he wouldn't have succeeded as the Washington correspon-dent of a New York daily newspaper. He lacked the reckisit fancy and imagination."

The book-oriented man has the illusion that the press would be better without ads and without the pressure from the advertiser. Reader surveys have astonished even publishers with the revelation that the roving eyes of newspaper readers take equal satisfaction in ads and news copy. During the Second War, the U.S.O. sent special issues of the principal American magazines to the Armed Forces, with the ads omitted. The men insisted on having the ads back again. Naturally. The ads are by far the best part of any magazine or newspaper. More pains and thought, more wit and art go into the making of an ad than go into any prose feature of press or magazine. Ads are *news*. What is wrong with them is that they are always *good* news. In order to balance off the effect and to sell good news, it is necessary to have a lot of bad news. Moreover, the newspaper is a hot medium. It has to have bad news for the sake of intensity and reader participation. *Real* news is *bad* news, as already noted, and as any newspaper from the beginning of print can testify. Floods, fires, and other communal disasters by land and sea and air outrank any kind of private horror or villainy as *news.* Ads, in contrast, have to shrill their happy message loud and clear in order to match the penetrating power of bad news.

Commentators on the press and the American Senate have noted that since the Senate began its prying into unsavory subjects it has assumed a role superior to Congress. In fact, the great disadvantage of the Presidency and the Executive arm in relation to public opinion is that it tries to be a source of good news and noble directive. On the other hand, Congressmen and Senators have the free of the seamy side so necessary to the vitality of the press.

Superficially, this may seem cynical, especially to those who imagine
that the content of a medium is a matter of policy and personal preference, and for whom all corporate media, not only radio and the press
but ordinary popular speech as well, are debased forms of human
expression and experience. Here I must repeat that the newspaper,
from its beginnings, has tended, not to the book form, but to the
mosaic or participational form. With the speed-up of printing and
news-gathering, this mosaic form has become a dominant aspect
of human association; for the mosaic form means, not a detached
"point of view," but participation in process. For that reason, the
press is inseparable from the democratic process, but quite expendable
from a literary or book point of view.

Again, the book-oriented man misunderstands the collective mosaic
form of the press when he complains about its endless reports on
the seamy underside of the social garment. Both book and press are,
in their very format, dedicated to the job of revealing the inside story,
whether it is Montaigne giving to the private reader the delicate con-
tours of his mind, or Hearst and Whitman resonating their barbaric
yawps over the roofs of the world. It is the printed form of public
address and high intensity with its precise uniformity of repetition
that gives to book and press alike the special character of public confessional.

The first items in the press to which all men turn are the ones about
which they already know. If we have witnessed some event, whether
a ball game or a stock crash or a snow-storm, we turn to the report
of that happening, first. Why? The answer is central to any understanding of media. Why does a child like to chatter about the events
of its day, however jerkily? Why do we prefer novels and movies about
familiar scenes and characters? Because for rational beings to see or
re-cognize their experience in a new material form is an unbought
grace of life. Experience translated into a new medium literally bestows
a delightful playback of earlier awareness. The press repeats the excitement we have in using our wits, and by using our wits we can
translate the outer world into the fabric of our own beings. This excitement of translation explains why people quite naturally wish to use
their senses all the time. Those external extensions of sense and faculty
that we call media we use as constantly as we do our eyes and ears,
and from the same motives. On the other hand, the book-oriented man
considers this nonstop use of media as debased; it is unfamiliar to
him in the book-world.

Up to this point we have discussed the press as a mosaic successor
to the book-form. The mosaic is the mode of the corporate or collective
image and commands deep participation. This participation is communal rather than private, inclusive rather than exclusive. Further

features of its form can best be grasped by a few random views taken from outside the present form of the press. Historically, for example, newspapers had waited for news to come to them. The first American newspaper, issued in Boston by Benjamin Harris on September 25, 1690, announced that it was to be "furnished once a month (or if any Glut of Occurrences happen, oftener)." Nothing could more plainly indicate the idea that news was something outside and beyond the newspaper. Under such rudimentary conditions of awareness, a principal function of the newspaper was to correct rumors and oral reports, as a dictionary might provide "correct" spellings and meanings for words that had long existed without the benefit of dictionaries. Fairly soon the press began to sense that news was not only to be reported but also gathered, and, indeed, to be made. What went *into* the press was news. The rest was not news. "He made the news" is a strangely ambiguous phrase, since to be in the newspaper is both to be news and to make news. Thus "making the news," like "making good," implies a world of actions and fictions alike. But the press is a daily action and fiction or thing made, and it is made out of just about everything in the community. By the mosaic means, it is made into a communal image or cross-section.

When a conventional critic like Daniel Boorstin complains that modern ghost-writing, teletype, and wire services create an insubstantial world of "pseudo-events," he declares, in effect, that he has never examined the nature of any medium prior to those of the electric age. For the pseudo or fictitious character has always permeated the media, not just those of recent origin.

Long before big business and corporations became aware of the image of their operation as a fiction to be carefully tattooed upon the public sensorium, the press had created the image of the community as a series of on-going actions unified by datelines. Apart from the vernacular used, the dateline is the only organizing principle of the newspaper image of the community. Take off the dateline, and one day's paper is the same as the next. Yet to read a week-old newspaper without noticing that it is not today's is a disconcerting experience. As soon as the press recognized that news presentation was not a repetition of occurrences and reports but a direct cause of events, many things began to happen. Advertising and promotion, until then restricted, broke onto the front page, with the aid of Barnum, as sensational stories. Today's press agent regards the newspaper as a ventriloquist does his dummy. He can make it say what he wants. He looks on it as a painter does his palette and tubes of pigment; from the endless resources of available events, an endless variety of managed mosaic effects can be attained. Any private client can be ensconced in a wide range of different patterns and tones of public affairs or human interest and depth items.

If we pay careful attention to the fact that the press is a mosaic, participant kind of organization and a do-it-yourself kind of world, we can
see why it is so necessary to democratic government. Throughout
his study of the press in *The Fourth Branch of Government,* Douglas
Cater is baffled by the fact that amidst the extreme fragmentation of
government departments and branches, the press somehow manages
to keep them in relation to each other and to the nation. He emphasizes
the paradox that the press is dedicated to the process of cleansing
by publicity, and yet that, in the electronic world of the seamless web
of events, most affairs must be kept secret. Top secrecy is translated
into public participation and responsibility by the magic flexibility of
the controlled news leak.

It is by this kind of ingenious adaptation from day to day that Western
man is beginning to accommodate himself to the electric world of total
interdependence. Nowhere is this transforming process of adaptation
more visible than in the press. The press, in itself, presents the contradiction of an individualistic technology dedicated to shaping and
revealing group attitudes.

It might be well now to observe how the press has been modified by
the recent developments of telephone, radio, and TV. We have seen
already that the telegraph is the factor that has done most to create
the mosaic image of the modern press, with its mass of discontinuous
and unconnected features. It is this group-image of the communal
life, rather than any editorial outlook or slanting, that constitutes the
participant of this medium. To the book-man of detached private
culture, this is the scandal of the press: its shameless involvement in
the depths of human interest and sentiment. By eliminating time and
space in news presentation, the telegraph dimmed the privacy of the
book-form, and heightened, instead, the new public image in the
press.

The first harrowing experience for the press man visiting Moscow is
the absence of telephone books. A further horrifying revelation is
the absence of central switchboards in government departments. You
know the number, or else. The student of media is happy to read a
hundred volumes to discover two facts such as these. They floodlight
a vast murky area of the pressworld, and illuminate the role of telephone as seen through another culture. The American newspaperman
in large degree assembles his stories and processes his data by telephone because of the speed and immediacy of the oral process. Our
popular press is a near approximation to the grapevine. The Russian
and European newspaperman is, by comparison, a littérateur. It is a
paradoxical situation, but the press in literate America has an intensely
oral character, while in oral Russia and Europe the press has a strongly
literary character and function.

The English dislike the telephone so much that they substitute numerous mail deliveries for it. The Russians use the telephone for a status symbol, like the alarm clock worn by tribal chiefs as an article of attire in Africa. The mosaic of the press image in Russia is felt as an immediate form of tribal unity and participation. Those features of the press that we find most discordant with austere individual standards of literary culture are just the ones that recommend it to the Communist Party. "A newspaper," Lenin once declared, "is not only a collective propagandist and collective agitator; it is also a collective organizer." Stalin called it "the most powerful weapon of our Party." Khrushchev cites it as "our chief ideological weapon." These men had more an eye to the collective form of the press mosaic, with its magical power to impose its own assumptions, than to the printed word as expressing a private point of view. In oral Russia, fragmentation of government powers is unknown. Not for them our function of the press as unifier of fragmented departments. The Russian monolith has quite different uses for the press mosaic. Russia now needs the press (as we formerly did the book) to translate a tribal and oral community into some degree of visual, uniform culture able to sustain a market system.

In Egypt the press is needed to effect nationalism, that visual kind of unity that springs men out of local and tribal patterns. Paradoxically, radio has come to the fore in Egypt as the rejuvenator of the ancient tribes. The battery radio carried on the camel gives to the Bedouin tribes a power and vitality unknown before, so that to use the word "nationalism" for the fury of oral agitation that the Arabs have felt by radio is to conceal the situation from ourselves. Unity of the Arab-speaking world can only come by the press. Nationalism was unknown to the Western world until the Renaissance, when Guttenberg made it possible to *see* the mother tongue in uniform dress. Radio does nothing for this uniform visual unity so necessary to nationalism. In order to restrict radio-listening to national programs, some Arab governments have passed a law forbidding the use of private headphones, in effect enforcing a tribal collectivism in their radio audiences. Radio restores tribal sensitivity and exclusive involvement in the web of kinship. The press, on the other hand, creates a visual, not-too-involved kind of unity that is hospitable to the inclusion of many tribes, and to diversity of private outlook.

If telegraph shortened the sentence, radio shortened the news story, and TV injected the interrogative mood into journalism. In fact, the press is now not only a telephoto mosaic of the human community hour by hour, but its technology is also a mosaic of all the technologies of the community. Even in its selection of the newsworthy, the press prefers those persons who have already been accorded some notoriety existence in movies, radio, TV, and drama. By this fact, we can test the nature of the press medium, for anybody who appears only in the newspaper is by that token, an ordinary citizen.

Wallpaper manufacturers have recently begun to issue wallpaper that presents the appearance of a French newspaper. The Eskimo sticks magazine pages on the ceiling of his igloo to deter drip. But even an ordinary newspaper on a kitchen floor will reveal news items that one had missed when the paper was in hand. Yet whether one uses the press for privacy in public conveyances, or for involvement in the communal while enjoying privacy, the mosaic of the press manages to effect a complex many-leveled function of group-awareness and participation such as the book has never been able to perform.

The format of the press—that is, its structural characteristics—were quite naturally taken over by the poets after Baudelaire in order to evoke an inclusive awareness. Our ordinary newspaper page today is not only symbolist and surreaiist in an *avant-garde way,* but it was the earlier *inspiration* of symbolism and surrealism in art and poetry, as anybody can discover by reading Flaubert or Rimbaud. Approached as newspaper form, any part of Joyce's *Ulysses* or any poem of T.S. Eliot's before the *Quartets* is more readily enjoyed. Such, however, is the austere continuity of book culture that it scorns to notice these *liaisons dangéreuses* among the media, especially the scandalous affairs of the book-page with electronic creatures from the other side of the linotype.

In view of the inveterate concern of the press with cleansing by publicity, it may be well to ask if it does not set up an inevitable clash with the medium of the book. The press as a collective and communal image assumes a natural posture of opposition to all private manipulation. Any mere individual who begins to stir about as if he were a public something-or-other is going to get into the press. Any individual who manipulates the public for his private good may also feel the cleansing power of publicity. The cloak of invisibility, therefore, would seem to fall most naturally on those who own newspapers or who use them extensively for commerical ends. May not this explain the strange obsession of the bookman with the press-lords as essentially corrupt? The merely private and fragmentary point of view assumed by the book reader and writer finds natural grounds for hostility toward the big communal power of the press. As forms, as media, the book and the newspaper would seem to be as incompatible as any two media could be. The owners of media always endeavor to give the public what it wants, because they sense that their power is in the *medium* and not in the *message* or the program.

American Society of Newspaper Editors
CODE OF ETHICS*

The primary function of newspapers is to communicate to the human race what its members do, feel and think. Journalism, therefore, demands of its practitioners the widest range of intelligence, or knowledge, and of experience, as well as natural and trained powers of observation and reasoning. To its opportunities as a chronicle are indissolubly linked its obligations as teacher and interpreter.

To the end of finding some means of codifying sound practice and just aspirations of American journalism, these canons are set forth:

I

Responsibility   The right of a newspaper to attract and hold readers is restricted by nothing but considerations of public welfare. The use a newspaper makes of the share of public attention it gains serves to determine its sense of responsibility, which it shares with every member of its staff. A journalist who uses his power for any selfish or otherwise unworthy purpose is faithless to a high trust.

II

Freedom of the Press   Freedom of the press is to be guarded as a vital right of mankind. It is the unquestionable right to discuss whatever is not explicitly forbidden by law, including the wisdom of any restrictive statute.

[Editors' Note: Referred to sometimes as "The Canons of Journalism."]

III

Independence   Freedom from all obligations except that of fidelity to the public interest is vital.

1. Promotion of any private interest contrary to the general welfare, for whatever reason, is not compatible with honest journalism. So-called news communications from private sources should not be published without public notice of their source or else substantiation of their claims to value as news, both in form and substance.

2. Partisanship, in editorial comment which knowingly departs from the truth, does violence to the best spirit of American journalism; in the news columns it is subversive of a fundamental principle of the profession.

IV

Sincerity, Truthfulness, Accuracy   Good faith with the reader is the foundation of all journalism worthy of the name.

1. By every consideration of good faith a newspaper is constrained to be truthful. It is not to be excused for lack of thoroughness or accuracy within its control, or failure to obtain command of these essential qualities.

2. Headlines should be fully warranted by the contents of the articles which they surmount.

V

Impartiality   Sound practice makes clear distinction between news reports and expressions of opinion. News reports should be free from opinion or bias of any kind.

1. This rule does not apply to so-called special articles unmistakably devoted to advocacy or characterized by a signature authorizing the writer's own conclusions and interpretation.

VI

Fair Play   A newspaper should not publish unoffical charges affecting reputation or moral character without opportunity given to the accused to be heard; right practice demands the giving of such opportunity in all cases of serious accusation outside judicial proceedings.

1. A newspaper should not invade private rights or feeling without sure warrant of public right as distinguished from public curiosity.

2. It is the privilege, as it is the duty, of a newspaper to make prompt and complete correction of its own serious mistakes of fact or opinion, whatever their origin.

Decency A newspaper cannot escape conviction of insincerity if while professing high moral purpose it supplies incentives to base conduct, such as are to be found in details of crime and vice, publication of which is not demonstrably for the general good. Lacking authority to enforce its canons the journalism here represented can but express the hope that deliberate pandering to vicious instincts will encounter effective public disapproval or yield to the influence of a preponderant professional condemnation.

Commission on Freedom of the Press
A FREE AND RESPONSIBLE PRESS

The "Report of the Commission on Freedom of the Press" was issued in 1947. Since then, it has stood as an ideal of the kind of press "we must have if we would have progress and peace." The following recommendations from the Report focus on the responsibilities of the press, the government, and the public in attaining such a goal.

THE principal aim of this section of our report is not to recommend more governmental action but to clarify the role of government in relation to mass communication.

1. *We recommend that the constitutional guarantees of the freedom of the press be recognized as including the radio and motion pictures.*

In view of the approaching advent of the broadcast facsimile newspaper and the development of the newsreel and the documentary film, constitutional safeguards for the radio and motion picture are needed more than ever. We believe that such regulation of these media as is desirable can and should be conducted within the limitations which the federal and state constitutions now place upon the regulation of newspapers and books.[1]

In the case of motion pictures this recommendation would not abolish state boards of review; it would require them to operate within the First Amendment as interpreted by the Supreme Court.

In the case of radio this recommendation would give constitutional support to the prohibition against censorship in the Communications Act. It would not prevent the Federal Communications Commission from denying a license on the ground that the applicant was unpre-

The new constitution of Missouri protects "freedom of expression by whatever means."

pared to serve the public interest, convenience, and necessity. Nor would it prevent the Commission from considering, in connection with an application for renewal, whether the applicant had kept the promises he made when the license was granted and had actually served the public interest, convenience, and necessity. This recommendation is intended to strengthen the prohibition against censorship, not to guarantee licensees a perpetual franchise regardless of their performance. The air belongs to the public, not to the radio industry.

2. *We recommend that government facilitate new ventures in the communications industry, that it foster the introduction of new techniques, that it maintain competition among large units through the antitrust laws, but that those laws be sparingly used to break up such units, and that, where concentration is necessary in communications, the government endeavor to see to it that the public gets the benefit of such concentration.*

We accept the fact that some concentration must exist in the communications industry if the country is to have the service it needs. People need variety and diversity in mass communication; they must also have service, a quantity and quality of information and discussion which can often be supplied only by large units.

The possibilities of evil inherent in concentration can be minimized by seeing to it that no artificial obstructions impede the creation and development of new units. In the communications industry it is difficult to start new units because of the large investment required and because of the control of the existing units over the means of distribution.

Little can be done by government or any other agency to reduce the cost of entering the industry except to adjust governmental charges, such as tax laws and postal rates, to facilitate new enterprises, and to prevent established interests from obstructing the introduction of new techniques. Tax laws and postal rates should be restudied with a view to discovering whether they do not discriminate against new, small businesses and in favor of large, well-established ones.

As for new techniques, an invention like FM radio offers the possibility of greatly increasing quantity and diversity in broadcasting. The cost of the equipment is low, and the number of frequencies large. We believe that the Federal Communications Commission should fully exploit the opportunity now before it and should prevent any greater concentration in FM radio than the service requires.

Government can stop the attempt by existing units of the press to monopolize distribution outlets. The types of governmental action called for range from police protection and city ordinances which would make it possible for new newspapers and magazines to get on the newsstands to antitrust suits against motion picture companies which monopolize theaters. The main function of government in relation to the communications industry is to keep the channels open, and this means, in part, facilitating in every way short of subsidy the creation of new units in the industry.

The Commission believes that there should be active competition in the communications industry. It inclines to the view that the issue of the size of the units competing is not one which can best be dealt with by law. The antitrust laws can be invoked to maintain competition among large units and to prevent the exclusion of any unit from facilities which ought to be open to all; their use to force the breaking-up of large units seems to us undesirable.

Though there can be no question that the antitrust laws apply to the communications industry, we would point out that these laws are extremely vague. They can be very dangerous to the freedom and the effectiveness of the press. They can be used to limit voices in opposition and to hinder the processes of public education.

Since the Commission looks principally to the units of the press itself to take joint action to provide the diversity, quantity, and quality of information and discussion which a free society requires, it would not care to see such action blocked by the mistaken application of the antitrust laws. Honest efforts to raise standards, such as we suggest elsewhere in this chapter, should not be thwarted, even though they result in higher costs.

Since the need for service is the justification for concentration, the government should see to it that, where concentration exists, the service is rendered; it should see to it that the public gets the benefit of the concentration. For example, the Federal Communications Commission should explore the possibilities of requiring the radio networks to increase the number of their affiliated stations and of using clear-channel licenses as a means of serving all the less populous regions of the country. The extension of radio service of the quality supplied by the networks and the maintenance and multiplication of local stations are of the first importance. There are only two ways of obtaining these results: they can be achieved by the acceptance of responsibility by the industry, or they can be achieved by government ownership. We prefer the former.

3. *As an alternative to the present remedy for libel, we recommend legislation by which the injured party might obtain a retraction or a restatement of the facts by the offender or an opportunity to reply.*

The only legal method by which a person injured by false statements in the press may vindicate his reputation is a civil action for damages.

The remedy is expensive, difficult, and encumbered with technicalities. Many injured persons hesitate to sue because of the "shadow of racketeering and blackmail which hangs over libel plaintiffs."[2]

The proposed remedy should operate quickly while the issue is before the public. It should lead to an increase in the practice, now common among the responsible members of the press, of voluntarily correcting misstatements. It ought to diminish lying in the press.

We are opposed to the group libel laws now under discussion in several states. We believe that an action for libel should be a civil suit brought by a person who can show that he, as an individual, was damaged by a false statement about him. We fear that, if an individual may sue or initiate a criminal prosecution, because a group he belongs to has been criticized falsely, the law might be used to suppress legitimate public controversy.

The Commission has given extensive consideration to numerous suggested methods of reducing lying in the press by law. We insist that, morally considered, the freedom of the press is a conditional right— conditional on the honesty and responsibility of writer, broadcaster, or publisher. A man who lies, intentionally or carelessly, is not morally entitled to claim the protection of the First Amendment. The remedy for press lying, however, must go deeper than the law can go. We are reluctant to suggest governmental interference with the freedom of the press; we see many difficulties of enforcement; we do not find in the present situation justification for stronger legislation than that which we here propose.

4. *We recommend the repeal of legislation prohibiting expressions in favor of revolutionary changes in our institutions where there is no clear and present danger that violence will result from the expressions.*

The Supreme Court has held that expressions urging the overthrow of the government by force are within the protection of the First Amendment unless there is a clear and present danger that these expressions will lead to violence. We believe that this sound principle is violated by the peacetime sedition clauses of the Alien Registration Act of 1940 and by the various state syndicalism acts which make it a crime to advocate the overthrow of the government by force, irrespective of the probable effect of the statements. The really dangerous persons within the scope of these laws can be reached by the conspiracy statutes and the general criminal law. As applied to other persons, which is most likely to be the case, these laws are of dubious constitutionality and unwise. Yet only a few of the agitators who are

---

2 Riesman, in *Columbia Law Review*, XLII, 1282, 1314–40. For a description of this remedy as well as for a more comprehensive discussion of the relation of government to the press, see the report to the Commission of one of its members, Zechariah Chafee, Jr., entitled *Government and Mass Communications*, to be published by the University of Chicago Press.

prosecuted can succeed in getting before the Supreme Court. Consequently, so long as this legislation remains on the statute-books, its
intimidating effect is capable of stifling political and economic discussion. These acts ought to be repealed.

5. *We recommend that the government, through the media of mass
communication, inform the public of the facts with respect to its
policies and of the purposes underlying those policies and that, to the
extent that private agencies of mass communication are unable or
unwilling to supply such media to the government, the government
itself may employ media of its own.*

*We also recommend that, where the private agencies of mass com-
munication are unable or unwilling to supply information about this
country to a particular foreign country or countries, the government
employ mass communication media of its own to supplement this
deficiency.*

We should not think it worth while to make these recommendations
if it were not for the fact that in recent years there have been increasingly strident charges that the government is exceeding its proper
functions and wasting the taxpayers' money when it undertakes to
inform the people in regard to its program or to supplement and correct the picture of this country which the press has projected to other
parts of the world or which results from misinformation or lack of
information.

Doubtless some governmental officers have used their publicity departments for personal or partisan aggrandizement. But this evil is
subject to correction by normal democratic processes and does not
compare with the danger that the people of this country and other
countries may, in the absence of official information and discussion,
remain unenlightened on vital issues.

In addition to supplying information at home and abroad, the government has special obligations in international communications,
which are elaborated in *Peoples Speaking to Peoples:* to use its
influence to reduce press rates all over the world; to obtain equal access to the news for all; to break down barriers to the free flow of
information; and to collaborate with the United Nations in promoting
the widest dissemination of news and discussion by all the techniques
which become available.

WHAT CAN BE DONE BY THE PRESS

The recommendations we have made for action by government,
though they are minimal, could be reduced still further in the domestic

field, at least, by the action of the press itself. Existing units of the press could abstain from attempts to monopolize distribution outlets; they could insist that new techniques be made available and freely used; the press could of its own motion make it a rule that a person injured by a false statement should have an opportunity to reply. We believe that these changes are bound to come through legislation if they do not come through the action of the press and that it would be the part of wisdom for the press to take these measures on its own initiative.

The communications industry in the United States is and, in the opinion of the Commission, should remain a private business. But it is a business affected with a public interest. The Commission does not believe that it should be regulated by government like other businesses affected with a public interest, such as railroads and telephone companies. The Commission hopes that the press itself will recognize its public responsibility and obviate governmental action to enforce it.

It may be argued that the variety, quantity, and quality of information and discussion which we expect from the press cannot be purveyed at a profit and that a business which cannot operate at a profit cannot last under a system of private enterprise. It has been said that, if the press is to continue as a private business, it can succeed only as other retailers succeed, that is, by giving the customers what they want. On this theory the test of public service is financial success. On this theory, too, the press is bound by what it believes to be the interests and tastes of the mass audience; these interests and tastes are discovered by finding out what the mass audience will buy. On this theory, if the press tries to rise higher than the interests and tastes of the mass audience as they are revealed at the newsstands or at the box office, it will be driven into bankruptcy, and its existence as a private business will be at an end.

We have weighed the evidence carefully and do not accept this theory. As the example of many ventures in the communications industry shows, good practice in the interest of public enlightenment is good business as well. The agencies of mass communication are not serving static wants. Year by year they are building and transforming the interests of the public. They have an obligation to elevate rather than to degrade them.

The gist of the recommendations in this section of our report is that the press itself should assume the responsibility of providing the variety, quantity, and quality of information and discussion which the country needs. This seems to us largely a question of the way in which the press looks at itself. We suggest that the press look upon itself as performing a public service of a professional kind. Whatever may be thought of the conduct of individual members of the older,

established professions, like law and medicine, each of these professions as a whole accepts a responsibility for the service rendered by
the profession as a whole, and there are some things which a truly
professional man will not do for money.

1. *We recommend that the agencies of mass communication accept
the responsibilities of common carriers of information and discussion.*

Those agencies of mass communication which have achieved a dominant position in their areas can exert an influence over the minds of
their audience too powerful to be disregarded. We do not wish to
break up these agencies, because to do so would break up the service
they can render. We do not wish to have them owned or controlled by
government. They must therefore themselves be hospitable to ideas
and attitudes different from their own, and they must present them to
the public as meriting its attention. In no other way can the danger to
the mind of democracy which is inherent in the present concentration
be avoided.

2. *We recommend that the agencies of mass communication assume
the responsibility of financing new, experimental activities in their
fields.*

Here we have in mind activities of high literary, artistic, or intellectual
quality which do not give promise of immediate financial return but
which may offer long-term rewards. Only in a few metropolitan areas
can the citizen easily gain access to a wide variety of motion pictures
and radio programs. Elsewhere discriminating, serious minorities are
prisoners of the estimate of mass taste made by the industry. Motion
pictures, radio programs, newspapers, and magazines aimed at these
minorities may not make money at the beginning. They require a considerable investment. They do not attract capital seeking quick profits.
Nonprofit institutions can do something in this field, but they should
not be expected to do the whole job. The responsibility of the industry
for diversity and quality means that it should finance ventures of this
kind from the profits of its other business.

3. *We recommend that the members of the press engage in vigorous
mutual criticism.*

Professional standards are not likely to be achieved as long as the
mistakes and errors, the frauds and crimes, committed by units of the
press are passed over in silence by other members of the profession.
As we indicated in chapter 5, the formal organization of the press into
a profession, with power in the organization to deprive an erring
member of his livelihood, is unlikely and perhaps undesirable. We have
repeatedly evidenced our desire that the power of government should

not be invoked to punish the aberrations of the press. If the press is to be accountable—and it must be if it is to remain free—its members must discipline one another by the only means they have available, namely, public criticism.

4. *We recommend that the press use every means that can be devised to increase the competence, independence, and effectiveness of its staff.*

The quality of the press depends in large part upon the capacity and independence of the working members in the lower ranks. At the present time their wages and prestige are low and their tenure precarious. Adequate compensation, adequate recognition, and adequate contracts seem to us an indispensable prerequisite to the development of a professional personnel.

Elsewhere in this chapter we shall refer to education for journalism. Here we would merely indicate that the press can do a good deal to improve the quality of its staff by promoting an intelligent educational program, both for young people and for men and women who are already at work in the field. The type of educational experience provided for working journalists by the Nieman Fellowships at Harvard seems to us to deserve extension, if not through private philanthropy, then with the financial assitance of the press itself.

5. *We recommend that the radio industry take control of its programs and that it treat advertising as it is treated by the best newspapers.*

Radio cannot become a responsible agency of communication as long as its programming is controlled by the advertisers. No newspaper would call itself respectable if its editorial columns were dominated by its advertisers and if it published advertising, information, and discussion so mixed together that the reader could not tell them apart. The importance and validity of this recommendation seem to us so obvious as not to require argument. Radio is one of the most powerful means of communication known to man. With the advent of facsimile and television, it will become more powerful still. The public should not be forced to continue to take its radio fare from the manufacturers of soap, cosmetics, cigarettes, soft drinks, and packaged foods.

WHAT CAN BE DONE BY THE PUBLIC

The people of this country are the purchasers of the products of the press. The effectiveness of buyers' boycotts, even of very little ones, has been amply demonstrated. Many of these boycotts are the wrong kind for the wrong purposes; they are the work of pressure groups seeking to protect themselves from justifiable criticism or to gain some special advantage. The success of their efforts indicates what a revolt of the American people against the service given them by the press might accomplish.

We are not in favor of a revolt and hope that less drastic means of improving the press may be employed. We cannot tell what direction a revolt might take; it might lead to government control or to the emasculation of the First Amendment. We want the press to be free, and a revolt against the press conducted for the purpose of giving the country a truly free press might end in less freedom than we have today.

What is needed, first of all, is recognition by the American people of the vital importance of the press in the present world crisis. We have the impression that the American people do not realize what has happened to them. They are not aware that the communications revolution has occurred. They do not appreciate the tremendous power which the new instruments and the new organization of the press place in the hands of a few men. They have not yet understood how far the performance of the press falls short of the requirements of a free society in the world today. The principal object of our report is to make these points clear.

If these points are clear, what can the people do about them? They have, or they can create, agencies which can be used to supplement the press, to propose standards for its emulation, and to hold it to its accountability.

1. *We recommend that nonprofit institutions help supply the variety, quantity, and quality of press service required by the American people.*

We have indicated our belief that the agencies of mass communication have a responsibility to the public like that of educational institutions. We now wish to add that educational institutions have a responsibility to the public to use the instruments employed by the agencies of mass communications. The radio, the motion picture, television, and facsimile broadcasting are most powerful means of molding the minds of men. That is why we worry about their exclusive appropriation by agencies engaged in the pursuit of profit. Not that educational institutions are free from financial problems and the pressures associated with them. But the nonprofit corporation does not exist for the purpose of making profits. It is peculiarly able to enlist the co-operation of all who are interested in the cultural development of the country. Hence it can render those services which commercial enterprise cannot offer on a profit-making basis.

It can restore an element of diversity to the information and discussion reaching the public by organizing the demand for good things and by putting out good things itself. A chain of libraries, schools, colleges, and universities, together with the various religious organizations, could establish the documentary film in mass communication. A chain of educational FM stations could put before the public the best thought of America and could make many present radio programs look as silly as they are.

The business of organizing demand requires nothing but realization of the importance of the opportunity and co-operation, to which educational institutions are notoriously averse. The business of putting out good things requires in addition a determined effort to acquire the professional skill that is needed if the efforts of nonprofit corporations are not to be scorned as the work of second-rate amateurs.

We cannot believe that nonprofit institutions will continue to fail to grasp the opportunity they have before them. It has always been clear that education is a process which goes on through the whole of life. It has always been clear that, as working hours diminished and leisure increased, a responsibility devolved upon educators to help people make wise use of their leisure. Now a new urgency is added to this duty. The world seems on the brink of suicide, and the ultimate catastrophe can be avoided only if the adult citizens of today can learn how to live together in peace. It will not be enough to educate the rising generation; the time is too short. The educators have the enormous task of trying to make the peoples of the earth intelligent now. It is fortunate that, as their task has grown greater and more pressing, technology has given them new instruments of incredible range and power.

2. *We recommend the creation of academic-professional centers of advanced study, research, and publication in the field of communications. We recommend further that existing schools of journalism exploit the total resources of their universities to the end that their students may obtain the broadest and most liberal training.*

The importance of the field of communications does not seem to us to have been adequately recognized by the educational institutions of the country. We doubt that new professional or technical training schools should be established in this area. We do see, however, a need for centers of investigation, graduate study, and critical publication. These are, in fact, so important that without them it is unlikely that the professional practices and attitudes which we recommend to the press can ever become characteristic of the communications industry.

Preparation for work in the press seems to us to require the best possible general education. It is important that students who enter schools of journalism should not be deprived of liberal education because they have made up their minds that they want to work on the press. Few schools of journalism can develop a liberal curriculum within their own faculties. It is therefore imperative that they associate themselves as closely as possible with other departments and schools of their universities.

3. *We recommend the establishment of a new and independent agency to appraise and report annually upon the performance of the press.*

The public makes itself felt by the press at the present time chiefly through pressure groups. These groups are quite as likely to have bad influence as good. In this field we cannot turn to government as the representative of the people as a whole, and we would not do so if we could. Yet it seems to us clear that some agency which reflects the ambitions of the American people for its press should exist for the purpose of comparing the accomplishments of the press with the aspirations which the people have for it. Such an agency would also educate the people as to aspirations which they ought to have for the press.

The Commission suggests that such a body be independent of government and of the press; that it be created by gifts; and that it be given a ten-year trial, at the end of which an audit of its achievement could determine anew the institutional form best adapted to its purposes.

The activities of such an agency would include:

1. Continuing efforts, through conference with practitioners and analysis by its staff, to help the press define workable standards of performance, a task on which our Commission has attempted a beginning.

2. Pointing out the inadequacy of press service in certain areas and the trend toward concentration in others, to the end that local communities and the press itself may organize to supply service where it is lacking or to provide alternative service where the drift toward monopoly seems dangerous.

3. Inquiries in areas where minority groups are excluded from reasonable access to the channels of communication.

4. Inquiries abroad regarding the picture of American life presented by the American press; and co-operation with agencies in other countries and with international agencies engaged in analysis of communication across national borders.

5. Investigation of instances of press lying, with particular reference to persistent misrepresentation of the data required for judging public issues.

6. Periodic appraisal of the tendencies and characteristics of the various branches of the communications industry.

7. Continuous appraisal of governmental action affecting communications.

8. Encouragement of the establishment of centers of advanced study, research, and criticism in the field of communications at universities.

9. Encouragement of projects which give hope of meeting the needs of special audiences.

10. The widest possible publicity and public discussion on all the foregoing.

The above recommendations taken together give some indication of methods by which the press may become accountable and hence remain free. We believe that if they are carried out, press performance will be brought much closer to the five ideal demands of society for the communication of news and ideas which were set forth in the second chapter: (1) a truthful, comprehensive, and intelligent account of the day's events in a context which gives them meaning; (2) a forum for the exchange of comment and criticism; (3) the projection of a representative picture of the constituent groups in the society; (4) the presentation and clarification of the goals and values of the society; (5) full access to the day's intelligence.

Plainly, each of these five ideals will be served by more than one of our recommendations. Instead of stating those relationships in detail, we think that it will be more helpful to point out how the various recommendations will supplement each other in remedying some aspects of the press as it now exists which have constantly disturbed the members of the Commission during our investigation.

The failure of radio to reach all citizens adequately can be relieved through the licensing policy of the F.C.C., while the international coverage of American news and opinions can be extended by various measures proposed in *Peoples Speaking to Peoples.*

Deliberate falsifications and reckless misstatements of fact will be lessened by a new legal remedy compelling the publication of a retraction or reply and, even more, by the assumption of a greater responsibility for accuracy on the part of the press, by the readiness of newspapers and other agencies of communication to criticize one another for gross departures from truthfulness, and by periodic appraisals of press accuracy issuing from a body of citizens.

The inclination of the press to adapt most of its output to the supposed desires of the largest possible number of consumers and the resulting trends toward sensationalism and meaninglessness can be reduced by similar periodical appraisals from citizens and by the initiation of new activities for the benefit of specialized audiences on the part of the press itself as well as nonprofit institutions. In the case of radio, the quality of output can be improved through organizations of listeners in the communities and through the determination of the industry to take control of its programs out of the hands of the advertisers and their agents.

The greatest difficulty in preserving free communications in a technical society arises from the concentration of power within the instruments of communication. The most conspicuous example of this is in the ownership of instrumentalities, but the concentration also exists in the power of advertisers, of labor organizations, of organized pressure groups—all capable of impairing the free interchange of news and ideas. The danger is that the entire function of communications will fall under the control of fewer and fewer persons.

Among the consequences of this concentration, the output of the press reflects the bias of owners and denies adequate expression to important elements in communities.

In order to counteract the evil effects of concentration, we have urged that newspapers and other agencies of mass communication regard themselves as common carriers of information and discussion, that the entry of new units into the field be facilitated, and that the government prevent monopolistic control of outlets by the sources of production.

Finally, members of the Commission were disturbed by finding that many able reporters and editorial writers displayed frustration—the feeling that they were not allowed to do the kind of work which their professional ideals demanded, that they were unable to give the service which the community needs from the press. A continuation of this disturbing situation will prevent the press from discharging its responsibilities toward society. As remedies we have urged the press to use every means that can be devised to increase the competence and independence of the staff, and we have urged universities and schools of journalism to train existing or potential members of the press in the exercise of judgment on public affairs. In many different ways the rank and file of the press can be developed into a genuine profession.

The outside forces of law and public opinion can in various ways check bad aspects of press performance, but good press performance can come only from the human beings who operate the instrumentalities of communication.

We believe that our recommendations, taken together, give some indication of methods by which the press may become accountable and, hence, remain free. The urgent and perplexing issues which confront our country, the new dangers which encompass our free society, the new fatefulness attaching to every step in foreign policy and to

38
FORM AND
TECHNIQUE
what the press publishes about it, mean that the preservation of democracy and perhaps of civilization may now depend upon a free and responsible press. Such a press we must have if we would have progress and peace.

Robert M. Hutchins
Zechariah Chafee, Jr.
John M. Clark
John Dickinson
William E. Hocking
Harold D. Lasswell
Archibald MacLeish

Charles E. Merriam
Reinhold Niebuhr
Robert Redfield
Beardsley Ruml
Arthur M. Schlesinger
George N. Shuster

Henry Justin Smith
THE DAY

"The fascination of news" probably began when the first caveman brought home with his first kill tales of his hunting trip. And so it has continued. Millions wait for the moment when they can open their daily newspaper and learn the latest news from all over the world. In this selection from his book, Deadlines, *Henry Justin Smith, former editor of the* Chicago Daily News, *traces the boredom, the excitement, the frenzy of a day in the life of a daily newspaper.*

I

IT IS still dark in the streets, still dark among the flat roofs of our block, when the day begins.

It is a winter morning before seven o'clock. Night clings to the city. Windows in some of the tall buildings burn with a radiance never extinguished; others spring into color ahead of the belated sun. On street cars and elevated trains that sail through the darkness like lighted ships the seven o'clock workers are arriving "downtown." They are shabbier, more morose, than those who come later. It is hard to be buoyant before seven o'clock in the morning.

In the newspaper office desks and long tables stand in a twilight due to glimmerings that penetrate through the windows. Typewriters, grotesquely hooded, lie in ranks. Waste-baskets yawn. The wires, clinging to the desks, are asleep; telephones have not yet found their tongues. The electric contact with the waking world is in suspension. What happened yesterday? What will happen today? The wires do not care.

A sleepy boy, shivering, his shoes trickling melted snow, enters the spectral room, carrying a bundle of morning newspapers which he lets fall upon a table. He sighs. He turns an electric switch, and the desks and tables spring into outline. The boy stares about him, stumbles over a waste-basket, kicks it away, sits in a battered chair in front of the mouth of a tarnished copper tube that runs through the ceiling, and drowses. He has barely settled down when he hears men coming in, and starts up. The men are two; young, but with greying hair. They have not much to say to each other. They do not even glance toward the boy. With a manner somewhat repressed, but alert enough, they go to desks, call out for the morning papers, and start slicing them up with scissors. Ten minutes go by, while the clock ticks serenely and the windows become grey with creeping daylight; daylight that sifts down among the roofs and through veils of smoke and fog, that comes cold and ashamed and reluctant. It envelops in new shadows the bowed shoulders of the two young men, touching their cheeks with its own pallor, casting pale reminders upon the papers they are cutting. One man glances over his shoulder at the clock. The clock presently strikes a puny but peremptory "Ping!" It is seven o'clock. The day has begun.

Now enter through the swinging door, which flies back and forth impatiently, the staff. For some time the tramping of their feet, the sound of their breathing, their low laughter, the swish and creak of the door, fill the room. There are ruddy, careless fellows in this company, sanguine youths to whom strain and difficulty are nothing. They tramp, tramp, past the desks and tables, doff overcoats, strip the typewriters of their hoods, whistle, wink at each other, take final puffs of forbidden cigarettes, chuckle together over amusing things in the morning papers, and meantime remain secretly alert—for what? Not merely for the calling of a name by the city editor (now established at his desk and scowling at clippings). Not merely for the chatter of a telephone bell, which may mean a day's work for some or all. The possibilities are vague. The tingling of blood means only that this is a new day. Something is bound to happen. They do not mention this to each other. It is against the code for one man to say to his mate: "John, this may be a momentous day. It may bring fame to someone. This may be our great opportunity." Instead, one reporter stretches and yawns: "Well, here we are again, boys; back in the old squirrel cage, to do a few more turns for the antique Press. What of it? Say, do you suppose such a thing could happen as that I'd get an interesting assignment? Where's the bird who said newspaper work was exciting? . . . "

They are like hunting dogs, pretending to be asleep, but with their ears cocked for the mysterious, the shapeless approaching event that is in the spirit of the day.

II

The room is now full. In this loft, some ninety feet long by thirty wide, place is found for nearly forty men. At one end, the end farthest from

the thunder of "L" trains, sits the city editor, surrounded by assistants,
tables, telephones, filing cases, wire baskets, spindles, and boys—in
that order of usefulness. Within elbow distance are the copy-readers,
whom the city editor both prizes and reviles. They bend over their long,
battered desk, some of them chewing tobacco unobtrusively, and jab
with their pencils at piles of manuscript, giving it an earnest and sar-
donic scrutiny. Just beyond them sit the telegraph editors, older men
and more solemn of face, as befits those whose judgment grapples
with majestic cables and Washington dispatches. The chief of these
worthies presides at a roll-top desk upon which boys periodically dump
a mess of Associated Press sheets, damp from their passage through
the tube. The desk has pigeon-holes crammed with dusty reports,
statistics, speeches not yet delivered, and biographies of men not
yet dead. The telegraph editor is just now arguing with the head proof-
reader over the spelling of a Russian name. The argument waxes hot.
We pass on.

There is a group of desks pertaining to the three men who attend to
the "make-up," two of the armchairs vacant because their owners are
in the composing room. And there is a large and excessively dusty
desk before which, with his back to its intricate recesses, sits the news
editor, from whom are supposed to issue ideas, solutions, and enthusiasm. None of them have issued from him thus far; but the day
is still young.

Behind all this is the ampler space occupied by the staff. Three reporters, sprawled over their typewriters and strings of clippings, are
doggedly pounding out "re-writes" of morning paper articles. Two
more are deciphering notes of matters they have just heard over the
telephone. Four others stand by a window, engaged in brisk discussion. Are they discussing politics, prurient plays, or prohibition? None
of these things. One overhears: "I doubt if Wells is such a scream in
England as he is in America. Now, when it comes to Compton
Mackenzie—"

A boy approaches one of these reporters and says, triumphantly:
"Wallace, Mr. Brown wants you."

"Right."

The literary causerie continues during Wallace's absence. He returns,
pulling on his gloves. A stir among the unassigned.

"I've got to interview Sir Scammon Scammonton. LaSalle station."

"Sorry for you. Must be dull day."

"It is," grimaces Wallace, swaggering off.

A dark-haired reporter sits penciling lines upon rough paper, and looking out dreamily into the hurly-burly of traffic and over the chaos of

cornices and water tanks visible from the window. He is far, far away from all this. The lines he scrawls are mystical, tender. He is a poet. And he is a very good reporter but his habits—

A stout man in a corner is writing: "It is understood that the non-partisan element in the country board—" but half his thoughts are upon Japanese prints. He is an amateur of Japanese prints.

In another corner a tall and slightly grey-haired reporter stabs with his cane at a vagrant cockroach, while shadows of reverie and discontent flit across his face. He was lately in Europe, whence he returned in disgust, shouting for the "good old life." Now he is yearning for Europe again. A novel that he began to write lies, yellowing, in a corner of his desk. He would like to go to Mexico, or to California. He applies every week for some trip or other. Meantime he meticulously does what he is told to do.

And then, there is a Cub, who sits bolt upright before his idle typewriter, eagerly, lovingly watching the distant city editor from whom today—yes, this very day—may come that "good assignment." Something exciting. Good Lord, if they would only let him—

It is a dull day, yet there is a resistless movement of the commonplace which at last pulls nearly all these men from their trifling or their brooding and sends them out into the city, out into the slushy and gloom-fast streets, out into the enormous glittering skyscrapers, to run down little events. They scatter, with their various moods of hope, disgust, scorn, or vivacity, to thread their way through the city.

The office, emptied of the staff, retains only the "desk men." These are now a little relaxed. Not only has the day's program been laid down, as far as possible, but the first edition, which has furnished a few minutes of tension, is on the presses. From regions far below there comes a muffled thunder, a jarring that faintly shakes the desks. In the news-room silence, compared with the recent pecking of typewriters and murmur of voices, prevails. The desk men straighten up in their chairs, sigh, and stretch. One of them pulls from a drawer a thick novel and reads.

It is a pause. But during this pause life goes on, climaxes prepare. Something draws nearer.

The managing editor, a heavily-built being with harsh spectacles, prowls into the room, gazes about and halts, watched apprehensively by a benchful of small boys. He disregards the juvenile array and swings heavily, thoughtfully, over toward the desk of the news editor.

"What's doing?" he demands, in that voice whose cadences can convey so much wrath, so much bitterness—and so much sweetness.

"Nothing special."

"Humph!" exclaims the Old Man, and retires to his den.

III

The Old Man has officially stigmatized the day as dull.

Boredom is the word.

Take a score of keenly sensitized men, confront them with routine, and the result is boredom. However, they can endure this, just as they are able to stand severe and long-continued excitement. To those who most tremble with suspense or burn with pride there comes the profoundest lethargy; but they have learned to swim in it without impairment of the spirit. Here is a faculty which they have in common with musicians, actors, and other artists. These men in the news-room have traces of the creative temperament, which hibernates, then springs up with new vigor. In some of them it is faded, grown old, or hidden behind stoicism. But in the oldest and most morose of the "desk men" there lives a spark of dramatic instinct, which lights the weariest face at the coming of a "good story."

Nothing of the kind now animates them. They labor on in an incessancy of tasks which must be done at once, even though scarcely worth doing. They must be rapid and skillful without being driven by interest. Throughout the newspaper plant a finely-timed engine, deftly blended of the human and mechanical, is turning, turning. Everything must move: The grotesque arms of the linotypes, the lumpishly-moving tables of the stereotypers, the gigantic, glistening coils of the presses, the rolling sidewalks upon which the finished papers slide toward the delivery wagons. All must turn with the clock-tick. It makes no difference whether the day be dull or thrilling. The relentless machinery waits for its injections of human intelligence. The world waits for the news. And always, among these men in the newsroom, there is a dim sense of the mechanism forever at work below them, a tinge of fear lest, through some fault, there be a break in the process, a dreadful pause in the endless tune. So, driven by habit and by their sub-conscious perception of their membership in the whole activity of the building, they contribute by pencil-strokes, by order, by corrections on proofs, to the flow of this activity.

As the half-hours pass and the day mounts to its meridian, there is a tensing of effort. Almost casually, two editions have already been issued, inspected, and forgotten. But now one can feel the climb toward a greater enterprise, the "home edition," the daily bugbear whose tradition is that it must be more comprehensive and correct than either of its predecessors. There is no more lassitude along the copy-desks; the piles of unread manuscript mount too fast. The staff is back, for the most part, and the spatter of typewriters deluges the silence. Boys run by with clumsy steps. Bells ring. The air hisses in the pneumatic tubes. The long, low room echoes to a thousand movements, a thousand utterances. Yet, despite the *forte* of the news-room, one is aware of the *fortissimo* of the city itself. For outside of the newspaper office, as well as within it, the day is at its height. Sky-scrapers now are belching out lunch-hour crowds, and the shopping streets are filled with joyous, vivid streams of people. Messages from this turbulence reach the newspaper office; cries come across the roof tops; the symphony of the city, with its roars, whistles, bellowings, arrives modified but clear. And if one puts his ear to the wires he can fancy that he hears the shrill and terrible voices of a hundred other cities where life seethes, even though "nothing is happening." One has a vision of potentialities of achievement or of disaster in these agitated centers of life. Straight out of the seeming commonplace of their movement in pursuit of tasks or fun will emerge the dramatic shock that the news-room is waiting for. Something is bound to happen.

IV

Something does happen.

First there is the sharp outcry of the Associated Press telephone, distinct from all the other bell-signals. The telegraph editor picks up the receiver and listens. Without a quiver of lips or eyebrows he reaches for paper, and scrawls. The vigilant news editor sees the rigidity of his shoulders, the slight gleam of his eyes, and rises. The copy-readers look up. An instinct awakened by tiny signs, too tiny for the eye of laity, warns "the desk" that this bulletin has a high voltage.

The news editor stands reading as the hand of the telegraph editor traces:

"Washtn . . . bomb on steps . . . treasury building . . . 2 killed."

The telegraph editor hangs up the receiver. For an instant he and his chief stare into each other's eyes. But nothing is said. The implications of this message are self-evident.

"Ask Mr. Barlow to come here," the news editor murmurs to a boy.

While the boy skates nonchalantly off, the editor, with a hand that cannot keep pace with his brain, is writing notes that fly from his pad to distant parts of the building. Simultaneously he is calling earnestly on the house telephone for the circulation department.

Barlow, the make-up editor, enters, heavy-set, frowning at being called from his nearly-complete pages of the home edition. At his heels treads easily but ominously the Old Man, whose presence pervades the room like fate.

The news editor flies at Barlow and mutters to him in a paraphrase of the bulletin, which by this time is being masticated by a linotype machine. Barlow's frown vanishes. He gives an eager nod, seizes a just-written sheet of paper headed "eight-column line, rush extra," and takes it with him as he makes long, heavy strides toward the composing-room door. His mind's eye has mapped out a new first page. At the door he stumbles against a boy and leaves behind him an echo of brief profanity.

The Old Man is told the news.

"I thought it would happen some day," he remarked. He eyes calmly "the telegraph desk" where now two men are working frantically, while another takes more bulletins from the telephone. Elsewhere in the room there is little commotion. The usual group of reporters is arguing the usual topics. "Peck-peck" goes the Cub's typewriter, grinding out some trifle or other.

Suddenly the young city editor emerges from his nest of telephones and comes down the room at a half-trot.

"They've tried to blow up the federal building here," he snaps, with a half-joyous, half-bitter gleam in his eyes. He dashes back to his desk, followed by the shadowy bulk of the Old Man.

The news editor begins to swear, and laughs instead, having in mind Barlow and his forms. "This will finish him," he thinks, as he speeds toward the composing room. Out there he finds Barlow and his assistant under full steam "breaking up the paper," ordering gleaming stacks of type about, shouting at printers above the perpetual clackety-swish of the linotypes, crossing out and writing in words upon the "schedules" that name the leading articles for various pages. The coatless printers paw the type with their blackened fingers, chew tobacco, and register unconcern. Type lies strewn, in bundles of lines, all over the "stone." Long galleys of brass are piled up like cordwood. Up to the high, glass-roofed ceiling resounds the turmoil of the "stone." The battered clock points imperturbably to 12:05. And at 12:25 all this puzzle must be cleared.

Taking Barlow by the elbow, the news editor speaks in his ear.

The color surges into Barlow's face. Still speechless, he darts to the half-complete first-page "form," and roars at the printer whose hands are flying over its columns. The printer hears and nods. He must change everything. What of it? All in the day's work. But the composing-room foreman, sauntering up, tosses in the remark. "Tearin' up again? You'll never make it," and with a wave toward the clock, passes on.

"We've got to make it, Jim," the news editor cries after him. Then, like a man watching two boiling kettles at once, he hastens back to the news-room.

Within the last two minutes the news-room has been transformed in spirit. Everybody has straightened; everybody has caught the stroke. Who said newspaper work was monotonous? seems to shine from the faces. It is gorgeous. The telegraph editor and the city editor are in two separate whirlpools of movement. Boys rush at the telegraph editor and slam sheets of copy upon his desk; the man at the telephone shoves scribbled slips toward him. He rapidly assembles and groups these, discarding some, piecing others together, laboring with his whole mind to form a story sequential and lucid. A series of flashes are passing through his mind: "Doubt if they'll get this bulletin in. . . . There'll be an awful mess for the next edition." And farther back in his mind occur thoughts more private, such as: "That rumor the other day about the reds was right," and "I suppose the wrong man will be caught, as usual." But his routine brain cells, his hands, go on shaping, shaping. And save for an out-thrust lower lip he betrays no agitation.

The city editor is twice as busy as this. He has had to scratch off a dozen lines of copy for the home edition, to dispatch six men to the federal building, answer (and get rid of) three persons wanting to know if he was "posted," listen to general orders from the Old Man, alter a headline that does not "fit," and map out a sort of program for the rest of the day. His mind is ablaze with enterprises and pierced with apprehensions. Who knows but a rival paper has already beaten him? He will not be beaten. He sends out to every part of himself a desperate signal to function, to be alive. His tongue is dry; his voice threatens to scream. He is at bay, fighting an invincible alliance of enemies: The clock, his rivals, the tangle of things to do, his own rebellious nerves, the nerve reactions of everybody else. He calls upon his uttermost reserve. He is four men in one. He is enraged at life—but he is deliriously happy. And there flits through him a wan joke: "I suppose the police will call it a sewer-gas explosion." The joke, which goes unspoken, is extinguished by a wave of perception, vaguer than these words, but suggesting to him that society is a brutal and turbulent thing, and bringing to him, like a passing flash of the cinema, a picture of the federal building portico in ruins, and the bodies lying there.

Through all this pierces the realization that the home edition has gone to press. The turmoil around him is no less, but here is the face of his friend, the news editor, emerging from the delirium.

"How's it goin', George?"

"All right," he hears himself reply.

Wallace, the reporter, leans up against the desk.

"Well, boss," inquires Wallace with a subdued twinkle, "how much on the great Sir Scammon Scammonton? He says—"

The city editor becomes aware of Wallace, and halts him with:

"John, jump down to federal building . . . take taxi . . . forget about that damned lord—"

Wallace is off, murmuring quaintly: "I obey, boss, I obey."

City editor to news editor: "They think there are six dead down there. A delivery wagon was blown up. There are pieces of horse all over the street. The district attorney says—"

"We'll have to make four separate stories of it for the First Final. At least four—"

"I know. It's a big plot, of course. Oh, is that Billy on the wire? Give him here."

The news editor moves on, devoting a glance to the bowed backs of the local copy-readers, to whom the fury begun with the telegraph desk has now been transmitted. Their eyes bulge with the interest, the horror, of what they are reading. One counts with his fingers the number of letters required for a certain heading. A book that another, a placid, grey-haired man, was reading, has fallen to the floor, and lies open at the title page, "Growth of the Soil."

Reporters who have come in already from the explosion are mauling their typewriters, slamming the cylinders back and forth with a rattle like rifle fire. A constant yell of "Boy!" Dust, colored by the pale noon-day sunlight, swims, serene and beautiful above their heads. Murmurs, chucklings, imprecations mingle in a flow of sound; the expressions of the fever that has seized the staff. They are painting, painting. The picture will be hurled out into the streets, seen, and lost. All are artists now, co-operating on the big canvas of the First Final. They are instinctively making art of it, discarding, heightening and coloring. Yes, they color some things, so that the hasty reader can tell them as more important than others. Maybe they do not distort facts; they do not so much distort as rearrange. They suggest perspectives, and introduce good lighting for this tale of tales.

All the while, into their hands is being poured more material, and more. The wires say that the nation is aroused. "The White House has let it be known that. . . . " The wires sing with theories, conjectures, revelations. The tragedy here at the federal building is in the foreground. A notebook has been found among the rags of one of the corpses, with code words in it. Wallace is reading sentences from this book over the 'phone. The district attorney is giving out a long statement. Every minute a member of the staff enters with details which he regards as "bigger stuff than anything." Evidently the mystery of this story is deeper than we thought. It will be unraveling itself for days. We shall be pestered with it for days. What a plague! But what joy!

Meantime, behold it is two o'clock, and the First Final stares us in the face. Ah, here comes the Old Man. "The composing room is swamped." We thought so. "Throw away everything except explosion stuff." The market reports must go in uncorrected. The speech of a distinguished guest at a luncheon goes on the floor. The Cub has written five hundred words about scenes at hospitals and is told he is a fool.

The inexorable clock—the damnable, gliding clock. The waiting machines. The waiting world.

We are desperate men.

We go to the "stone" to make up the First Final. Once more, chaos; bigger heaps of galleys, greater muddles of type. Parts of stories are lost; parts of others are still lagging on the linotypes. We lose our heads, and quarrel. We become children, and say: "Who's blaming me for it?" "I told him to do it." "Good God, this gang is going to pieces."

The type pours to the "stone" from all sides. The pages lie, broken, hopeless.

This time we shall never "get out."

And suddenly we find that it is all done. The forms are full. The last one is being locked up, and slid into the outstretched hands of the stereotypers.

We glance at each other, wipe off sweat, and grin.

V

This is a splendid product of ours, after all. The boys are bringing in papers, staggering under the bundles. We spread them out on the desks, admire and criticize. It is scarcely possible we did this. Thirty minutes, twenty minutes, ago we were writing the words that now peer at us from the pages, faintly familiar creations that have arrayed themselves in a manner distinctively their own. It is all there as we planned it in our frenzy. The house has risen from that chaos at the "stone." The event that has shaken the country's nerves lies there embodied in types of varying blackness and size, making a structure with girders and gables, with foundations and flourishes. A structure nevertheless built to last but a day, to outlast scarcely even our pride in it.

Our pride in it is momentary. We are conscious that we have con-
quered. This feeling is confirmed when our rivals are brought in, and
their paltry efforts to keep pace with us are seen. But we are too wise,
or too weary, to gloat more than for that moment. Tomorrow may
snatch this triumph away from us. And besides—

It is the Old Man's voice:

"Look here, we say in this head that three wheels of the wagon were
blown off; but in the eye-witness account it says—"

And he lays a broad thumb upon the column.

Two or three men, among them the city editor, respectfully examine
the discrepancy.

"There's always something to spoil it all," grumbles the Old Man, and
bears his newspaper away, grasped in both hands, while the staff
exchanges rueful winks. The city editor slips on his coat and says
savagely to the news editor: "If I don't show up tomorrow you can
guess why." His eyes burn in his pale young face. He flings himself
out, biting off the end of a cigar. The eyes of the grey-haired copy-
reader follow him humorously, tenderly.

The news editor turns to the disposal of matters for the afternoon.
The greater part of the afternoon still remains. There are still "late
developments." There will be a "rush hour extra." The news editor
walks back through the room, remarking to the "desk" as he goes:
"Nobody off early today. We'll need all hands."

They look up, unamazed. Were it to go on forever, they would still
be unamazed.

VI

But at last it is five o'clock, and the very last extra of all has been
patched up, and there is nothing more to do.

Darkness has come again. It seems now to have been scarcely ten
minutes since the first of those alert figures entered through the
swinging door; but the evidences of a complete day are all about:
waste-paper ankle deep around the desks; waste-baskets crammed
with torn newspaper sheets; pencil-butts, proofs, crumpled notes.

The men, the last of them, are putting on hats and coats and de-
parting. They go wearily and sulkily. The emotional storm in which
they have been tossed has left them chilled. The more thrilling the
day, the more leaden its close. This product, conceived with such
skill and speed and evolved with such a fury of zeal, is already scarcely
more than waste-paper. The men tramp gloomily into the hall, turning
up the collars of their overcoats and peering into the shadows of the

gloomy corridor. They go down the elevator, grumbling, but still with a vestige of elation.

"Well, that was *some* day," they mutter.

"*Some* day," echo the dying voices of the linotypes.

"*Some* day," groan the presses from the basement.

The men, slackened in spirit, cynical about it all, exuding revolt, are happy in spite of everything. "*Some* day," to be sure. They will tell their wives and children about it. They will meet acquaintances who will respectfully ask their opinions, because they are newspaper men.

There are new furrows in their faces; but their youth is inextinguishable.

The grey-haired copy-reader, who is last to leave, watches them go, turns out a light or two, and slowly prepares for the street. And he thinks about these men, whom, in a way, he loves:

"I wonder what draws them into this game? I wonder why they keep at it, the game being what it is. I wonder what the fascination of news is. I wonder what news really is. . . .

"The continuousness of it all; the knowledge that no matter what we do today, we must do better tomorrow. . . .

"The unendurable boredom; the unendurable excitement. . . .

"Maybe we stay on because life is like that, and we get more of life here than somewhere else."

VII

The only lights remaining are two that burn dispiritedly at either end of the long room. The wires sleep again, oblivious of the sparkling but dreadful world. The battlefield is deserted.

Now enter two sad-faced, elderly males in soiled and shapeless clothing, carrying large sacks. Into these they dump contents of wastebaskets, and bundles of scraps. They seem very, very old and depressed. In and out among the desks they go, muttering to themselves, and clearing away the dull traces of the splendid task. These specters know nothing of the efforts or the victories just recorded. The voices of the city, the cries of newsboys, the tootings and tinklings of the streets, are nothing at all to these aged scavengers. Outlived . . . all outlived.

Having finished their funereal task, they go out, and the room is left to its memories, the wires to their slumber.

So ends the day.

A FREE PRESS

Can we have a "free press" when newspaper owners are millionaires and large employers of labor? A. J. Liebling, whose long-running section "The Wayward Press" appeared frequently in the New Yorker, *asks this and other questions of our newspapers. His perceptive, witty articles on the press are generally considered the finest collection of journalism criticism of our time.*

I THINK almost everybody will grant that if candidates for the United States Senate were required to possess ten million dollars, and for the House one million, the year-in-year-out level of conservation of those two bodies might be expected to rise sharply. We could still be said to have a freely elected Congress: anybody with ten million dollars (or one, if he tailored his ambition to fit his means) would be free to try to get himself nominated, and the rest of us would be free to vote for our favorite millionaires or even to abstain from voting. (This last right would mark our continued superiority over states where people are compelled to vote for the government slate.)

In the same sense, we have a free press today. (I am thinking of big-city and middling-city publishers as members of an upper and lower house of American opinion.) Anybody in the ten-million-dollar category is free to buy or found a paper in a great city like New York or Chicago, and anybody with around a million (plus a lot of sporting blood) is free to try it in a place of mediocre size like Worcester, Mass. As to us, we are free to buy a paper or not, as we wish.[1]

---

[1] *A Free and Responsible Press,* the published report of a committee headed by Robert Maynard Hutchins in 1947, says, "Although there is no such thing as a going price for a great city newspaper, it is safe to assume that it would cost somewhere between five and ten million dollars to build a new metropolitan daily to success. The investment required for a new newspaper in a medium-sized city is estimated at three-quarters of a million to several million." Prices have gone up very considerably since this was written. The rise underlines my thesis.

In a highly interesting book, *The First Freedom,* Morris Ernst has told the story of the increasing concentration of news outlets in the hands of a few people. There are less newspapers today than in 1909, and less owners in relation to the total number of papers. In 1909 there were 2,600; today 1,750.[2] Ernst refrains from any reflection on the quality of the ownership; he says merely that it is dangerous that so much power should be held by so few individuals. I will go one timid step further than Ernst and suggest that these individuals, because of their economic position, form an atypical group and share an atypical outlook.

The newspaper owner is a rather large employer of labor. I don't want to bore you with statistics, but one figure that I remember unhappily is 2,867, the number of us who lost jobs when the Pulitzers sold the *World* for salvage in 1931. He is nowadays forced to deal with unions in all departments of his enterprise, and he is as unlikely as any other employer to be on their side. As owner of a large and profitable business, he is opposed to government intervention in his affairs beyond the maintenance of the subsidy extended to all newspapers through second-class-mail rates. As an owner of valuable real estate, he is more interested in keeping the tax rate down than in any other local issue. (Newspaper crusades for municipal "reform" are almost invariable tax-paring expeditions.) A planned economy is abhorrent to him, and since every other nation in the world has now gone in for some form of economic planning, the publisher has become our number-one xenophobe. His "preference" for Socialist Britain over Communist Russia is only an inverse expression of relative dislike.[3] Because of publishers' wealth, they do not have to be slugged over

---

Earl L. Vance, in an article in the *Virginia Quarterly Review* (Summer 1945) cited in "Survival of a Free, Competitive Press," a publication of the Senate Committee on Small Businesses, says, "Even small-newspaper publishing is big business. *Time* magazine recently reported sale of the Massillon, Ohio, *Independent* (circulation 11,858 for 'around $400,000,' the Spartanburg, S.C. *Herald* (17,351) and *Journal* (8,678) for $750,000—all smaller dailies. In contrast, William Allen White paid only $3,000 for the Emporia *Gazette* in 1892. A metropolitan daily now represents an investment of many millions. Scripps-Howard in 1923 paid $6,000,000 for the same newspaper that had been offered in 1892 for $51,000; the Philadelphia *Inquirer* sold for $18,000,000 in 1930; the Kansas City *Star* for $11,000,000 in 1926."

I hadn't seen either of these publications before I wrote my Alumni Magazine article; I cite them here to show I wasn't dreaming my figures. The only recent instance I know of a man buying a newspaper for under five figures and making it go occurred in Las Vegas, Nevada. There in 1950, the typographical union struck the only paper. It was a long stubborn strike, and the unions started a small paper of their own, which lost so much money, for such a small strike, that they agreed to sell it to a young publicity man for gambling halls named Hank Greenspun for $1,000. Hank bought it and then found a bank account with $2,500 in it among the cash assets. He thus made an immediate profit of $1,500, which must be a record. Within three years Greenspun built it into a rough, spectacularly aggressive and quickly profitable newspaper, the *Sun,* and it is, or should be, a mighty moneymaker today. This was, however, possible only because Las Vegas, in a decade, has quadrupled its population, and the older paper remains without interest, a smalltown sheet. There was therefore created an instantaneous vacuum, and the *Sun* filled it. The same thing could happen in another boom town, as it used to in the Gold Rush days, but there has been only one Las Vegas in a half century.

2 Now 1,763 but the number of ownerships has decreased.

3 He likes Conservative Britain rather better, except for its Socialized Medicine.

the head by "anti-democratic organizations" to force them into using
their properties to form public opinion the N.A.M. approves. The gesture would be as redundant as twisting a nymphomaniac's arm to get her into bed.[4] I am delighted that I do not have to insinuate that they consciously allow their output to be shaped by their personal interests. Psychoanalytical after-dinner talk has furnished us with a lovely word for what they do: they rationalize. And once a man has convinced himself that what is good for him is good for the herd of his inferiors, he enjoys the best of two worlds simultaneously, and can shake hands with Bertie McCormick, the owner of the Chicago *Tribune.*[5]

The profit system, while it insures the predominant conservative coloration of our press, also guarantees that there will always be a certain amount of dissidence. The American press has never been monolithic, like that of an authoritarian state. One reason is that there is always important money to be made in journalism by standing up for the underdog (demogogically or honestly, so long as the technique is good). The underdog is numerous and prolific—another name for him is circulation. His wife buys girdles and baking powder and Literary Guild selections, and the advertiser has to reach her. News-papers as they become successful and more to the right leave room for newcomers to the left. Marshall Field's Chicago *Sun,* for example, has acquired 400,000 readers in five years, simply because the *Tribune,* formerly alone in the Chicago morning field, had gone so far to the right.[6] The fact that the *Tribune's* circulation has not been much affected indicates that the 400,000 had previous to 1941 been availing themselves of their freedom not to buy a newspaper. (Field himself illustrates another, less dependable, but nevertheless appreciable, factor in the history of the American press—the occasional occurrence of that economic sport, the maverick millionaire.) E. W. Scripps was the outstanding practitioner of the trade of founding newspapers to stand up for the common man. He made a tremendous success of it,

4 *A Free and Responsible Press,* that result of the collaboration of thirteen bigwigs, which I again cite lest you think I am flippant, says:

"The agencies of mass communication are big business, and their owners are big businessmen. . . . The press is a large employer of labor. . . . The newspapers alone have more than 150,000 employees. The press is connected with other big business through the advertising of these businesses, upon which it depends for the major part of its revenue. The owners of the press, like the owners of other big businesses, are bank directors, bank borrowers, and heavy taxpayers in the upper brackets.

"As William Allen White put it: 'Too often the publisher of an American newspaper has made his money in some other calling than journalism. He is a rich man seeking power and prestige. . . . And they all get the unconscious arrogance of conscious wealth.'

"Another highly respected editor, Erwin D. Canham of the *Christian Science Monitor,* thinks upper-bracket ownership and its big-business character important enough to stand at the head of his list of the 'shortcomings of today's American newspapers.'"

A Free and Responsible Press was published after the appearance of my article.

5 McCormick died in 1955. If he is not in Heaven he is eternally astonished.

6 The *Sun-Times,* having become almost equally prosperous, has by now, 1964, gone almost equally as far. Poor Mr. Field is dead and his son is a Republican. Mavericks seldom breed true.

owning about twenty of them when he died. The first James Gordon Bennett's *Herald* and Joseph Pulitzer's *World,* in the eighties and nineties, to say nothing of the Scripps-Howard *World-Telegram* in 1927, won their niche in New York as left-of-center newspapers and then bogged down in profits.

Another factor favorable to freedom of the press, in a minor way, is the circumstances that publishers sometimes allow a certain latitude to employees in departments in which they have no direct interest— movies, for instance, if the publisher is not keeping a movie actress, or horse shows, if his wife does not own a horse. Musical and theatrical criticism is less rigorously controlled than it is in Russia.[7]

The process by which the American press is pretty steadily revivified, and as steadily dies (newspapers are like cells in the body, some dying as others develop), was well described in 1911 by a young man named Joseph Medill Patterson, then an officer of the Chicago *Tribune,* who was destined himself to found an enormously successful paper, the *Daily News* of New York, and then within his own lifetime pilot it over the course he had foreshadowed. The quotation is from a play, *The Fourth Estate,* which Patterson wrote in his young discontent.

"Newspapers start when their owners are poor, and take the part of the people, and so they build up a large circulation, and, as a result, advertising. That makes them rich, and they begin most naturally, to associate with other rich men—they play golf with one, and drink whisky with another, and their son marries the daughter of a third. They forget all about the people, and then their circulation dries up, then their advertising, and then their paper becomes decadent."

Patterson was not "poor" when he came to New York eight years later to start the *News;* he had the McCormick-Patterson *Tribune* fortune behind him, and at his side Max Annenberg, a high-priced journalist condottiere who had already helped the *Tribune* win a pitched battle with Hearst in its own territory. But he was starting his paper from scratch, and he did it in the old dependable way, by taking up for the Common Man—and sticking with him until 1942, by which time the successful-man contagion got him and he threw his arms around unregenerated Cousin Bertie's neck. The *Tribune* in Chicago and the *News* in New York have formed a solid front ever since. Patterson was uninfluenced by golf, whisky, or social ambitions (he was a parsimonious, unsociable man who cherished an illusion that he had already hit the social peak). I think it is rather the complex of age, great wealth, a swelled head, and the necessity to believe in the

---

7 There is, however, no theater to write about, except in New York, and provincial critics of music lean over backward to be kind, because it is hard enough to get people to subscribe for concerts without underlining their deficiencies.

Heaven-decreed righteousness of a system which has permitted one to possess such power that turns a publisher's head. The whisky, weddings, yachts, horse shows, and the rest (golf no longer sounds so imposing as it did in 1911)[8] are symptoms rather than causes.

Unfortunately, circulations do not "dry up" quickly, nor advertising fall away overnight. Reading a newspaper is a habit which holds on for a considerable time. So the erstwhile for-the-people newspaper continues to make money for a while after it changes its course. With the New York *Herald* this phase lasted half a century. It would, moreover, be difficult to fix the exact hour or day at which the change takes place: it is usually gradual, and perceptible to those working on the paper before it becomes apparent to the outside public. At any given moment there are more profitable newspapers in being than new ones trying to come up, so the general tone of the press is predominantly, and I fear increasingly, reactionary. The difference between newspaper publishers' opinions and those of the public is so frequently expressed at the polls that it is unnecessary to insist on it here.

Don't get me wrong, though. I don't think that the battle is futile. I remember when I was a freshman, in 1920, listening to a lecture by Professor Mecklin in a survey course called, I think, Citizenship, in which he told how most of the newspapers had misrepresented the great steel strike of 1919. The only one that had told the truth, he said, as I remember it, was the old *World*. (I have heard since that the St. Louis *Post-Dispatch* was good, too, but he didn't mention it.) It was the first time that I really believed that newspapers lied about that sort of thing. I had heard of Upton Sinclair's book *The Brass Check*, but I hadn't wanted to read it because I had heard he was a "Bolshevik." I came up to college when I was just under sixteen, and the family environment was not exactly radical. But my reaction was that I wanted someday to work for the *World*, or for some other paper that *would* tell the truth. The *World* did a damned good job, on the strikes and on the Ku Klux Klan and on prohibition and prison camps (in Florida, not Silesia), and even though the second-generation Pulitzers let it grow namby-pamby and then dropped it in terror when they had had a losing year and were down to their last sixteen million, it had not lived in vain.

I think that anybody who talks often with people about newspapers nowadays must be impressed by the growing distrust of the information they contain. There is less a disposition to accept what they say than to try to estimate the probable truth on the basis of what they

There has been a revival since the first Eisenhower inaugural. I attribute it to the invention of the electric go-cart, in which, I am informed, the golfers now circulate, obviating ambulation. It sounds like the most fun since the goat-wagon.

say, like aiming a rifle that you know has a deviation to the right. Even a report in a Hearst newspaper can be of considerable aid in arriving at a deduction if you know enough about (a) Hearst policy, (b) the degree of abjectness of the correspondent signing the report.[9]

Every now and then I write a piece for the *New Yorker* under the heading of the Wayward Press (a title for the department invented by the late Robert Benchley when he started it early in the *New Yorker's* history). In this I concern myself not with big general thoughts about Trends (my boss wouldn't stand for such), but with the treatment of specific stories by the daily (chiefly New York) press. I am a damned sight kinder about newspapers than Wilcott Gibbs[10] is about the theater, but while nobody accuses him of sedition when he raps a play, I get letters calling me a little pal of Stalin when I sneer at the New York *Sun.* This reflects a pitch that newspaper publishers make to the effect that they are part of the great American heritage with a right to travel wrapped in the folds of the flag like a boll weevil in a cotton boll. Neither theatrical producers nor book publishers, apparently, partake of this sacred character. I get a lot more letters from people who are under the delusion that I can Do Something About It All. These reflect a general malaise on the part of the newspaper-reading public, which I do think will have some effect, though not, God knows, through me.

I believe that labor unions, citizens' organizations, and possibly political parties yet unborn are going to back daily papers. These will represent definite, undisguised points of view, and will serve as controls on the large profit-making papers expressing definite, ill-disguised points of view. The Labor Party's *Daily Herald,* in England, has been of inestimable value in checking the blather of the Beaverbrook-Kemsley-Rothermere newspapers of huge circulation. When one cannot get the truth from any one paper (and I do not say that it is an easy thing, even with the best will in the world, for any one paper to tell all the truth), it is valuable to read two with opposite policies to get an idea

---

9 Albert Camus, the brilliant and versatile young French novelist, playwright, and critic, who was also editor of *Combat,* a Paris daily, once had an idea for establishing a "control newspaper" that would come out one hour after the others with estimates of the percentage of truth in each of their stories, and with interpretation of how the stories were slanted. The way he explained it, it sounded possible. He said, "We'd have complete dossiers on the interests, policies, and idiosyncrasies of the owners. Then we'd have a dossier on every journalist in the world. The interest, prejudices, and quirks of the owner would equal Z. The prejudices, quirks, and private interests of the journalist, Y. Z times Y would give you X, the probable amount of truth in the story." He was going to make up dossiers on reporters by getting journalists he trusted to appraise men they had worked with. "I would have a card-index system," he said. "Very simple. We would keep the dossiers up to date as best we could, of course. But do people really want to know how much truth there is in what they read? Would they buy the control paper? That's the most difficult problem." Camus died without ever learning the answer to this question. His energies were dissipated in creative writing and we lost a great journalist.

10 Gibbs is dead too. Shortly after his funeral I got a letter from a *New Yorker* reader in Hico, Texas, previously unknown to me, that began: "Well, Gibbs is dead and soon the whole damn lot of you will be."

of what is really happening. I cannot believe that labor leaders are so stupid they will let the other side monopolize the press indefinitely.[11]

I also hope that we will live to see the endowed newspaper, devoted to the pursuit of daily truth as Dartmouth is to that of knowledge. I do not suppose that any reader of the *Magazine* believes that the test of a college is the ability to earn a profit on operations (with the corollary that making the profit would soon become the chief preoccupation of its officers). I think that a good newspaper is as truly an educational institution as a college, so I don't see why it should have to stake its survival on attracting advertisers of ball-point pens and tickets to Hollywood peep shows. And I think that private endowment would offer greater possibilities for a free press than state ownership (this is based on the chauvinistic idea that a place like Dartmouth can do a better job than a state university under the thumb of a Huey Long or Gene Talmadge). The hardest trick, of course, would be getting the chief donor of the endowment (perhaps a repentant tabloid publisher) to (*a*) croak, or (*b*) sign a legally binding agreement never to stick his face in the editorial rooms. The best kind of an endowment for a newspaper would be one made up of several large and many small or medium-sized gifts (the Dartmouth pattern again). Personally, I would rather leave my money for a newspaper than for a cathedral, a gymnasium, or even a home for streetwalkers with fallen arches, but I have seldom been able to assemble more than $4.17 at one time.[12]

■   ■   ■

To reread this paragraph makes me glum. Mergerism has hit Britain with a sudden rush; the *News-Chronicle* is gone and the *Herald* looks to be for it.

Professor Michael E. Choukas, of the Dartmouth faculty, summing up after the last article of the Public Opinion in a Democracy series, commented: "Mr. Liebling's 'endowed newspaper' would probably be free from direct pressure, but it would be unable to avoid the indirect efforts of the propagandists." I think that Professor Choukas, a sociologist who has specialized in the study of propaganda, has developed an exaggerated respect for the opposition. Albert Camus's plan for the "control newspaper," which I have briefly described in another footnote, is an example of the ingenuity a good newspaperman can bring to bear, and men like Vic Bernstein, Paul Sifton, and Edmund Taylor in this country (to cite only a few—there are hundreds of others) would certainly bring into the ring with them more perspicacity than anybody the National Association of Manufacturers could hire. A man who thinks he can fool other men is always a little a fool himself. His assumption that he can do it presupposes a foolish vanity— like that of the recidivist con man who spends most of his life in jail. His contempt for the truth marks him as a bit sub-human. Professor Choukas did not mention my hopes for strong labor papers.

The professor's own remedy for the dilemma, however, is worthy of citation. I hope somebody makes a good hard try at it.

"I frankly do not believe that any indirect assault would have much effect as a check against those who deliberately set out to mislead us," he wrote. "A direct attack could be launched against them by a privately endowed, independent agency whose main task would consist of compiling a list of all the propaganda groups in the country, analyzing their techniques, discovering their goals, and releasing the available information to government officials, to men responsible for our channels of communication, to men who measure public opinion, to colleges and universities, and to those pathetically few groups in the country who have undertaken to fight the battle of Democracy in a positive manner.

"This I feel should be done before our crisis reaches climactic proportions—before the next depression."

The above piece, written 14 years ago, was in manner laboriously offhand, but represented my serious thought. I erred badly on the side of optimism. The postwar euphoria that lingered in the air like fall-out must have trapped me. There has been no new competition in any large American city since the piece was written, and now it seems infinitely less likely that there ever will be.

The period between the two wars, while it marked a great diminution in the number of newspapers in New York, had brought at least one tremendously successful newcomer, the *Daily News,* which changed the whole physiognomy of Metropolitan journalism. When I wrote in 1947 the two Marshall Field entries, *PM* in New York and the *Sun* (the *Sun-Times* to be) in Chicago, were both still in there battling. *PM,* which was destined to fail, had been founded in 1940, and the *Sun,* fated to succeed financially, had begun in 1942. It did not seem to me, therefore, that the times already precluded new starts, although, as I noted, they were harder than before.

The suggestions I made about where new papers might find sponsors now sound infantile, but at the time I thought, wrongly, that labor retained some of the intelligence and coherence of the Roosevelt days, and it seemed to me not inconceivable that some financial Megabelodon might fancy a good newspaper as a more distinctive memorial than the habitual foundation for research into some disease that had annoyed the testator during life. (These bequests always seem to me to mark a vengeful nature, and the viruses they are aimed at profit by them almost as much as the doctors. They eat tons of cultures, play with white rats, and develop resistance by constant practice, as slum children learn to get out of the way of automobiles.) Megabelodon, however, although a huge creature, had a brain cavity about as big as the dime slot on a telephone coin box, and most men who could afford to endow a newspaper seeem to be rigged the same way.

Silliest of all, as I read back now, is the line about the profit system guaranteeing a certain amount of dissidence. This shows, on my part, an incurable weakness for judging the future by the past, like the French generals who so charmed me in 1939. I still believe that "there is always important money to be made by standing up for the under-dog," but the profit system implies a pursuit of *maximum profit*—for the shareholders' sake, distasteful though it may be. That it is theoretically possible to make money by competition in the newspaper field is therefore immaterial, since there is a great deal more money to be made by

a) Selling out and pocketing a capital gain

b) Buying the other fellow out and then sweating the serfs. . . .

Warren Breed
SOCIAL CONTROL IN THE NEWS ROOM

*Is the news we read in our daily papers slanted? If so, who is responsible for
the slanting? The owner? The editor? The reporter himself? Dr. Warren Breed,
a sociologist at Tulane University, examines the complexities of newspaper
objectivity and contends that slanting, if any, is usually the result of subtle
rather than overt pressures.*

TOP leaders in formal organizations are makers of policy, but they
must also secure and maintain conformity to that policy at lower
levels. The situation of the newspaper publisher is a case in point.
As owner or representative of ownership, he has the nominal right
to set the paper's policy and see that staff activities are coordinated
so that the policy is enforced. In actuality the problem of control is
less simple, as the literature of "human relations" and informal group
studies and of the professions[1] suggests.

Ideally, there would be no problem of either "control" or "policy" on
the newspaper in a full democracy. The only controls would be the
nature of the event and the reporter's effective ability to describe it.
In practice, we find the publisher does set news policy, and this policy
is usually followed by members of his staff. Conformity is *not* automatic, however, for three reasons: (1) the existence of ethical journalistic norms; (2) the fact that staff subordinates (reporters, etc.)
tend to have more "liberal" attitudes (and therefore perceptions) than
the publisher and could invoke the norms to justify anti-policy writing;
and (3) the ethical taboo preventing the publisher from commanding

See, for instance, F. J. Roethlisberger and William J. Dickson, *Management and the Worker*
(Cambridge: Harvard University Press, 1947), and Logan Wilson, *The Academic Man* (New
York: Oxford University Press, 1942).

subordinates to follow policy. How policy comes to be maintained, and where it is bypassed, is the subject of this paper.

Several definitions are required at this point. As to personnel, "newsmen" can be divided into two main categories. "Executives" include the publisher and his editors. "Staffers" are reporters, rewrite men, copyreaders, etc. In between there may be occasional city editors or wire editors who occupy an interstitial status. "Policy" may be defined as the more or less consistent orientation shown by a paper, not only in its editorial but in its news columns and headlines as well, concerning selected issues and events. "Slanting" almost never means prevarication. Rather, it involves omission, differential selection, and preferential placement, such as "featuring" a pro-policy item, "burying" an anti-policy story in an inside page, etc. "Professional norms" are of two types: technical norms deal with the operations of efficient news-gathering, writing, and editing; ethical norms embrace the newsman's obligation to his readers and to his craft and include such ideals as responsibility, impartiality, accuracy, fair play, and objectivity.[2]

Every newspaper has a policy, admitted or not.[3] One paper's policy may be pro-Republican, cool to labor, antagonistic to the school board, etc. The principal areas of policy are politics, business, and labor; much of it stems from considerations of class. Policy is manifested in "slanting." Just what determines any publisher's policy is a large question and will not be discussed here. Certainly, however, the publisher has much say (often in veto form) in both long-term and immediate policy decisions (which party to support, whether to feature or bury a story of imminent labor trouble, how much free space to give "news" of advertisers' doings, etc.) Finally, policy is covert, due to the existence of ethical norms of journalism; policy often contravenes these norms. No executive is willing to risk embarrassment by being accused of open commands to slant a news story.

While policy is set by the executives, it is clear that they cannot personally gather and write the news by themselves. They must delegate these tasks to staffers, and at this point the attitudes or interests of staffers may—and often do—conflict with those of the executives.[4]

2 The best-known formal code is The Canons of Journalism, of the American Society of Newspaper Editors.

3 It is extremely difficult to measure the extent of objectivity or bias. One recent attempt is reported in Nathan B. Blumberg, *One-Party Press?* (Lincoln: University of Nebraska Press, 1954), which gives a news count for 35 papers' performance in the 1952 election campaign. He concluded that 18 of the papers showed "no evidence of partiality," 11 showed "no conclusive evidence of partiality," and 6 showed partiality. His interpretations, however, are open to argument. A different interpretation could conclude that while about 16 showed little or no partiality, the rest did. It should be noted, too, that there are different areas of policy depending on local conditions. The chief difference occurs in the deep South, where frequently there is no "Republican" problem and no "union" problem over which the staff can be divided. Color becomes the focus of policy.

4 This condition, pointed out in a lecture by Paul F. Lazarsfeld, formed the starting point for the present study.

Of 72 staffers interviewed, 42 showed that they held more liberal views than those contained in their publisher's policy; 27 held similar views, and only 3 were more conservative. Similarly, only 17 of 61 staffers said they were Republicans.[5] The discrepancy is more acute when age (and therefore years of newspaper experience) is held constant. Of the 46 staffers under 35 years of age, 34 showed more liberal orientations; older men had apparently "mellowed." It should be noted that data as to intensity of attitudes are lacking. Some staffers may disagree with policy so mildly that they conform and feel no strain. The present essay is pertinent only insofar as dissident newsmen are forced to make decisions from time to time about their relationship to policy.[6]

We will now examine more closely the workings of the newspaper staff. The central question will be: How is policy maintained, despite the fact that it often contravenes journalistic norms, that staffers often personally disagree with it, and that executives cannot legitimately command that it be followed? The frame of reference will be that of functional analysis, as embodied in Merton's paradigm.[7]

The present data come from the writer's newspaper experience and from intensive interviews with some 120 newsmen, mostly in the northeastern quarter of the country. The sample was not random and no claim is made for representativeness, but on the other hand no paper was selected or omitted purposely and in no case did a newsman refuse the request that he be interviewed. The newspapers were chosen to fit a "middle-sized" group, defined as those with 10,000 to 100,000 daily circulation. Interviews averaged well over an hour in duration.[8]

There is an "action" element inherent in the present subject—the practical democratic need for "a free and responsible press" to inform citizens about current issues. Much of the criticism of the press stems

5 Similar findings were made about Washington correspondents in Leo C. Rosten, *The Washington Correspondents* (New York: Harcourt, Brace, 1937). Less ideological conflict was found in two other studies: Francis V. Prugger, "Social Composition and Training of the Milwaukee Journal News Staff," *Journalism Quarterly*, 18 (September, 1941), 231–44, and Charles E. Swanson, "The Mid-City Daily" (Ph.D. Dissertation, State University of Iowa, 1948). Possible reasons for the gap is that both papers studied were perhaps above average in objectivity; executives were included with staffers in computations; and some staffers were doubtless included who did not handle policy news.

6 It is not being argued that "liberalism" and objectivity are synonymous. A liberal paper (e.g., *PM*) can be biased too, but it is clear that few liberal papers exist among the many conservative ones. It should also be stressed that much news is not concerned with policy and is therefore probably unbiased.

7 Robert K. Merton, *Social Theory and Social Structure* (Glencoe: Free Press, 1949), esp. pp. 49–61. Merton's elements will not be explicitly referred to but his principal requirements are discussed at various points.

8 The data are taken from Warren Breed, "The Newspaperman, News and Society" (Ph.D. dissertation, Columbia University, 1952). Indebtedness is expressed to William L. Kolb and Robert C. Stone, who read the present manuscript and provided valuable criticisms and suggestions.

from the slanting induced by the bias of the publisher's policy.[9] This criticism is often directed at flagrant cases such as the Hearst press, the *Chicago Tribune,* and New York tabloids, but also applies in lesser degree, to the more conventional press. The description of mechanisms of policy maintenance may suggest why this criticism is often fruitless, at least in the short-run sense.

HOW THE STAFFER LEARNS POLICY

The first mechanism promoting conformity is the "socialization" of the staffer with regard to the norms of his job. When the new reporter starts work he is not told what policy is. Nor is he ever told. This may appear strange, but interview after interview confirmed the condition. The standard remark was "Never in my ____ years on this paper, have I ever been told how to slant a story." No paper in the survey had a "training" program for its new men; some issue a "style" book; but this deals with literary style, not policy. Further, newsmen are busy and have little time for recruit training. Yet all but the newest staffers know what policy is.[10] On being asked, they say they learn it "by osmosis." Sociologically, this means they become socialized and "learn the ropes" like a neophyte in any subculture. Basically, the learning of policy is a process by which the recruit discovers and internalizes the rights and obligations of his status and its norms and values. He learns to anticipate what is expected of him so as to win rewards and avoid punishments. Policy is an important element of the newsroom norms, and he learns it in much the following way.

The staffer reads his own paper every day; some papers *require* this. It is simple to diagnose the paper's characteristics. Unless the staffer is naïve or unusually independent, he tends to fashion his own stories after others he sees in the paper. This is particularly true of the newcomer. The news columns and editorials are a guide to the local norms. Thus a southern reporter notes that Republicans are treated in a "different" way in his paper's news columns than Democrats. The news about whites and Negroes is also of a distinct sort. Should he then write about one of these groups, his story will tend to reflect what he has come to define as standard procedure.

Certain editorial actions taken by editors and older staffers also serve as controlling guides. "If things are blue-pencilled consistently," one

---

9 For a summary description of this criticism, see Commission on the Freedom of the Press, *A Free and Responsible Press* (Chicago: University of Chicago Press, 1947), chap. 4.

10 While the concept of policy is crucial to this analysis, it is not to be assumed that newsmen discuss it fully. Some do not even use the word in discussing how their paper is run. To this extent, policy is a latent phenomenon; either the staffer has no reason to contemplate policy or he chooses to avoid so doing. It may be that one strength of policy is that it has become no more manifest to the staffers who follow it.

reporter said, "you learn he [the editor] has a prejudice in that re-gard."[11] Similarly an executive may occasionally reprimand a staffer for policy violation. From our evidence, the reprimand is frequently oblique, due to the covert nature of policy, but learning occurs never-theless. One staffer learned much through a series of incidents:

I heard [a union] was going out on strike, so I kept on it; then the boss said something about it, and well—I took the hint and we had less coverage of the strike forming. It was easier that way. We lost the story, but what can you do?

We used a yarn on a firm that was coming to town, and I got dragged out of bed for that. The boss is interested in this industrial stuff—we have to clear it all through him. He's an official in the Chamber. So . . . after a few times, it's irritating, so I get fed up. I try to figure out what will work best. I learn to try and guess what the boss will want.

In fairness it should be noted that this particular publisher was one of the most dictatorial encountered in the study. The pattern of control through reprimand, however, was found consistently. Another staffer wrote, on his own initiative, a series about discrimination against Jews at hotel resorts. "It was the old 'Gentlemen's Agreement' stuff, docu-mented locally. The boss called me in . . . didn't like the stuff . . . the series never appeared. You start to get the idea. . . ."

Note that the boss does not "command"; the direction is more subtle. Also, it seems that most policy indications from executives are nega-tive. They veto by a nod of the head, as if to say, "Please don't rock the boat." Exceptions occur in the "campaign" story, which will be discussed later. It is also to be noted that punishment is implied if policy is not followed.

Staffers also obtain guidance from their knowledge of the charac-teristics, interests, and affiliations of their executives. This knowledge can be gained in several ways. One is gossip. A reporter said: "Do we gossip about the editors? Several of us used to meet—somewhere off the beaten path—over a beer—and talk for an hour. We'd rake 'em over the coals."

Another point of contact with executives is the news conference (which on middle-sized papers is seldom *called* a news conference), wherein the staffer outlines his findings and executives discuss how to shape the story. The typical conference consists of two persons, the reporter and the city editor, and can amount to no more than a few words. (Reporter: "One hurt in auto accident uptown." City editor: "Okay, keep it short.") If policy is at stake, the conference

---

1 Note that such executives' actions as blue-pencilling play not only the manifest function of preparing the story for publication but also the latent one of steering the future action of the staffer.

may involve several executives and require hours of consideration. From such meetings, the staffer can gain insight through what is said and what is not said by executives. It is important to say here that policy is not stated explicitly in the news conference nor elsewhere, with few exceptions. The news conference actually deals mostly with journalistic matters, such as reliability of information, newsworthiness, possible "angles," and other news tactics.

Three other channels for learning about executives are house organs (printed for the staff by syndicates and larger papers), observing the executive as he meets various leaders and hearing him voice an opinion. One staffer could not help but gain an enduring impression of his publisher's attitudes in this incident:

I can remember [him] saying on election night [1948], when it looked like we had a Democratic majority in both houses, "My God, this means we'll have a labor government." [Q. How did he say it?] He had a real note of alarm in his voice; you couldn't miss the point that he'd prefer the Republicans.

It will be noted that in speaking of "how" the staffer learns policy, there are indications also as to "why" he follows it.

REASONS FOR CONFORMING TO POLICY

There is no one factor which creates conformity-mindedness, unless we resort to a summary term such as "institutionalized statuses" or "structural roles." Particular factors must be sought in particular cases. The staffer must be seen in terms of his status and aspirations, the structure of the newsroom organization and of the larger society. He also must be viewed with reference to the operations he performs through his workday, and their consequences for him. The following six reasons appear to stay the potentially intransigent staffer from acts of deviance—often, if not always.[12]

1. Institutional authority and sanctions. The publisher ordinarily owns the paper and from a purely business standpoint has the right to expect obedience of his employees. He has the power to fire or demote for transgressions. This power, however, is diminished markedly in actuality by three facts. First, the newspaper is not conceived as a purely business enterprise, due to the protection of the First Amendment and a tradition of professional public service. Secondly,

12 Two cautions are in order here. First, it will be recalled that we are discussing not all news, but only policy news. Secondly, we are discussing only staffers who are potential non-conformers. Some agree with policy; some have no views on policy matters; others do not write policy stories. Furthermore, there are strong forces in American society which cause many individuals to choose harmonious adjustment (conformity) in any situation, regardless of the imperatives. See Erich Fromm, *Escape from Freedom* (New York: Farrar and Rinehart, 1941), and David Riesman, *The Lonely Crowd* (New Haven: Yale University Press, 1950).

firing is a rare phenomenon on newspapers. For example, one editor said he had fired two men in 12 years; another could recall four firings in his 15 years on that paper. Thirdly, there are severance pay clauses in contracts with the American Newspaper Guild (CIO). The only effective causes for firing are excessive drunkenness, sexual dalliance, etc. Most newspaper unemployment apparently comes from occasional economy drives on large papers and from total suspensions of publication. Likewise, only one case of demotion was found in the survey. It is true, however, that staffers still fear punishment; the myth has the errant star reporter taken off murders and put on obituaries —"the Chinese torture chamber" of the newsroom. Fear of sanctions, rather than their invocation, is a reason for conformity, but not as potent a one as would seem at first glance.

Editors, for their part, can simply ignore stories which might create deviant actions, and when this is impossible, can assign the story to a "safe" staffer. In the infrequent case that an anti-policy story reaches the city desk, the story is changed; extraneous reasons, such as the pressure of time and space, are given for the change.[13] Finally, the editor may contribute to the durability of policy by insulating the publisher from policy discussion. He may reason that the publisher would be embarrassed to hear of conflict over policy and the resulting bias, and spare him the resulting uneasiness; thus the policy remains not only covert but undiscussed and therefore unchanged.[14]

2. Feelings of obligation and esteem for superiors. The staffer may feel obliged to the paper for having hired him. Respect, admiration, and gratitude may be felt for certain editors who have perhaps schooled him, "stood up for him," or supplied favors of a more paternalistic sort. Older staffers who have served as models for newcomers or who have otherwise given aid and comfort are due return courtesies. Such obligations and warm personal sentiments toward superiors play a strategic role in the pull to conformity.

3. Mobility aspirations. In response to a question about ambition, all the younger staffers showed wishes for status achievement. There was agreement that bucking policy constituted a serious bar to this goal. In practice, several respondents noted that a good tactic toward advancement was to get "big" stories on Page One; this automatically

Excellent illustration of this tactic is given in the novel by an experienced newspaperwoman: Margaret Long, *Affair of the Heart* (New York: Random House, 1953), chap. 10. This chapter describes the framing of a Negro for murder in a middle-sized southern city, and the attempt of a reporter to tell the story objectively.

The insulation of one individual or group from another is a good example of social (as distinguished from psychological) mechanisms to reduce the likelihood of conflict. Most of the factors inducing conformity could likewise be viewed as social mechanisms. See Talcott Parsons and Edward A. Shils, "Values, Motives and Systems of Action," in Parsons and Shils (eds.), *Toward a General Theory of Action* (Cambridge: Harvard University Press, 1951), pp. 223–30.

means no tampering with policy. Further, some staffers see news-papering as a "stepping stone" job to more lucrative work: public relations, advertising, free-lancing, etc. The reputation for troublemaking would inhibit such climbing.

A word is in order here about chances for upward mobility. Of 51 newsmen aged 35 or more, 32 were executives. Of 50 younger men, 6 had reached executive posts and others were on their way up with such jobs as wire editors, political reporters, etc. All but five of these young men were college graduates, as against just half of their elders. Thus there is no evidence of a "break in the skill hierarchy" among newsmen.

4. Absence of conflicting group allegiance. The largest formal organization of staffers is the American Newspaper Guild. The Guild, much as it might wish to, has not interfered with internal matters such as policy. It has stressed business unionism and political interests external to the newsroom. As for informal groups, there is no evidence available that a group of staffers has ever "ganged up" on policy.

5. The pleasant nature of the activity.

a. *In-groupness in the newsroom.* The staffer has a low formal status vis-à-vis executives, but he is not treated as a "worker." Rather, he is a co-worker with executives; the entire staff cooperates congenially on a job they all like and respect: getting the news. The newsroom is a friendly, first-namish place. Staffers discuss stories with editors on a give-and-take basis. Top executives with their own offices sometimes come out and sit in on newsroom discussions.[15]

b. *Required operations are interesting.* Newsmen like their work. Few voiced complaints when given the opportunity to gripe during interviews. The operations required—witnessing, interviewing, briefly mulling the meanings of events, checking facts, writing—are not onerous.

c. *Non-financial perquisites.* These are numerous: the variety of experience, eye-witnessing significant and interesting events, being the first to know, getting "the inside dope" denied laymen, meeting and sometimes befriending notables and celebrities (who are well-advised to treat newsmen with deference). Newsmen are close to big decisions without having to make them; they touch power without being re-

---

15 Further indication that the staffer-executive relationship is harmonious came from answers to the question, "Why do you think newspapermen are thought to be cynical?" Staffers regularly said that newsmen are cynical because they get close enough to stark reality to see the ills of their society and the imperfections of its leaders and officials. Only two of 40 staffers took the occasion to criticize their executives and the enforcement of policy. This displacement, or lack of strong feelings against executives, can be interpreted to bolster the hypothesis of staff solidarity. (It further suggests that newsmen tend to analyze their society in terms of personalities, rather than institutions comprising a social and cultural system.)

sponsible for its use. From talking with newsmen and reading their books, one gets the impression that they are proud of being newsmen.[16] There are tendencies to exclusiveness within news ranks, and intimations that such near out-groups as radio newsmen are entertainers, not real newsmen. Finally, there is the satisfaction of being a member of a live-wire organization dealing with important matters. The newspaper is an "institution" in the community. People talk about it and quote it; its big trucks whiz through town; its columns carry the tidings from big and faraway places, with pictures.

Thus, despite his relatively low pay, the staffer feels, for all these reasons, an integral part of a going concern. His job morale is high. Many newsmen could qualify for jobs paying more money in advertising and public relations, but they remain with the newspaper.

6. News becomes a value. Newsmen define their job as producing a certain quantity of what is called "news" every 24 hours. This is to be produced *even though nothing much has happened.* News is a continuous challenge, and meeting this challenge is the newsman's job. He is rewarded for fulfilling this, his manifest function. A consequence of this focus on news as a central value is the shelving of a strong interest in objectivity at the point of policy conflict. Instead of mobilizing their efforts to establish objectivity over policy as the criterion for performance, their energies are channelled into getting more news. The demands of competition (in cities where there are two or more papers) and speed enhance this focus. Newsmen do talk about ethics, objectivity, and the relative worth of various papers, but not when there is news to get. News comes first, and there is always news to get.[17] They are not rewarded for analyzing the social structure, but for getting news. It would seem that this instrumental orientation diminishes their moral potential. A further consequence of this pattern is that the harmony between staffers and executives is cemented by their common interest in news. Any potential conflict between the two groups, such as slowdowns occurring among informal work groups in industry, would be dissipated to the extent that news is a positive value. The newsroom solidarity is thus reinforced.

The six factors promote policy conformity. To state more exactly how policy is maintained would be difficult in view of the many variables contained in the system. The process may be somewhat better under-

16 There is a sizable myth among newsmen about the attractiveness of their calling. For example, the story: "Girl: 'My, you newspapermen must have a fascinating life. You meet such interesting people.' Reporter: 'Yes, and most of them are newspapermen.'" For a further discussion, see Breed, *op. cit.*, chap. 17.

17 This is a variant of the process of "displacement of goals," newsmen turning to "getting news" rather than to seeking data which will enlighten and inform their readers. The dysfunction is implied in the nation's need not for more news but for better news—quality rather than quantity. See Merton, *op. cit.*, "Bureaucratic Structure and Personality." pp. 154–55.

stood, however, with the introduction of one further concept—the reference group.[18] The staffer, especially the new staffer, identifies himself through the existence of these six factors with the executives and veteran staffers. Although not yet one of them, he shares their norms, and thus his performance comes to resemble theirs. He conforms to the norms of policy rather than to whatever personal beliefs he brought to the job, or to ethical ideals. All six of these factors function to encourage reference group formation. Where the allegiance is directed toward legitimate authority, that authority has only to maintain the equilibrium within limits by the prudent distribution of rewards and punishments. The reference group itself, which has as its "magnet" element the elite of executives and old staffers, is unable to change policy to a marked degree because first, it is the group charged with carrying out policy, and second, because the policy maker, the publisher, is often insulated on the delicate issue of policy.

In its own way, each of the six factors contributes to the formation of reference group behavior. There is almost no firing, hence a steady expectation of continued employment. Subordinates tend to esteem their bosses, so a convenient model group is present. Mobility aspirations (when held within limits) are an obvious promoter of inter-status bonds as is the absence of conflicting group loyalties with their potential harvest of cross pressures. The newsroom atmosphere is charged with the related factors of in-groupness and pleasing nature of the work. Finally, the agreement among newsmen that their job is to fasten upon the news, seeing it as a value in itself forges a bond across status lines.

As to the six factors, five appear to be relatively constant, occurring on all papers studied. The varying factor is the second: obligation and esteem held by staffers for executive and older staffers. On some papers, this obligation-esteem entity was found to be larger than on others. Where it was large, the paper appeared to have two characteristics pertinent to this discussion. First, it did a good conventional job of news-getting and news-publishing, and second, it had little difficulty over policy. With staffers drawn toward both the membership and the reference groups, organization was efficient. Most papers are like this. On the few smaller papers where executives and older staffers are not respected, morale is spotty; staffers withhold enthusiasm from their stories, they cover their beats perfunctorily, they wish for a job on a better paper, and they are apathetic and sometimes hostile to policy. Thus the obligation-esteem factor seems to be the

18 Whether group members acknowledge it or not, "if a person's attitudes are influenced by a set of norms which he assumes that he shares with other individuals, those individuals constitute for him a reference group." Theodore M. Newcomb, *Social Psychology* (New York: Dryden, 1950), p. 225. Williams states that reference group formation may segment large organizations; in the present case, the reverse is true, the loyalty of subordinates going to their "friendly" superiors and to the discharge of technical norms such as getting news. See Robin M. Williams, *American Society* (New York: Knopf, 1951), p. 476.

active variable in determining not only policy conformity, but morale and good news performance as well.

SITUATIONS PERMITTING DEVIATION

Thus far it would seem that the staffer enjoys little "freedom of the press." To show that this is an oversimplification, and more important, to suggest a kind of test for our hypothesis about the strength of policy, let us ask: "What happens when a staffer *does* submit an anti-policy story?" We know that this happens infrequently, but what follows in these cases?

The process of learning policy crystallizes into a process of social control, in which deviations are punished (usually gently) by reprimand, cutting one's story, the withholding of friendly comment by an executive, etc. For example, it is punishment for a staffer when the city editor waves a piece of his copy at him and says, "Joe, don't *do* that when you're writing about the mayor." In an actual case, a staffer acting as wire editor was demoted when he neglected to feature a story about a "sacred cow" politician on his paper. What can be concluded is that when an executive sees a clearly anti-policy item, he blue-pencils it, and this constitutes a lesson for the staffer. Rarely does the staffer persist in violating policy; no such case appeared in all the interviews. Indeed, the best-known cases of firing for policy reasons— Ted O. Thackrey and Leo Huberman—occurred on liberal New York City dailies, and Thackrey was an editor, not a staffer.

Now and then cases arise in which a staffer finds his anti-policy stories printed. There seems to be no consistent explanation for this, except to introduce two more specific subjects dealing first, with the staffer's career line, and second, with particular empirical conditions associated with the career line. We can distinguish three stages through which the staffer progresses. First, there is the cub stage, the first few months or years in which the new man learns techniques and policy. He writes short, non-policy stories, such as minor accidents, meeting activity, the weather, etc. The second, or "wiring-in" stage, sees the staffer continuing to assimilate the newsroom values and to cement informal relationships. Finally there is the "star" or "veteran" stage, in which the staffer typically defines himself as a full, responsible member of the group, sees its goals as his, and can be counted on to handle policy sympathetically. [19]

To further specify the conformity-deviation problem, it must be understood that newspapering is a relatively complex activity. The newsman

[9] Does the new staffer, fresh from the ideals of college, really "change his attitudes"? It would seem that attitudes about socio-economic affairs need not be fixed, but are capable of shifting with the situation. There are arguments for and against any opinion; in the atmosphere of the newsroom the arguments "for" policy decisions are made to sound adequate, especially as these are evoked by the significant others in the system.

is responsible for a range of skills and judgments which are matched only in the professional and entrepreneurial fields. Oversimplifications about policy rigidity can be avoided if we ask, *"Under what conditions can the staffer defy or bypass policy?"* We have already seen that staffers are free to argue news decisions with executives in brief "news conferences," but the arguments generally revolve around points of "newsiness," rather than policy as such.[20] Five factors appear significant in the area of the reporter's power to bypass policy.

1. The norms of policy are not always entirely clear, just as many norms are vague and unstructured. Policy is covert by nature and has large scope. The paper may be Republican, but standing only lukewarm for Republican Candidate A who may be too "liberal" or no friend of the publisher. Policy, if worked out explicitly, would have to include motivations, reasons, alternatives, historical developments, and other complicating material. Thus a twilight zone permitting a range of deviation appears.[21]

2. Executives may be ignorant of particular facts, and staffers who do the leg (and telephone) work to gather news can use their superior knowledge to subvert policy. On grounds of both personal belief and professional codes, the staffer has the option of selection at many points. He can decide whom to interview and whom to ignore, what questions to ask, which quotations to note, and, on writing the story, which items to feature (with an eye toward the headline), which to bury, and in general what tone to give the several possible elements of the story.

3. In addition to the "squeeze" tactic exploiting executives' ignorance of minute facts, the "plant" may be employed. Although a paper's policy may proscribe a certain issue from becoming featured, a staffer, on getting a good story about that issue may "plant" it in another paper or wire service through a friendly staffer and submit it to his own editor, pleading the story is now too big to ignore.

4. It is possible to classify news into four types on the basis of source of origination. These are: the policy or campaign story, the assigned story, the beat story, and the story initiated by the staffer. The staffer's autonomy is larger with the latter than the former types. With the campaign story (build new hospital, throw rascals out, etc.), the staffer is working directly under executives and has little leeway. An assigned story is handed out by the city editor and thus will rarely hit policy head on, although the staffer has some leverage of selection. When we come to the beat story, however, it is clear that the function of the re-

20 The fullest treatment of editor-reporter conferences appears in Swanson, *op. cit.*

21 Related to the fact that policy is vague is the more general postulate that executives seek to avoid formal issues and the possible damaging disputes arising therefrom. See Chester I. Barnard, *Functions of the Executive* (Cambridge: Harvard University Press, 1947).

porter changes. No editor comes between him and his beat (police department, city hall, etc.), thus the reporter gains the "editor" function. It is he who, to a marked degree, can select which stories to pursue, which to ignore. Several cases developed in interviews of beat men who smothered stories they knew would provide fuel for policy— policy they personally disliked or thought injurious to the professional code. The cooperation of would-be competing reporters is essential, of course. The fourth type of story is simply one which the staffer originates, independent of assignment or beat. All respondents, executives, and staffers averred that any employee was free to initiate stories. But equally regularly, they acknowledged that the opportunity was not often assumed. Staffers were already overloaded with beats, assignments, and routine coverage, and besides, rewards for initiated stories were meager or non-existent unless the initiated story confirmed policy. Yet this area promises much, should staffers pursue their advantage. The outstanding case in the present study concerned a well-educated, enthusiastic reporter on a conventional daily just north of the Mason-Dixon line. Entirely on his own, he consistently initiated stories about Negroes and Negro-white relations, "making" policy where only void had existed. He worked overtime to document and polish the stories; his boss said he didn't agree with the idea but insisted on the reporter's right to publish them.

5. Staffers with "star" status can transgress policy more easily than cubs. This differential privilege of status was encountered on several papers. An example would be Walter Winchell during the Roosevelt administration, who regularly praised the President while the policy of his boss, Mr. Hearst, was strongly critical of the regime. A *New York Times* staffer said he doubted that any copyreader on the paper would dare change a word of the copy of Meyer Berger, the star feature writer.

These five factors indicate that given certain conditions, the controls making for policy conformity can be bypassed. These conditions exist not only within the newsroom and the news situation but within the staffer as well; they will be exploited only if the staffer's attitudes permit. There are some limitations, then, on the strength of the publisher's policy.

Before summarizing, three additional requirements of Merton's functional paradigm must be met. These are statements of the consequences of the pattern, of available alternative modes of behavior, and a validation of the analysis.

CONSEQUENCES OF THE PATTERN

To the extent that policy is maintained, the paper keeps publishing smoothly as seen both from the newsroom and from the outside, which is no mean feat if we visualize the country with no press at all. This is the most general consequence. There are several special consequences. For the society as a whole, the existing system of power relationships is maintained. Policy usually protects property and class interests, and thus the strata and groups holding these interests are better able to retain them. For the larger community, much news is printed objectively, allowing for opinions to form openly, but policy news may be slanted or buried so that some important information is denied the citizenry. (This is the dysfunction widely scored by critics.) For the individual readers, the same is true. For the executives, their favorable statuses are maintained, with perhaps occasional touches of guilt over policy. For newsmen, the consequences are the same as for executives. For more independent, critical staffers, there can be several modes of adaptation. At the extremes, the pure conformist can deny the conflict, the confirmed deviate can quit the newspaper business. Otherwise, the adaptations seem to run in this way: (1) Keep on the job but blunt the sharp corners of policy where possible ("If I wasn't here the next guy would let *all* that crap go through . . . "); (2) Attempt to repress the conflict amorally and anti-intellectually ("What the hell, it's only a job; take your pay and forget it . . . "); (3) Attempt to compensate, by "taking it out" in other contexts: drinking, writing "the truth" for liberal publications, working with action programs, the Guild, and otherwise. All of these adjustments were found in the study. As has been suggested, one of the main compensations for all staffers is simply to find justification in adhering to "good news practice."

POSSIBLE ALTERNATIVES AND CHANGE

A functional analysis, designed to locate sources of persistence of a pattern, can also indicate points of strain at which a structural change may occur. For example, the popular recipe for eliminating bias at one time was to diminish advertisers' power over the news. This theory having proved unfruitful, critics more recently have fastened upon the publisher as the point at which change must be initiated. Our analysis suggests that this is a valid approach, but one requiring that leverage in turn be applied on the publisher from various sources. Perhaps the most significant of these are professional codes. Yet we have seen the weakness of these codes when policy decisions are made. Further leverage is contained in such sources as the professional direction being taken by some journalism schools, in the Guild, and in sincere criticism.

Finally, newspaper readers possess potential power over press performance. Seen as a client of the press, the reader should be entitled to not only an interesting newspaper, but one which furnishes significant news objectively presented. This is the basic problem of democracy: to what extent should the individual be treated as a member of a mass, and to what extent fashioned (through educative measures) as an active participant in public decisions? Readership studies show that readers prefer "interesting" news and "features" over penetrating analyses. It can be concluded that the citizen has not been sufficiently motivated by society (and its press) to demand and apply the information he needs, and to discriminate between worthwhile and spurious information, for the fulfillment of the citizen's role. These other forces—professional codes, journalism schools, the Guild, critics, and readers—could result in changing newspaper performance. It still remains, however, for the publisher to be changed first. He can be located at the apex of a T, the crucial point of decision making. Newsroom and professional forces form the base of the T, outside forces from community and society are the arms. It is for the publisher to decide which forces to propitiate.

■   ■   ■

Thus we conclude that the publisher's policy, when established in a given subject area, is usually followed, and that a description of the dynamic socio-cultural situation of the newsroom will suggest explanations for this conformity. The newsman's source of rewards is located not among the readers, who are manifestly his clients, but among his colleagues and superiors. Instead of adhering to societal and professional ideals, he redefines his values to the more pragmatic level of the newsroom group. He thereby gains not only status rewards, but also acceptance in a solidary group engaged in interesting, varied, and sometimes important work. Thus the cultural patterns of the newsroom produce results insufficient for wider democratic needs. Any important change toward a more "free and responsible press" must stem from various possible pressures on the publisher, who epitomizes the policy making and coordinating role.

Robert J. Manning
FOREIGN POLICY AND THE PRESS

Assistant Secretary for Public Affairs when he made the following speech to the National Editorial Association on March 13, 1964, Robert J. Manning is currently Editor of The Atlantic. *Recognizing that the importance of "the separation of journalism and government is as basic and as advisable as separation of church and state," Mr. Manning questions the journalist's basic responsibilities in the reporting of the nation's foreign affairs.*

ONE in my line of government work, when he faces an audience of journalists, has the difficult choice of talking directly about his own work or dabbling more generally in foreign affairs.

The second alternative is probably easier, and certainly less risky. But I would prefer to talk tonight mostly about our business—journalism and foreign affairs. I think there is much we can discuss; so I'll take the risk that before the night is out, I'll have proved myself akin to the Mark Twainian Daniel whom God, as the story goes "ordered forth into the lion's den, but he slipped and came in tenth."

Information gaps are probably inevitable in the best informed societies, and ours is no exception, however clearly defined the issues of foreign policy may be. What I have been struck by in the past few years are the special reasons for such a gap today—and the special peril it holds.

The reasons lie, of course, in the nature of our world. We live at the floodtide of change in all the continents. We are confronted with a totalitarian ideology that seeks our destruction. And we are riding the crest of a revolution in science and technology.

Each of the challenges we face would tax the wisdom, the ingenuity, and the patience of any generation of Americans. Together they pose a test greater than any our nation has confronted. Most acutely, they pose a test of public understanding.

This is a test made difficult by our history. We Americans are the product of a century of precious isolation. We developed our nation behind the protective shield of great oceans. In the mid-19th century Alexis de Tocqueville wrote that the American system of government was the best ever invented by man. He predicted it would be adequate to meet the needs of our society for many generations, unless the United States became actively involved in foreign affairs. The perceptive Frenchman did not try to predict what would happen in that eventuality because he considered it unlikely. Needless to say, it has happened, and with a vengeance.

Since World War II we have catapulted to a position of world leadership and full world responsibility. Yet our training as a nation for such leadership and responsibility has been minimal. The great and complex problems of this age are difficult enough for our policymakers to comprehend. How then are they to be adequately explained to and contributed to by the general public?

This Republic is in great peril when the public is inadequately informed. We see in many parts of our country today the results of public confusion on questions of foreign policy—a growing sense of frustration, among some groups, that has given rise to extremism; a quest for easy, quick "answers"; a search for scapegoats; a demand for such contradictory "solutions" as smaller budgets and "total victory," higher tariffs and freer trade, cheap security and reckless venturesomeness.

Without question, the subject matter of foreign policy is growing more complex. A great deal is happening all the time in foreign affairs all around our planet and, with the advent of rockets, in outer space as well.

We have our own national interest, our own set of foreign policies and foreign crises. These are diverse and complicated to a degree that frequently agonizes the most knowledgeable experts. But ours is a world of 120 other countries, of 120 other foreign policies, of 120 other sets of national goals or national appetites. Keeping track of what is going on, and translating it into terms understandable by large numbers of citizens, is a task that challenges both the press and the government departments concerned with foreign policy, primarily, of course, the Department of State and the White House.

The relationship of you, the press, and us in government in our open society is not a simple thing. It is at least as variegated as human nature and vulnerable to human frailty. The traditional stance of the press confronting government is the adversary relationship; its heraldic sign is crossed swords with bar sinister on a field of spilled ink. In domestic political matters excessive coziness between any element of the press and a reigning political group quickly and properly draws criticism.

In foreign affairs, however, I question whether the old-fashioned adversary relationship is sufficient to the delicate task our nation faces these days on the world scene. When you print the news, to an important extent you make the larger facts. What the press chooses to emphasize frequently becomes the postulates of public opinion (though I have some reservations on this point) and as such can become an important ingredient of policy. In such a situation is the public interest best served when the press and government stand on separate pedestals and snipe at each other across a mythical abyss? I think you will agree that the answer is no—and that journalism as well as government is aware of the need for something more. I suggest that accurate reporting perhaps requires a closer relationship than may have been traditional, perhaps a closer one than some here tonight would consider wise or possible.

On the basis of long experience in journalism and two years' experience in government, I suggest a direct cross-fertilization between American journalism and American government. Let me be as precise as possible, so as to avoid misunderstanding: The separation of journalism and government is as basic and as advisable as separation of church and state. Government intrusion into the functioning of journalism—whether by censorship, by regulatory controls, by economic penetration, or political manipulation—would represent serious jeopardy to our political system.

That accepted, there is more to be said about the subject. Countless times in these last two years I have wished that officials in government knew more about journalism, its needs, its practices, its uses, and its shortcomings. Even more convinced am I that journalists—most of them—need to know more, much more, about government, how it works, why it works and, sometimes, does not work; how decisions are made and how they are not made; what are the facts as against the myths and misconceptions.

There is one direct way to accomplish this. Journalism should encourage some of its top established hands, and some of its more promising new hands, to take leave for intervals of a year or two in government service. The government would profit from the infusion of versatility, energy, and enterprise that makes a good newspaperman. The newspaperman would become a wiser and more valuable craftsman. On his return, the newspaper reader would be better served and better informed.

The opportunities for newspapermen in government are not by any means confined to information work (which in many ways is the least demanding and least rewarding of the many activities for which a competent newsman is fitted). The governmental careers of men like Carl Rowan, William Attwood, and John Bartlow Martin, to name a few, suggest the high quality of service and imagination that a journalistic background can produce.

I suppose there are still some editors and publishers who, while sipping at the 19th hole with leaders of industry, banking, and commerce, will shake their heads and maintain that a newspaperman who enters into public service somehow taints himself for further journalism. It seems unfortunate that such thinking should survive the kerosene lamp and the automobile crank. I can think literally of no activity that has been more educational to me as a journalist than these past two years in government. In a time when, as H. G. Wells says, "human history becomes more and more a race between education and catastrophe," I heartily recommend a few semesters in Washington or at an embassy overseas.

Whatever steps might be taken to alter or improve the old adversary relationship, one point must be emphasized from the outset: It should neither suggest nor require any abdication of the critical faculties of the reporter and editor. Quite the contrary, the more thorough knowledge which skilled reporters today accumulate about what is happening in foreign affairs serves to invigorate, not weaken, the function of responsible criticism. On a subject like South Viet Nam—unquestionably one of the most difficult and sensitive issues confronting us—the access to information within the government that has been available to the press has provided the basis for the considerable number of well-informed and critical editorials that have appeared in recent weeks.

Irresponsible criticism is, of course, a different matter, but there is a very high correlation between misinformation, or lack of information, and the kind of wild criticism that graces the "hate sheets" of the right and reveals itself in the latent paranoia of a few newspapers and correspondents around the country. The reckless charges that pass for comment in these forums cannot survive exposure to information. It is no coincidence that with rare exceptions the writers (I hesitate to dignify them, and besmirch the craft, by calling them reporters) who regularly produce the most startling accusations about the State Department do not call my office or any other section of the Department to ask questions or check conclusions. Apparently they feel their concoctions will clang more loudly if not muted by the facts.

Leaving aside this category—in which, by the way, I place none of the regular State Department correspondents—it does seem to me that on the whole the job of communicating information about foreign policy is one that the press and the government have in common, not one in which our interests are opposed. The basic elements of my present job are remarkably similar to that of a reporter: to get out the news—fast, accurate, and as complete as possible. Nearly always my associates—several of whom are also former newsmen— and I are in the position of working with, not against, the reporters who cover foreign news and call us daily, if not hourly.

Information flows from the State Department in many ways. In testimony last year before Congressman [John E.] Moss's subcommittee on government information, James Reston of the New York *Times* described the Department as a "gabby outfit." Ours is a house with many windows, and its daily information output is enormous. Anyone who, as I have, has served as a correspondent in a foreign capital will vouch for the truth of the statement that nowhere in the world are reporters given such complete and unfettered access to the makers and shapers of foreign policy. As a practical matter, every State Department reporter has a government telephone directory which tells him what every officer in the Department does and who's in charge of what desk, area, or section. A reporter is not confined to a few known sources. Whatever the subject that arises, he can quickly pinpoint the individuals with responsibility and can call them directly, by direct dial, without having to filter through a central switchboard. Even home telephone numbers are provided—and are regularly used by reporters with late-breaking deadlines. The newsmen assigned to the State Department make wide use of this access-by-telephone every day. It is a source of information at least as important as the regular press briefings by the Department spokesman and the Secretary of State. Naturally, as in any area, he has to build his own network of sources who are able and willing to serve him. But the sources are there to be cultivated.

In addition, considerable use is made of background briefings. This is the device, treasured by reporters everywhere, whereby a high official will discuss subjects but not for direct quotation and not for attribution. The stories that result are generally authoritative and accurate, and they contribute greatly to the supply of information publicly available about United States foreign relations. They provide important guidance on the government's thinking on a given topic.

I have listened to a lot of nonsense about the so-called iniquity of the background briefing, but most of it comes from distant critics who make me agree with Josh Billings that "it is better to know nothing than to know what ain't so." Anybody with experience in reporting knows two things. One is that a reporter is only as good as his ability to separate fact from fancy, bogus from real. Another is that there is no such thing as goldfish-bowl diplomacy. Show me a businessman who conducts his business in a high-pitched voice at noon on Main

Street, and I'll show you a diplomat who does his work by talking out loud on the front page of the Washington *Post.*

Heisenberg's principle of uncertainty in nuclear physics has a close analogy in foreign relations: It is usually not possible to describe a diplomatic situation publicly, however accurately, without changing it and making it different. The public comment itself becomes part of the situation. An on-the-record statement by the Secretary of State, be it a prepared speech or a response to a question, is instantly filmed, recorded, printed, and otherwise communicated, with all the speed of modern telecommunications, to a mixed audience of friends, partners, skeptics, and enemies all around the globe. Many are ready to seize on a single ill-considered word and blow it up for propaganda purposes. As a consequence, important comments issued formally on the record by high officials often must be planned as carefully as a surgical operation so that no listeners anywhere can have reason to misunderstand or abuse what is said.

That is why most newsmen highly value the background device, which permits a policy officer to speak freely and informally to let reporters in on his thinking without giving our cold-war adversaries the same access. At the briefing conferences conducted twice a year at the Department for the press and other media a mixture of on-record and background discussion have been used. After the most recent conference, we asked the participants to comment on this point; the 800 replies we received favored background briefings by four to one.

In a sense the background rule makes it possible for the government to take a reporter into its confidence. This calls for good faith on both sides, and it is nearly always present. The exceptions are happily infrequent, though no less irritating when they occur. It is a procedure that can be abused. It is an abuse, for example, for the government to use this method to float trial balloons, as a way to sample public opinion without choosing sides in advance, or in any way to mislead or misinform. It can be abused by reporters who fail to maintain the distinction between it and on-the-record briefings. But despite these pitfalls, its overall utility is great. The fact that a knife can be used to kill is no reason to eat with our fingers. The best safeguard against misuse of backgrounders lies in the skill and integrity of the reporters themselves. What is said on background or not for quotation is subject to the same acid tests of accuracy and relevancy as any other government pronouncement, and rightly so.

Let me examine another aspect of the government-press relationship. It is frequently argued that it is the government's responsibility to keep secrets, the responsibility of the press to get them and print them. "The press lives by disclosure," opined the *Times* of London in 1851. If a foreign agent came into the State Department and managed to procure secret information, he would be liable to prosecution and a heavy sentence. When a reporter does the same thing, he wins praise from his editor and gets nominated for prizes. The story is printed, and either way our enemies can read it.

In the year 1964 I think that this simplified, traditional view of the role of the government and the role of the press is out of date. I prefer to think that the responsibility both for informing the public and for maintaining certain areas of nondisclosure is one which is shared by the press and the government. To be sure, the press's responsibility is heavily weighted toward full disclosure: I would not wish it otherwise. But I believe, and I think I speak for the majority of reporters, that we would lose an important ingredient of the relationship of trust that is basic to how the press gets along with government if the press did not recognize its responsibility in circumstances of great national importance to help us keep some secrets.

I feel that I am on solid ground when I say this because I know from my experience in the past year that with rare exceptions the reporters who regularly cover the Department of State do recognize this responsibility. I know one reporter, for example, who is still sitting on a dramatic first-person story of his involvement in a recent great international crisis. Many others have happened upon or otherwise uncovered information which if immediately divulged would have caused us serious difficulties. They did not immediately rush it into print, recognizing that to do so would not serve their own interests as responsible journalists seeking to report the news accurately and fully, and might seriously prejudice American foreign policy objectives or national security.

THIRST FOR FOREIGN POLICY INFORMATION RISING

The responsibility for getting the news out is also one that we share. A great many things happen each day, only a few of which come to public attention—not because they are kept secret but because they are not considered news. The press itself is highly selective. Only a fraction of the information that pours into a typical city room survives the cutting and paring process called editing and makes its way into print. Douglass Cater has written that the power of the press,

. . . stems from its ability to select—to define what is news and what isn't. In Washington on an average day, a good many hundreds of thousands of words are spoken, tens of dozens of "events" occur. The press decides which of those words and events shall receive the prompt attention of millions and which, like timber falling in a deep and uninhabited forest, shall crash silently to the ground.

Several independent studies show that an average of 3 to 8 percent of general news space in American newspapers is devoted to foreign affairs items. The average daily newspaper content of foreign news is four to eight columns. Foreign news actually sent by the Associated Press on its main ticker averages 22,000 words per day, or 27 columns. If nonduplicating items from other wire services plus special reports are included, it can be calculated that the average American daily newspaper provides its readers with well under 20 percent of the foreign news actually reported each day. I simply do not think that is enough.

The problem of making manageable the vast outpouring of news on foreign policy that becomes available each day challenges journalism in many ways. The press often still practices methods of makeup, construction, and play that were in use half a century ago. As a result, editors often seem to be overwhelmed by the torrent of events and their readers have served up to them a daily collection of fragments. That approach to foreign affairs may have made sense when the United States was involved in only one crisis at a time. It no longer suffices today, when we are participants or ringside spectators to 15 to 20 crises at a time. The frequent result is that each day's news on each topic is apt to be so brief, so fragmentary, as to be more misleading than no news at all. Too often, each day's fragment remains a fragment. As a result, in the words of the late Joe Liebling:

> Our present news situation, in the United States, is breaking down to something like the system of water distribution in the Casbah, where peddlers wander about with goatskins of water on small donkeys, and the inhabitants send down an oil tin and a couple of pennies when they feel thirst.

Ironically this comes at a time when the national thirst for foreign policy information is rising. The American people want to know what is happening, how it affects them, what we are doing about it. By any indication, including public opinion polls, more people are concerned about foreign policy than at any time in our history. Still one hears editors insisting that "the people" don't want to read a lot of foreign affairs guff. I do not believe it.

The inability of the daily media to keep abreast of this rising level of interest is reflected in the success of other enterprises, particularly magazines, which give at least the impression of providing a fuller, connected account of foreign news. Volume of information is not the problem; what is needed rather is a more reflective approach to foreign news which relates the snippets to one another, which locates an event in history as well as geography, and which takes more profound account of the fact that other people's domestic politics often influence their foreign policies.

SOME WORDS OF CRITICISM

I do not want to abuse your hospitality, and I therefore hope that some words of criticism will not be taken amiss; they come from a deep sense of involvement in the profession of journalism and a desire to see improvements. I do not presume to tell you how to behave—for I recognize that there is no mightier potentate than the proprietor of an independent newspaper. Many of you, I know, are editors or publishers of weekly newspapers, and I understand there is solid backing to the claim that weeklies are more extensively and carefully read than many dailies. I understand also that in many cases the weekly is the only newspaper its readers read. On both these counts, therefore, it is depressing to know that so many editors of weeklies disdain to provide their readers with much coverage of national and foreign affairs. I realize there are staffing and money problems, but in this age of communications wizardry, joint efforts, and speedy travel, the weekly community could easily and cheaply build up a service providing solid, well-written, and well-thought-out material on the big world issues.

Another more general characteristic of journalism today should cause more concern than it seems to be causing. The press today suffers from a bad case of complacency and self-righteousness and is noteworthy among all fraternities that perform public services for its lack of self-criticism.

Our press today is keenly, sometimes even stridently, assertive of its rights and prerogatives, but it has a bad case of laryngitis when it is time to talk about its responsibilities. If Congressman Moss will excuse me, I would like to say that the intellectual quality of a great deal of the testimony delivered to his subcommittee after the Cuban crisis was so low as to remind some of us of the old description of the Platte River in midsummer—two inches deep and a mile wide at the mouth.

When it comes to actual performance, I think the press in this country can be described as not only the freest and most imaginative but also the most responsible and best in the world. (One could make some reservations; for example, I would say that the very best in British journalism surpasses most of the best in ours.) But we cannot afford to stop where we are and be satisfied. There is still too much tendency among editors to operate on the old-fashioned presumption that the reader has the IQ of a 12-year-old child. There is still that ancient reflex that is mindful of the old Chicago city editor who once in anger called his staff together and said, "What this newspaper needs is some new cliches." There is great truth in the indictment that the press is generally too greatly preoccupied by entertainment, by what it takes to reach the easier side of reader interest.

I have the impression that journalism is not doing enough to recruit and properly train top-level people. I have been struck in years since the war to find that newspapers and magazines, even some very good ones, have to go out and cajole people into journalism. The tendency to call it a profession and pay as if it weren't is still strong, once you get away from the metropolitan areas.

As for the long vaunted "power of the press," where does that stand today? I confess that I am in a somewhat ambiguous state of mind; there are moments when I believe too many in government attach too much power of influence to the press; then there are mornings when I question that this is so. I think we have to concede that the power is indeed very great but that in general the press today is powerful more as an exciter than a provoker, and for the most part a channeler of other people's ideas and arguments. There has been a vast increase in analytical and interpretive reporting since the war, but still not a great deal of political, intellectual, theological, or philosophical inspiration comes with the average newspaper in America.

So the power of the press directly to influence is in great part a negative power, as it is exerted today; it stems in large part from others' ideas. This is also related to the power of omission that comes from the fact that each day the writers and the editors have to choose which large segments of a very large news budget they are *not* going to pass on to the public. I don't mean to suggest that there is not still in our press the power to do great good (and bad)—great power to make or break careers or ideas—but it is clearly limited, and the chief limit is set by the ability and the willingness of the possessors of this power to use it.

HANDLING OF FOREIGN POLICY NEWS

Coming back to my home ground, the handling of foreign policy news, I would like to comment, if I may, on two other tendencies that seem to me to create problems for all three elements—the newspapers, the readers, and the government.

One is the newspapers' feverish preoccupation not with what has happened but what is going to happen tomorrow. I know State Department correspondents who spend literally hours trying to learn the names of new ambassadorial or other appointees before candidates have even been selected. One prestigious newspaper over a period of several months had two separate "exclusive" stories reporting that a certain official had been picked as ambassador to two different capitals. The diplomat did not go to any one of those posts, and when he was actually appointed to his present post the newspaper neglected to report it. This overpreoccupation with getting ahead of events, to be the first to report what is *going* to happen, results in a lot of wasted motion, a lot of incorrect or highly premature stories, and any number of woes for government officials. More than that, however, it takes journalism's eye off the big part of the game—what *has* happened, what does it mean—to the detriment of us all.

Even the best writers and reporters—and I believe that the corps that covers the Department of State and foreign affairs in Washington is by and large the most diligent and most talented group in journalism—are not always able to rise above the mixture of bugaboo and custom that dictates the structure and the play of stories. They are seriously handicapped by their editors' assumption that it is still possible to report the world's major convolutions as if they are innings in a ball game. This frequently leads to the scorecard wrap-up of a number of otherwise unrelated episodes in foreign affairs, a device that few reporters like but one that many editors cannot resist. Usually the attempt is made to summarize a series of events around the world as "victories" or "defeats" for U.S. policy.

Nothing is easier, and few things are more misleading, than to chart the tides of foreign relations with a limited set of phrases taken from the vocabulary of the sports page. The relations of nations in the world arena are not like a ball game; victory and defeat are not determined by the number of times a ball goes out of the park. Evaluating progress in the cold war—forward, backward, sideways, up or down—is a subtle process, one which the most penetrating analysts usually avoid. They see all too clearly the folly of trying to pick out who's ahead from day to day or week to week.

In a world where ideology confronts ideology, and both face the quickening tides of nationalism; where foreign policy pronouncements by the leader of a nonaligned state may be motivated by his domestic politics, and may in fact conflict with firm private assurances to the contrary—and are understood as such by all concerned; where around the globe nations and peoples above all are seeking their own form of development, their own definitions of progress; where Communist states swap insults and plot their own, nationally oriented paths in foreign and domestic policy; where our own alliances experience the natural retrenchments that must occur in a changing world—in such a world "victory" and "defeat" are usually no more than words to be played with.

One of the occupational hazards of trying to keep score in foreign affairs is that it sometimes makes the practitioner look silly. Not even on the AP's weekly top-ten listings do teams plunge from victory to defeat and back again with the erratic swiftness ascribed to U.S. policy.

About three months ago a prominent weekly publication put together a scorecard roundup which opened with the sentence: "Russia, the facts are showing, has lost the cold war." Two months later it printed a similar wrap-up which began: "Troubles of the world look somewhat less alarming than at any time in many years." A third installment, four weeks later, was summed up with this opening sentence: "America is going from defeat to defeat in almost every corner of the world." It even carried a map pinpointing the "defeats." Surely this must have strained the credulity of some of the magazine's readers. I venture to suggest that the world has not changed that much in three months, and to deal with the matter in such a sophomoric manner verges on insult. The cold war goes on, neither won nor lost, but invariably changing in its manifestation. America is not "going from defeat to defeat" (nor does a globe have corners).

A reporter must always guard against reporting the plausible as the actual, and this is certainly true in foreign affairs. What is likely or logical does not always happen in foreign policy; reporting likelihoods as facts before they come true is not far removed, it seems to me, from other kinds of misreporting.

There is an important difference, it seems to me, between the right of a reporter to pursue information about foreign policy, or any other subject, and the responsibility of his newspaper to print all the data thus uncovered. The right of the reporter to try to find out what is happening is limited only by his enterprise. I do not think any check beyond present security restrictions should be placed on a reporter's right to cover the news, which should be limited solely by his enterprise. But the obligation to disclose by publication is not so absolute.

The press discloses in the name of the public's right to know. But the public also has a right to have its interests defended and advanced in the field of foreign policy and national security. These two rights may come in conflict, and when they do, the public may well prefer success to disclosure. There have been many episodes in the past two years —of which the Cuban missile crisis was the most dramatic—where the success of American policy depended very directly on the preservation of a period of privacy during which the policy could be formulated and carried out, where disclosure would have spelled defeat.

Where in these cases does the public interest lie? The public, I submit, has a right *not* to know when knowledge can gravely compromise our security or damage our foreign policy. Many reporters, among them the most able, respect both these rights. But their responsibility is less great than that of their editors, who are the ones who finally select what is printed—and is thus disseminated to the world at large, as well as the American people. It is not an easy responsibility to live with; it raises questions to which no single answer is right.

It is not for a government official to presume the right or the wisdom to settle this problem; it is journalism's to contemplate, and I am sure that many of you have pondered it.

PARTNERSHIP BETWEEN JOURNALISM AND GOVERNMENT

I have devoted much time to criticism because I have assumed that you share with me a belief that healthy criticism is always needed among those who labor in the world of ideas. I have not taken pains to reiterate the obvious—that the American press today is indeed the "fourth branch of government," in some ways the branch that is least captive of custom and least fearful to tread where the timid fear to enter.

A revelation of government service has been the discovery that this great partnership between responsible journalism and responsible government—wary, sometimes abrasive, sometimes argumentative —works, and it works for the country.

A great nation devoid of intelligence, wrote Horace Mann, is "an obscene giant," destined despite its power and capacities, to "rush with the speed of a whirlwind to an ignominious end." We are together in striving to assure that this does not become our epitaph.

The perils we live with today are perhaps more subtle than those of World War II or the early days of the cold war. But they are no less real and probably more pernicious. Undeclared warfare backed by the challenge of thermonuclear weapons is a greater danger than we ever faced in the past. These are problems for all of us in press and government. To a very real extent we are partners in adversity.

I. F. Stone
WHEN THE GOVERNMENT LIES, MUST THE PRESS FIB?

To whom and to what should the press be responsible? What is the responsibility of the press when the government lies? I. F. Stone, one of America's leading independent, liberal voices, examines these critical questions in this selection which originally appeared in I. F. Stone's Weekly.

AS A boy in small town America, February 22 was made memorable for us small fry by red-white-and-blue cardboard hatchets and candied cherries, symbols of the Father of Our Country, who could not tell a lie, even if the consequence were a painful loss of prestige in the paternal woodshed. Now it seems the Parson Weems story about the cherry tree may no longer be regarded as quite the right upbringing for American youth. Now it seems that no truly patriotic American, especially if a newspaperman, is supposed to tell the truth once our government has decided that it is more advantageous to tell a lie. This is the real meaning of President Kennedy's appeal to the American Newspaper Publishers Association for self-censorship in the handling of the news. Mr. Kennedy put it more tactfully. He asked editors to ask themselves not only "Is it news?" but "Is it in the national interest?" But the national interest in a free society is supposed to lie in the fullest dissemination of the facts so that popular judgment may be truly informed. It is the mark of a closed or closing society to assume that the rulers decide how much the vulgar herd shall be told.

The President's real meaning was clearer to those who attended the two-day secret mass briefing, or official brainwashing, for the press at the State Department earlier in the week. There Assistant Secretary of State for Public Affairs Roger Tubby seemed to be implying that the Cuban invasion might have worked if the press had not printed so much about it in advance. He wanted newspaper editors to ask themselves whether a particular bit of news might help the enemy, and to call the State Department and ask if they were in doubt. One newspaperman present who had the spirit to challenge this was Richard Dudman of the *St. Louis Post-Dispatch* who objected that Tubby assumed the only thing wrong with the Cuban invasion was that it didn't work. Assuming, Dudman asked, that it was poorly conceived whether it worked or not, wouldn't it have been better to have had more information and more public discussion? This elicited only a polite mumble from Tubby, an old State Department hand now back in service who shares its ineradicable view that Papa Knows Best. This was not just post mortem since Mr. Kennedy himself told the briefing that there would be other situations, not similar he hoped, when our preparations would have to be made in secret. (I see no reason why American readers should not be allowed to know this since Soviet bloc reporters present were allowed to hear it and since I was not invited I am not bound to secrecy.) This opens the wider prospect of more adventures in which we make war without declaring it and brings us to the incident over which officials at the briefing expressed the greatest irritation.

This incident illustrates the dangers of hastily sweeping the Cuban affair under the rug without a full investigation.[1] The incident was the bombing of Camp Libertad, the military airport near Havana on April 14, just before the invasion began. This bombing was "covered" not only by a false story but by a false plane landing in Miami. The false story, quickly scented by several newspapers, was that the bombing was done by defecting Castro airmen stationed on the field. The false plane landing story was fully told in *Time* magazine April 28. It said the operation against Cuba started "with a surprise attack by B-26 light bombers on Cuban airports" to destroy Castro's air force. "To lend credence to a cover story that the bombings were by pilots defecting from Castro's air force," *Time* reported, "a few 30-caliber bullets were fired into an old Cuban B-26. A pilot took off in the crate and landed it at Miami. . . . A reporter noted that dust and undisturbed grease covered bomb-bay fittings . . . guns were uncorked and unfired. The planes that actually did the bombing never were seen." Officials at the briefing sessions made it clear they think the newspapers should not have exposed the falsity of this story. This goes beyond the standard of asking editors to ask themselves whether a story is in the national interest. It asks them to print as true whatever

1 Eisenhower who managed to go through the years of McCarthyism without ever uttering the term "witch hunt," suddenly discovers this term and advises against a "witch hunt" into the Cuban debacle. Obviously a full inquiry would also open up the story of the Guatemalan affair during his Administration.

the government may think expedient in a given situation. It says that when the government lies, the press should fib. This is how *Izvestia* and *Pravda* are edited, but it hardly fits Jefferson's idea of a free press.

91
I. F. Stone
WHEN THE
GOVERNMENT
LIES, MUST
THE PRESS
FIB?

This incident calls for further examination. A B-26 raid on Cuba's military airports is quite an operation. We still don't know the full story. Was it by Cuban or American pilots? Where did the planes come from and where did they land afterwards? Were U.S. facilities used? These are the questions Cuba could raise if the incident were ever brought before an international tribunal. We are constantly talking of the "infamy" of Pearl Harbor, but here we had a hand in a sneak attack without a declaration of war on a neighboring country with which we are still legally at peace. The false story which covered it could not hide the truth from the Cubans; they knew they had not been bombed by planes from their own airfields. The false story—*and this is the important point*—was designed to hide the truth from the American press and the American public. It was not the enemy, it was our own people, this story was intended to deceive. Was it in the national interest to let the government deceive the American people? Is it ever in the national interest to let a government deceive, not a supposed enemy, but ourselves?

What if this sneak attack were on a larger country than Cuba, with a big air force of its own, able to return to bomb our cities? What if Castro had retaliated by bombing Miami? To raise these questions is to see the danger of allowing such agencies as CIA secretly to make war on its own, in violation of law, treaty and Constitution. To raise them is to see how indispensable it is to preserve some check upon them through a free press. To raise them is also to see on how dangerous and slippery a road we are proceeding.

The danger will not be met by the currently fashionable proposal to take cloak-and-dagger activities out of the CIA and put them in the Pentagon. The danger will be worse if authorization for secret warmaking shenanigans is put in the hands of the military, with the far greater resources at its disposal; in any case the Cuban affair was a joint enterprise of CIA and the armed forces. The danger lies in these "para-military" activities themselves on which Mr. Kennedy suddenly sets so much store. To embark on secret warlike activities against peoples whose governments we dislike, is to set out on a course destructive of free government and of peace.

Joseph Pulitzer, Jr.
THE PRESS LIVES BY DISCLOSURES

Bearer of a famous name in journalism history, Joseph Pulitzer, Jr., discusses President John F. Kennedy's proposal of voluntary censorship of the press in the following remarks delivered during Pulitzer's twenty-fifth reunion at Harvard in 1961.

A CENTURY ago when an external threat to the survival of the nation was undreamed of, Wilbur Fisk Storey, editor of the *Chicago Times*, declared: "It is a newspaper's duty to print the news and raise hell." This incisive judgment on one journalistic purpose was questioned recently by President Kennedy when he expounded before an audience of American publishers the problems of a free press in the cold war. Mr. Kennedy proposed a voluntary censorship of news on matters involving the national security. He called for more self-restraint or self-discipline in such matters by the press. At the same time the president recognized the responsibility of newspapers to inform the public, in his words, "to arouse, to reflect, to state our dangers and our opportunities, to indicate our crises and our choices, to lead, mold, educate and sometimes even anger public opinion." The dilemma, as he defined it, concerns "a free and open society in a cold and secret war." Speaking of the monolithic and ruthless conspiracy which confronts the free world, Mr. Kennedy said:

Its preparations are concealed, not published. Its mistakes are buried, not headlined. Its dissenters are silenced, not lionized. No expenditure is questioned, no rumor is printed, no secret is revealed. It conducts the cold war, in short, with a wartime discipline no democracy would ever hope or wish to match. Nevertheless, every democracy recognizes the necessary restraints of national security—and the question remains whether those restraints need to be more strictly observed if we are to oppose this kind of attack as well as outright invasion.

The occasion for suggesting consideration of voluntary censorship was the ill-fated Cuban invasion, in which operation some newspapers, as you know, disclosed active participation by the Central Intelligence Agency. While one may sympathize with the busy public servants who were harassed by newspaper reports of CIA activity, one must weigh against such inconvenience or interference the traditional safeguard of press freedom, protected by the constitution as a fundamental bulwark of our free society. One may respectfully assert that the editor in Chicago uttered a cogent and wise maxim when he declared that "it is a newspaper's duty to print the news and raise hell."

Admitting the roughness of the language, this is not a frivolous conception of a newspaper's responsibility to the public it serves. On the contrary, the statement implies the essence of a free, inquiring, critical press. It recognizes, I suggest, a newspaper's obligation to print a full and accurate account of the news, to interpret its significance or meaning in the broader context of the issues of the day, and to comment on events with vigor, sound reasoning and moral purpose irrespective of the popularity of the views expressed or any denunciations that might thunder from high places of authority.

"The press lives by disclosures," as the London *Times* observed in a wise assessment of the role of the press. More than a century ago, 1851, British officials were agitating for censorship after Lord Palmerston had been disclosed as backing a clandestine operation by Louis Napoleon to become emperor of France. In reply, the *Times* disagreed that the purpose of a newspaper is "to share the labors of statesmanship, or that it is bound by the same duties, the same liabilities as Ministers of the Crown."

The purposes and duties of the two powers are constantly separate, generally independent, sometimes diametrically opposite. The dignity and freedom of the press are trammelled from the moment it accepts an ancillary position. . . . The press can enter into no close or binding alliances with the statesmen of the day, nor can it surrender its permanent interests to the convenience of the ephemeral power of any Government. The first duty of the press is to obtain the earliest and most correct intelligence of the events of the time, and instantly, by disclosing them, to make them the common property of the nation. . . . The Press lives by disclosures.

If the foregoing consensus means that the press must serve no master but the public interest, and that the disclosure of the truth is indispensable to an informed public opinion on which rest sound public policies, it is my view that editors can best contribute to the public welfare by the exercise of each individual conscience in covering the news and commenting on it. If the editorial opinions of a newspaper are to be sound, meaningful, and influential in shaping the great potentialities of American life in a free society, those declarations of opinion must rely on the most complete, unrestrained, accurate account of the consequential events of the day. Self-imposed censorship, voluntarily agreed to—conformity to a code of suppression designed to protect the general welfare—would warp the integrity of the news on which sound opinions rely.

Voluntary censorship has been accepted during periods of war as a temporary abridgment of a protected right in order to safeguard American lives engaged on the fighting fronts. But wars have involved a controlled press for only a limited duration. The competitive challenge of the Communist world, it is widely accepted, may threaten the nation for decades. Not with open war but with covert means, our opponents may be expected to test the foundations of freedom.

An ever-widening circle of news suppression over an extended period would merit the people's loss of confidence in the press, deepening as the suppressions or distortions inevitably came to light. Could we accept the decline of an informed public opinion after editorial debate had become an empty ceremonial dependent on a pale replica of the facts? Voluntary censorship in the cold war under government tutelage would, in time, I suggest, stifle the initiative, the curiosity, the skepticism which goad responsible editors to ferret out the facts of important news situations. Valid interpretations and informed discussion of the issues would falter. Enlightened public opinion would languish in a twilight of half-truths. The "collision of adverse opinions," in John Stuart Mill's phrase, would no longer supply the "remainder of the truth" which men must share with their government to ensure that sound decisions are taken and constructive policies are supported.

The press is a tribune to defend the undefended, a chronicle to record its times, an examiner of controversies; it monitors the economy and the social progress of its age, it is a journal of man's successes and failures, a fighter for progress and reform; it is a herald of events, an observer of the tides of change, a commentator on the great issues confronting the nation, a reporter of happenings in public life, a review of the policies—good and bad—of its leaders; the newspaper is a challenge to the policy makers, a guardian of man's liberties; it is a mirror of man's aspirations; a sentinel to protect the public. If the press is all these things—if it offers enlightenment to guide a free society toward a more noble destiny—could it serve unimpaired for long under the restraints of even self-imposed censorship? Would not the honored institution become enfeebled and decline in its capacity to support the nation's struggle against tyranny or, conversely, to challenge decisions which, in a climate of moderation, might be recognized as inimical to America's best interests? A free institution would slowly lose its character and abandon its tradition. If "the press lives by disclosures," a muted journalism would debase the truth and be undeserving of the trust imposed in it by the writers of the constitution.

Surely nothing involving human judgment is absolute or perfect. Flaws of character, errors by prejudice, weakness, unconscious bias, any of these would prevent perfection in the exercise of sound news and editorial judgment in deciding what facts an editor who is also a patriotic citizen should suppress in the interest of military security. If we can agree that no responsible editor would deliberately injure the nation's security, would it not be wise to accept the damage caused by a mistaken judgment rather than acquiesce in a code of censorship administered by men of good will but no less fallible? Mr. Kennedy recognized the need for vitality in public discussion of national affairs when he told the publishers, "Without debate, without criticism, no administration can succeed—and no republic can survive . . . that is why our press was protected by the First Amendment."

In May the president conferred with a group of newspaper executives at the White House. It was reported that the government and the press will continue to study the objective of protecting security without censorship and will meet again in several months.

In conclusion may I quote from an editorial carried in the *St. Louis Post-Dispatch* which summarizes the problem we have been examining:

In the case of the Cuban affair, many newspapers of Florida agreed among themselves to say nothing about the training of refugees for the invasion. The *New York Times,* on the other hand, sent Latin American experts to Miami to obtain and publish as much information as they could obtain from refugee leaders.

Obviously, the editors of the New York and Florida papers differed in their judgment, as was their right. But it seems also obvious that if all of the newspapers had agreed to conform to a code, in cooperation with a government agency, the American people would be less able to evaluate the Cuban adventure and use its lessons to decide their future course. They might never have learned of the failure; they might not be in a position to demand an accounting.

There is no doubt that the existence of an agressive and inquiring press is and will be an inhibiting factor in the sort of operation the CIA attempted in Cuba. But it would be better to conclude that maneuvers of this sort should not be undertaken by an open society than that our society should become less open. Perhaps a choice need not be made. This much, however, is quite clear: a free, aggressive, inquiring and above all pluralistic press is indispensable to a free society. In full knowledge that some newspapers may abuse their trust, the free society must rely upon the discretion and sense of responsibility of individual editors and publishers instead of trying to impose upon them all a monolithic uniformity like that of the totalitarian press.

Mr. Kennedy himself gave a partial answer to his own argument for considering press restraints. He said: "Even today, there is little value in opposing the threat of a closed society by imitating its arbitrary restrictions. Even today, there is little value in insuring the survival of our nation if our traditions do not survive with it."

With that we fully agree.

S. George Little
THE RESPONSIBILITY OF
A NEWSPAPER SYNDICATE

Often maligned, the newspaper syndicate can, according to S. George Little, President of the General Features Corporation, play a vital, positive role in the shaping of today's newspaper. In the following article Mr. Little outlines what he considers to be "the function of a responsible newspaper syndicate."

LIKE the jet plane, space satellites, electronic typesetters, television, and motion pictures, newspaper syndicates are children of the twentieth century—an age when improvements and new developments in all media of communications have advanced at a tremendous rate. Although the first press service in America was established in 1848 by a group of six papers in New York—primarily to handle shipping news—it was not until after the turn of the century that newspaper syndicates began to come into their own and become an important part of the world-wide communications network.

Newspaper syndicates have multiplied and flourished to the extent that today there are more than 275 organizations in the business of distributing features to newspapers all over the world. There are almost fifty categories of features, ranging from political commentary, to the care of children, to crossword puzzles; and, while most of the syndicates have only a few features, fully eighty percent of syndicated material found in newspapers throughout the world is serviced by no more than the top dozen or so leading syndicates. Obviously it is imperative that these largest newspaper syndicates realize their tremendous responsibilities to the public; it is no less imperative that the smaller syndicates be fully aware of their responsibility too.

To the typical newspaper reader, there is one criterion alone by which he judges the content of his newspaper: *Is it worth reading?* The goal of every editor and writer deserving of his position as a member of the Fourth Estate is to provide a positive answer to that question. He does it by offering readers features that are informative and entertaining. But, more significantly, a feature must also be *important* and *interesting* before a reader will be completely satisfied that it is *worth reading.*

Here, in a nutshell, is the key to what I feel is the function of a responsible newspaper syndicate: to offer readers information and entertainment that are worth reading, that are important and interesting, and *that are available only through the medium of his local newspaper.* Generally speaking, the obligations of a newspaper syndicate embrace four areas of responsibility: (1) to the newspaper-reading public; (2) to the newspapers themselves; (3) to the authors and artists who produce the features (and who are, of course, an inherent part of any syndicate); and (4) to itself (its officers and other employees who are directly involved in the business of feature syndication).

Before it can possibly serve the best interests of the reading public, a syndicate must first examine its own linen. It must be dead certain that its material is the best available and is without the blemish of vicious ideas, impropriety, or unprincipled and irresponsible opinion that may, however well disguised, be disseminated among an unsuspecting public.

To accomplish even this much sounds like an impossible job. But is it? Difficult, yes; but not impossible.

First of all, in its development of features, a syndicate is limited only by its own values and rules—its own integrity. Ideally, it should not be the dupe of any political or religious group, but should strive to produce features that reflect the highest ideals of whatever point of view is expressed. (In this respect, large syndicates are better able to research and present opposing ideas more freely and accurately because of their access to unlimited information in every field.)

As the syndicate involves itself with these problems of what has been called "The Narrow Range of Opinion," the question of censorship naturally arises. To what extent should a syndicate censor its material?

I think it is self-evident that if a syndicate selects features produced only by highly *responsible* writers and artists, the problem of censorship partially resolves itself. The responsible columnist will not indulge in wanton vilification or scurrilous diatribe; the responsible artist will avoid jokes that are in bad taste and will keep the cleavage of his voluptuous comicstrip heroine within acceptable bounds.

There should be a distinction made between features that are meant to entertain and those that are meant to inform. For example, the so-called "sob sister" columns which are a polyglot of the pseudo-scientific and of synthetic humor patently based on real human problems should not be condoned by the ethical syndicate. Not only can such "advice" seriously confuse many readers with similar problems, but, wrapped in its veneer of indelicate quips, can also do irreparable harm.

This is not to say that entertainment and information cannot be combined successfully and in a responsible manner. It can, and it is. But humorous entertainment is best confined to comic strips and panels and those columns that are obviously humorous in intent. Advice or information, especially in the areas of mental and physical health, should be factual and carefully distinguished from any humor that might be imparted within a given column.

No less important than producing the best features possible for a newspaper-reading public is the syndicate's special obligation to the newspapers themselves.

According to the late Dean of U.S. Journalism Historians, Frank Luther Mott, there are eight concepts of news which invite the attention of readers. They are 1) news as timely report; 2) news as record; 3) news as objective fact; 4) news as interpretation; 5) news as pictures; 6) news as sensation; 7) news as human interest; and 8) news as prediction. The role of the syndicate is to satisfy each and every one of these aspects in order to complement and strengthen a newspaper's own locally produced news.

Since few newspapers can alone afford the services of the top authorities in every field of interest, it is up to the syndicate to marshal just as much of the best available talent as possible through their syndication process. In this regard, it is a syndicate's *obligation* to pioneer and create for the benefit and improvement of newspapers—not imitating what has gone before, but originating new and dynamic features to help build greater newspaper readership and responsible standards.

It is important to note at this point that a newspaper syndicate's efforts toward producing unique and significant features are necessarily limited and largely shaped by the demands of newspaper editors and, as a matter of course, their readers. The most successful syndicates realize that newspapers are controlled by subscribers, that advertising is there because of readership and circulation, and that subscribers often buy a second newspaper solely for certain features that they regularly read. The editors of the most successful newspapers realize this, too, and choose carefully in their selection of features. Many rely heavily upon readership surveys, others upon their own knowledge of and feeling for their readers' interest in their particular circulation areas.

Thus, a syndicate's "pioneering" efforts are tempered by newspapers and succeed in direct proportion to prevailing demand. Yet the responsible syndicate resists fashioning its features to the dictates of questionable opinion and goes ahead with news programs, all the while seeking to provide the best in entertainment and factual reporting. Also, these syndicates should be aware that good features make big names instead of big names making good features!

Worth mentioning here is the fact that the ethical organization does not pirate away the talent of a competing syndicate without due regard for all existing obligations. To do so often results in a kind of professional suicide to the reputations and future success of both syndicate and its acquisition. It may be true that the practice of "pirating features" is sometimes the fault of the columnists or artists as well as of the unscrupulous syndicate, but a responsible syndicate should no more go seeking a competitor's talent without leave than a man go in search of a new mate in his neighbor's backyard. Business ethics and morals are fundamental to the activity of responsible newspaper editors.

The rules which govern the activities of the responsible newspaper syndicate ultimately involve, then, a system of values and an integrity not unlike those rules which determine a man's personal conduct. The main distinction is that, because of its greater potential influence in shaping the lives of men and affairs, the syndicate has a responsibility different more in degree than in kind. To preserve its integrity, a syndicate must not be dominated by any one group and must work independently of, but in harmony with all segments of the people and the press. It should, and does, function to complement the work of every newspaper, from the smallest to the largest metropolitan daily.

Significantly, the extent to which its function is performed is a measure of the virtue of any agency. The ethical, responsible newspaper syndicate should therefore do everything possible to live up to those basic obligations mentioned above.

Insofar as a newspaper syndicate has done this much, it has performed its function; insofar as it has fulfilled its peripheral obligations to the public, to newspapers and to itself, it has done its duty.

Thomas Pepper
GROWING RICH ON THE HIPPIE

Big City dailies merge or fail; the one-press city becomes the norm; only the underground press expands. Catering to subcultural groups, the underground publishers find their audience hungry for words and ideas not found in the "establishment" press. From issues printed on ditto machines in basement offices to the professional Village Voice, *the underground press is read and felt across the land. Thomas Pepper is a former reporter on the Winston-Salem* Journal.

THE underground press has come of age. It is no longer underground and it isn't much of a press, but it does have fanfare—lots of it. In issue after issue in different cities around the country, underground editors proclaim that what they represent is the wave of the future, and that the future will be significantly better because of what they represent. As Allan Katzman, an editor of New York's *East Village Other*, told a correspondent for the ("establishment") *San Francisco Chronicle*, "America now finds itself split into two camps, two life cycles. A cultural evolution is taking place that will sweep the grey-haired masters into the garbage heap. Wisdom and time are on the side of youth." In similar vein, when *Open City* of Los Angeles announced a "national" edition last September, it explained in an editorial: "We feel that it is time that each of the groups now in revolt against an increasingly monolithic social system learns that it has much more in common with the other groups than it previously knew. Perhaps this way the separate, isolated rebellions which the Establishment finds comparatively easy to put down could be joined into one truly effective social and political uprising."

This self-generated excitement was made semi-official last month when *Newsweek* and *The Wall Street Journal* ran survey stories. Both reported increasing circulation and increasing financial success for underground papers, and both elicited the customary hyperbolic quotes from the subjects of any such feature stories. Peter Werbe, co-editor of Detroit's *The Fifth Estate*, assured *Newsweek* readers that success would not spoil the underground press. "I still view it as the first step in the guerrilla movement," the 27-year-old Werbe allowed. "Here we can begin to question the legitimacy of the System." Another underground editor, Marvin Garson, predicted: "It's going to get bigger all the time. There are going to be more and more papers that will give people coverage they're not getting—and will never get—from the daily papers."

Adding substance to such predictions is the appearance of at least two underground news agencies, roughly comparable to the Associated Press and United Press International of the regular world. One, the Underground Press Syndicate (UPS), is a kind of cooperative that permits some sixty papers to reprint one another's stories with a credit line attached. The other, Liberation News Service (LNS), sells its news articles, reviews and essays to subscribers for $180 a year. Based in Washington, LNS has recently advanced beyond the mails and introduced teletype machines.

Estimates of the number of underground papers and readers vary widely. *The Wall Street Journal* counted "more than 50," *Newsweek* "more than 150"; Marshall Bloom, an LNS executive, told *The New York Times* that nearly 200 underground papers had begun publication in the last two years. On the other hand, Bloom told *The Nation* that LNS services some 280 publications, of which 125 were "underground" in a general sense, some eighty were "peace" papers, and the rest were college papers not controlled by an administration. Readership estimates vary from 333,000 (by *The Wall Street Journal*) to 4.6 million (by Bloom). Right now, with the whole underground movement in flux, no figure could be accurate for long.

What do these papers print, and what needs do they fulfill? Are they what they say they are? And are they affecting anyone, particularly their declared enemies, the established press and in turn established society?

In a real sense, the underground papers have brought home to everyone the fact that regular metropolitan dailies do not communicate with subcultures—those small, identifiable groups who remain interested in affairs too local even for a city paper. Instead, the metropolitan papers write for a mass audience, which to them means a middle-class audience, or at least an audience that is presumed to have middle-class mores. When big-city dailies do single out small, identifiable groups, they are careful not to upset existing social rankings. Whether in gossip columns, food recipes, feature stories, or in the moral tone of editorials, local "out groups" have learned not to expect much from their city desks. There are exceptions but, as often as not, attempts to include such "out-groups" are artificial, as in the "zone" editions that alter a few pages, or superficial, as in the coverage of sacraments like obituaries and high school sports.

The callousness of standardized news coverage has long been apparent to its victims—such groups as Bible Belt Southerners (who are pre-middle class), poor Negroes and unassimilated, ethnic white Northerners. Hence the vitality of ethnic radio stations which publicize the stories, the events, the songs and the concerns of America's subcultures, and which counterbalance the mass appeal of big papers by an exclusive appeal to special interests. The suburban newspapers —including all their drivel—fulfill an identical need for yet another subculture. By its success, the underground press has brought all these facts into the open, to a point where "intellectuals" are now aware of them, and to a point where an ordinary, predictable communications gap is transformed into big news—or as some people put it, into a sign of "sickness" in American Society.

One should give credit where credit is due: By making both a financial and a cultural hit with their appeal to a rich and identifiable market, the underground papers have awakened virtually all concerned to a real deficiency in American newspaper journalism. But that is about all the underground press has done. It has certainly not improved the quality of journalism.

Indeed, the underground press has become a kind of suburban press all its own—a suburban press for the hippie and dropout set. The three basic commodities in today's underground newspaper—the advertising, the calendar of events and the artistic and political commentary—all have a parallel in the suburban press. Because the mores of the two audiences are different, the content of the ads, the calendars and the commentaries is different too; in the underground papers, the ads are vulgar, the calendars refer to love-ins rather than Little League, and the commentaries are critical and left wing rather than laudatory and conservative. But the difference between the underground and the suburban press is entirely one of content. The functions of both—to entertain and reinforce their audience—are the same. Suburban and underground editors give virtually the same justification for one-sided, sometimes polemical journalism—that the overwhelming influence of big-city dailies must be countered, and can be countered only if other voices are heard alone, crying in the wilderness with all their purity. Underground papers, like their suburban cousins, give readers what they want to read; they are a great new business, and far from representing a fundamental critique of American society, are actually full-fledged participants in it.

The formula for success in the journalistic underground was invented by *The Village Voice,* a tabloid with offices in Greenwich Village. Started in 1955, the *Voice* didn't turn a profit, according to a *Wall Street Journal* story, until 1963. Today, profit figures are withheld—probably because they are so large. Even before 1963, the secret to whatever appeal the *Voice* had was its technique of always outdoing the rest of the New York press: It stood to the left of the regular press politically, and to the imaginative side artistically. These were not difficult tasks, and there was an eager audience in those New Yorkers who—from a sense of duty or from a vested interest—feel permanently and gnawingly dissatisfied with American public life. With the demise of the New York *Herald Tribune,* the *Voice* has found it even easier to attract local readers who search for alternatives to reading only *The New York Times.* The *Voice,* a weekly, does not run news as such. It has sections devoted to reviews of music, movies, theatre, books and the press, and it regularly carries as filler material announcements that don't make the regular papers. In a typical issue, the *Voice* will run three or four long personal, sometimes narcissistic commentaries on recent social or political events, with considerable emphasis on the abstract issues or moral principles thought to be relevant, and very little on the technical or bureaucratic aspects of fitting means to ends. The *Voice* prints a prodigious quantity of advertising, including retail shops, entertainment, books, off-beat fashions and classifieds. For the audience involved, the ads are informative and useful; they unquestionably pull well for the advertisers. Apart from everything else, the *Voice* is chic, as essential a piece of equipment to some New Yorkers as the *Trib* used to be to others.

The *Voice's* formula—always feed the reader something that outdoes the regular, local press—has now been copied throughout the country. The content may have changed—the *Voice* now seems conservative by comparison with some of the later entrants to the field—but the process and the significance remain the same. Like their innovative "enemies" in the business world, their avowed "enemies" in the established press, and their dominant ancestor, *The Village Voice,* today's underground papers are meeting previously latent consumer needs, catering uncritically to the tastes of their consumers, and prospering from a shrewd analysis of the contemporary leisure-time market. The Berkeley *Barb,* the *East Village Other,* and the Los Angeles *Free Press* led the way in classified ads, for example, by opening their columns to advertisers soliciting sex partners, nude models and drugs. The demand for similar papers has snowballed. In every case, the local appeal of ads and calendars is mixed with the national appeal of underground revolt. Helped along by low operating costs, permissive court decisions on pornography, and the fortunate coincidence that today's social rebels happen to be sons and daughters of relatively wealthy parents, the underground papers have flourished by making themselves useful to a select group of advertisers.

Local conditions do produce some substantive differences. In Los Angeles, a relatively new paper, the *Underground*, has attacked the *Free Press* for making an "'in' thing of sick sex and drugs." In North Carolina, the *Anvil* shuns vulgarity and tries, in a somewhat tortured way, to present serious political and economic analysis. But because of the overwhelming sameness in most underground papers, the best of them all probably wouldn't qualify as "underground" today. It is the Pittsburgh *Point*, a well-produced weekly, whose response to the modern world is more than an outraged scream. Its political reporting, while reflecting concern about war, race and moral principles, is also strikingly detached. In covering a conference on organizing the poor, for example, the *Point* managed to take some shots at the participants without feeling obliged to disagree with their overall aims. In other words, the *Point* noticed a nuance or two that its more frenzied counterparts could hardly afford to describe. After quoting speaker Nicholas Von Hoffmann complaining about "wasted oratory" in community organization, *Point* editor Charles C. Robb wrote: "Von Hoffmann wasted some oratory himself in a long, rambling talk that was half ad lib, half read from scribbled notes." Later in the same article, Robb described one panelist as "the Negro grocer from Homewood who has become the loudest established black militant in the city." The *Point* also declared its preferences in last November's county election, but did not feel called upon to blame a conspiracy for their subsequent defeat.

Surprising as it might seem from the tone of the underground press, its writers are not the only people unhappy with the accomplishments of America's regular papers. There are plenty of critics—Irving Kristol, James Reston and McGeorge Bundy among them—who offer publishers both critiques and suggested reforms. And while the underground press may not realize it, the deficiencies of regular newspapers are only partly ideological. After all, the practices of the big-city papers, like those of the underground papers, make good economic sense. There is a limit to what can be done, and papers tend naturally to their most obvious, short-range tasks and stick naturally to traditional ways of doing things. Only the most ethically minded publishers seek quality for its own sake, whether in coverage of foreign affairs, city hall, or subcultures. And even among these publishers, an economic constraint will establish an outer limit to what is possible. Ironically, the most visible force for reform of big-city papers is neither the serious critics nor the underground critics but the new, slick city magazines. These magazines have demonstrated, by their own success, that the *nouveau riche* want and will buy more stimulating artistic commentary than is provided by the daily papers. Lately, the papers have been following suit.

The underground papers are not a quality press because they pander to their readers with a dexterity befitting the establishment papers they criticize so bitterly. In their own pages, instead of stimulating political and social discussion worthy of the society they say they seek, the underground papers offer nothing more than a stylized theory of protest. Indeed, by the definitions it now prescribes, the underground movement not only requires protest as an end in itself; it depends on protest. For without a dogged concentration on perpetual antagonism, some people might admit to improvements, "sell-out," and leave the movement. Then where would the underground papers be and what would they write about? This theme of "selling out" is a new and a hip variant of an old and inadequate form of social protest—one that was rejected both by the incremental reformers of civics-book America and by the professional revolutionaries of Russia, China and Africa, all of whom realized, sooner or later, that some positive program is needed to translate general goals into concrete benefits.

Instead of bringing much needed reforms to the established press, the underground papers have inspired their rich, fat, corporate enemies to enter the underground market themselves, and thus to cash in on yet another fad. This bears out the verdict of the London *Economist,* which wrote some nineteen months ago that "much of the new left's judgement of contemporary society is based on aesthetic rather than political or even moral criteria." It is helpful to separate the life style of the underground subculture from its claim to superior morality and from the specific political ideas buried beneath the psychedelic art work. One can then see that with an unholy mess like the Vietnamese War to provide a base for indignation, it has been all too easy for the movement to condemn everybody else. If things are less simple from now on—with equally moral politicians disagreeing over policies and judgments and hunches—the underground press may find that a tone of outrage, supplemented by ads for beads and uninhibited roommates, will not hold its profitable audience together.

Mark F. Ethridge
THE NEWSPAPER THAT WILL ENDURE—
A SUMMING UP

Noting the enormous changes in American society and the implication of these changes for the nation's press, Mark F. Ethridge, then editor of the Long Island Newsday, *comments on his belief in the survival of the newspaper as a viable force. His remarks were delivered in 1964 on the two-hundredth anniversary of the* Hartford Courant, *one of the country's oldest papers.*

MOST of what has been said today about communications, particularly newspapers, should be put against the background of a sociological revolution which the United States is undergoing.

When he was inaugurated as president of Yale University, Kingman Brewster, the speaker of last night, said, among other things, "The next decade of our trusteeship must cope with three revolutions: the explosion of knowledge, the burgeoning population and the uncanny development of automated machines and mechanized intelligence." Dr. Brewster would now undoubtedly like to add as the fourth revolution which we are witnessing and in which we are living, the fight for civil rights.

I don't know of any industry that has been more affected by the sociological revolution that has taken place since World War II than the newspaper business. It manifests itself in many ways as far as we are concerned:

In the decline of the number of newspapers. In the past ten years, 202 dailies have died, or reverted to weeklies. In the same time 171 have been started, most of them suburban. No new newspapers have been started in cities of more than 100,000 in the past 15 years, except in Portland, Oregon; Phoenix, Arizona; Jackson, Mississippi, Atlanta and Oklahoma City. The first three have died. Since I entered newspaper work 35 percent of the dailies have disappeared.

In the trend toward monopoly, merger, printing corporations and 24-hour newspapers. Ninety-six percent of the cities in the United States have no daily newspaper competition. Chains, or groups, as some of them prefer to be called, control 50 percent of the circulations of daily newspapers. There are 23 states with cities that have no daily newspaper competition, several more with only one competing newspaper situation. The trend toward monopoly, merger and 24-hour operations will continue, I venture.

This sociological revolution manifests itself in the fact that 20 percent of the American population moves each year, chiefly to the cities and the suburbs. Dr. Gallup said today that whereas 80 percent of the American people were farmers a century ago, only a tenth of that number, 8 percent, are on the farms now.

The mass migration has created a host of problems: the decay of the core of the cities, the creation of slums, the disruption of tax structures, the extreme employment sensitivity to the shifting of defense industries, the demands of the urban and suburban counties for greater and fairer representation in their state legislatures and in the lower House of the national Congress, shifting the balance of power from the rural to urban and suburban areas of the country and in the demand for a greater measure of civil rights, sometimes leading to riots.

It has affected newspapers, too. There has been a decline in the number of metropolitan newspapers and a great increase in suburban papers. Department stores and shopping centers in metropolitan areas have followed their customers to the suburbs and have created new shopping habits. The young marrieds of whom Dr. Gallup spoke shop together in large part. Where they don't the woman can wear shorts to the stores, get free parking and put her baby in a shopping cart. These changing habits have been a boon to suburban newspapers. Since I know it best, I shall use *Newsday* as an example.

When Harry Guggenheim and Alicia Patterson founded *Newsday* in a garage in Hempstead, L.I., the population of the two counties in which we circulate, Nassau and Suffolk, was 604,000. Today, that population is 2,400,000. The circulation of *Newsday* has just passed 400,000 and it is the eighth largest evening paper in the country— the 17th largest of all dailies. Obviously, since it carries a bigger weekday advertising linage than any New York paper, it has drained off enormous revenues from the New York newspapers. It is the biggest, but only one of the 106 newspapers in the two counties. Our situation is not unique. In the two counties which Los Angeles claims as the metropolitan area there are 26 daily newspapers, one of them with more than 150,000 circulation. What is indicated is that there will be further rationalization of metropolitan newspaper situations. In ten metropolitan areas which he studied, Dr. Ken Byerly of the University of North Carolina found that suburban newspapers had more circulation than their metropolitan counterparts.

This sociological revolution has also manifested itself in the phenomenal growth of television as an advertising medium and as a medium of news accepted by the people and as an instrument of public communication and public service. Television's effect upon newspapers can be demonstrated by two or three figures. In the past five years there has been a decline of more than 16 percent in national advertising in newspapers, almost all of it going to television. Since 1956, the peak year of newspapers, the decline has been more than 25 percent. Last year, for instance, the top 100 national advertisers spent 56 percent of their money on television, 20 percent in general magazines, 17 percent in newspapers and the other 7 percent in radio and other media. Television combined with suburbanization has made it more difficult to keep up the circulation of afternoon papers. A man used to get two papers; now he gets a morning paper and usually his community paper which gives him the news of schools, sewers, tax rates, etc.—the things by which he lives.

There is one other factor in the sociological revolution which has been mentioned by speakers here today as affecting all branches of communications. That is the measurable rise in the intellectual level of our people, a rise which Dr. Gallup stressed. It exists; it was stimulated undoubtedly by the GI bill and sputnik. But it is a factor with which all media of communication must reckon. Speaking at Marquette three years ago, Wally Carroll told of Willie Stevens, the so-called "idiot boy" of the Hall-Mills murder case. Wally said that pasted on the typewriter of a foreign correspondent was a picture of Willie. Asked why, the correspondent answered, "I have to remind myself that this is my average reader."

"Today," said Wally, "the world of Willie Stevens is behind us. Whatever the newspaper reading public of that time may have been, it is no longer so today. . . . It is to these readers of new tastes and interests and their new sense of responsibility that we in the newspapers must give more serious attention."

I grew up in a newspaper generation that, if it did not regard Willie Stevens as the average reader, was certainly taught that we must write for the twelve-year-old mind. What I am afraid of today is that the mirror is being turned back toward us and that too many of our readers regard newspapermen as the twelve-year-olds; that too many of us have been mired in the old-fashioned concepts of the functions of newspapers while the intelligence level of the American people has risen. I frequently think that too many of us regard our methods as unalterable as the laws of the Medes and the Persians. Then I wonder where the hell the Medes are.

If in what I have said you are listening to a Jeremiah, let me disclaim pessimism. Hamilton Basso in "The View From Pompey's Head" had one of his characters say that he was "still a little blinded by the dust of wonder that had got into my eyes." That happened to me more than 50 years ago when I first discovered newspapering. As a realist I have tried to diagnose the disease; as one who believes strongly that newspapers will endure, let me suggest a few ways in which that may be assured.

What I believed when I became a publisher 30 years ago, I still hold to: not only the best, but the cheapest box office attraction a newspaper has is its editorial and news content. Give me a newspaper that prints the news fully, fairly and fearlessly, interprets it intelligently and comments upon it vigorously and I will take my chances on survival.

I believe strongly that newspapers are indispensable to the full enlightenment of the American people and that in altered form they will survive through any period in which we may be interested. Television is capable of excellent documentaries and spot coverage of major stories, but inherent in its structure is the necessity for a great measure of entertainment. But neither television, which must paint with a broad brush, nor radio, no matter how local, can give extended coverage or satisfy the hunger of people to know about their schools, sewers, free-ways, local tax rates, juvenile delinquency and other problems closer to them than Baghdad or Moscow. Nor can they compete with metropolitan newspapers in depth coverage of significant stories, national, international or local.

If we of newspapers are to endure—and we will—we must recapture our editorial pages from the columnists and write in the vigorous tradition of Greeley, Cobb of the *World*, Watterson, Grady and other giants of the editorial pages.

We must recognize that there has been a lift in the intellectual level and a change in the habits and tastes of our readers—a more serious concern for things that affect their survival. There has been, in my time, a change for the better in the newspapers' concept of their responsibility to the public. There is less cheapness, less tawdriness, less pandering to the baser emotions and fewer newspapers that do it than when I came along. There is more sober and generally more independent discussion of issues; less blatant partisanship.

There is better reporting; more background information, more reporting in depth, more interpretation of the news, more graphic aids for the reader, a keener awareness that eternal vigilance is indeed the price of good government, as Monty Curtis said. I have never known an administration, national, local or state, that did not try to manage the news when the news was unfavorable and I don't suppose there will ever be one. The newspaper is still the best weapon against concealment of civic wrongs of all sorts.

When I think of public service, I think of young fellows with whom I have worked or who have worked for me: of Mike Johnson, who won a Pulitzer prize for exposing the dock racket in New York; of Dick Berger, who voluntarily went to jail in Kentucky and helped reform the prison system; of Buford Boone, who defied the mob at Tuscaloosa; of Bob Caro of *Newsday,* who broke up the mail order land schemes that were fleecing older people who wanted to retire and those dozens of others of whom Monty Curtis knows. There can be no underemphasis on the newspaper that wants to endure of its obligation to its role of public protector.

We must, I think, look to our manpower and its constant improvement. We must develop specialists: science writers, business writers, competent critics and specialists in public affairs. We must hire men who know as much or more than the people to whom they are writing, or know how to find out. Journalism schools can contribute mightily to that. Since Neil Luxon of North Carolina sent his cry into the wilderness—a cry for fewer and better schools of journalism—the first faint echo has been transformed into an insistent demand for better education, not in the techniques, but in the content of journalism, in the problems with which newspaper men have to deal.

We must keep up with production techniques, with automation. Newspapers are at least a generation behind in the sort of research that would make production more efficient. I am glad to say that the ANPA has in recent years greatly stepped up its own research. Many small newspapers are going to offset printing; many larger ones are embracing all sorts of labor-saving electronic devices, including about 10 which have computers. "Automate or die!" has become almost a slogan among newspaper managers. Needless to say, in a great many places, notably New York, automation is meeting with the bitterest resistance on the part of the unions and more trouble can be anticipated. But automation must come if more newspapers are not to die, and with it perhaps facsimile transmission of whole news pages as has now been instituted in Japan.

But when all the things I have mentioned have been done, the newspaper that will endure must stay with the fundamentals. A cub reporter's techniques are no substitute for informed counsel of able and fearless editors willing to combat bigotry and fanaticism wherever they occur. Our stake in the world is too high for us to be playing from ignorance and prejudice. Every newspaper which hopes to survive in a contracting field, every editor who is worth his salt, must deal with the problems of his region, his country and the world.

For the newspaper that endures, a fitting masthead might be Pulitzer's injunction, "Never be satisfied with merely printing news; always be drastically independent, never be afraid to attack wrong by predatory plutocracy, or predatory poverty."

And above all, in the spirit of what Monty Curtis has said, but in the words of Harry Ashmore, we must remember that "The free press was conceived not only for the protection of the verities, but as the cutting edge of change."

AUDIENCE AND EFFECT

James Reston
A LETTER TO SANTA

One of America's most influential journalists, James Reston talks about his newspaper, the New York Times, *and what it means to him. The following article was written during the lengthy newspaper strike of 1962–1963 and reflected the feelings held by many readers for whom the newspaper is an integral part of their daily lives.*

DEAR SANTA: All I want for Christmas is *The New York Times.* I don't ask for any of these new fur bed sheets, or electric socks or automatic spaghetti winders, but a man is entitled to have old friends around at a time like this.

Somebody struck the *Times* in the belief that it's a newspaper, but that is obviously ridiculous. The *Times* is a public institution, like the Yankees or Barney Baruch. When everything else is changing, the *Times* remains the same—typographical errors and all.

Reading the *Times* is a life career, like raising a family—and almost as difficult. But I've become accustomed to its peculiar ways and can't break the habit. It is a community service, like plumbing. It will light more fires and line more shelves and cover up more rugs on a snowy day than any other publication in the world, and I need it, Mister, especially at Christmas.

This is the season of peace and somehow—I don't know why—peace seems to have a better chance in the *Times.* Everybody else seems to be shouting at us and giving the human race six weeks to get out. But the *Times* is always saying that there was trouble in the sixteenth century, too. It never seems to think anything is quite as good or as bad as others make it out to be. It is always saying "on the one hand" and "on the other hand" and in the confusion it manages to give the impression that if things are *that* complicated, nobody will quite know how to start a war.

One of the great things about a newspaper, especially on Sunday, is that you can split the thing up and let everybody in the family settle into a quiet trance with the section he likes best. This cuts down on the noise. You can throw away what you don't want, and the ads don't sing.

The television makes newspapermen feel a little obsolescent once in a while, but it stuns the mind. It makes you listen to all the news you don't want to hear in order to get around to the news you do want to hear. You can't split up Chet Huntley or throw away part of Dave Brinkley—not at least without a fight.

This is one of the great advantages of the *Times:* you get so much more to throw away. It is impenetrable but indispensable. Other papers cover the news and the *Times* smothers it, but the reader benefits. People are always dying in the *Times* who don't seem to die in other papers, and they die at greater length and maybe even with a little more grace.

If a good professor is promoted to the head of the English department at Tufts, or even has the bad luck to be stuck with the presidency of Rutgers, the event is duly recorded—complete with ten-year-old one-column photograph—and is read with pride or sympathy on every campus in the land.

All this, Dear Santa, makes it hard, I know, to get the *Times* down the chimney, but striking the *Times* is like striking an old lady and deprives the community at Christmas of all kinds of essential information. If some recklessly beautiful girl gets married at the Waldorf this week, the television may let us see her gliding radiantly from the church and tossing her bouquet to some lucky member of the Hasty Pudding Club, but what about all those ugly girls who get married every Sunday in the *Times?*

Are they to be ignored just at their unlikely moment of triumph? The pretty girl may marry again, temptation and pretty girls being what they are, but the ugly girl hits the center aisle but once, and the event must be recorded then in the annals of human hope.

Without newspapers the procedures of life change. Tired men, sick of the human race after a long gabby day at the office, cannot escape on the train into the life story of Y.A. Tittle or the political perils of Harold Macmillan, but must go on talking to strangers all the way to Westport. Once home, they are bereft of excuses to avoid fixing that dripping tap or shoveling the walk.

Even history and geography seem different. Yemen was in deep trouble in the *Times* when the strike started, and things weren't very jolly in Afghanistan or Kashmir, but we never discovered how the thing came out.

So please do what you can to get the papers back. It's bad enough on the public but think of a reporter. I've been fielding the *Times* on the first bounce on my front stoop every morning for twenty-five years and it's cold and lonely out there now. Besides, how do I know what to think if I can't read what I write?

P.S.—Don't forget the *Herald Tribune,* too.

Harry Golden
THE NEWSPAPER GAME AND THE BIG STORY

What is it that the public wants to read about? What is the "Big Story"? Harry Golden, long-time editor of the Carolina Israelite, *provides some surprising or perhaps not so surprising answers.*

EACH generation believes that the news events of its time are the most world-shaking of all history, but the Big Story remains the same.

It is the story of a bride, of the winner on an Irish Sweepstakes ticket, of an ax murder, of a child killed by fire, of villainy and courage, of Don Larsen's perfect game in the World Series, of the so-called "love triangle," of the death of a man who lived down the street. . . .

It is the story of the human heart.

And the newspaperman, whose job it is to seek out this story, is much misunderstood.

Many a newspaperman winces when a layman refers to him as a "writer." Actually a writer is a novelist. This is not to say that we do not have many brilliant journalists, reporters, editors, analysts, economists, muckrakers, pamphleteers, sociologists, and propagandists—all writers in the sense that they communicate their ideas and their experiences through the printed word, in books, newspapers, pamphlets, broadsides, and magazines; but "writer" is really a designation which belongs to the creative artist.

The layman looks with awe on the by-line in his newspaper. Some of our great reporters and editors have their names attached to their material, but on most daily newspapers the by-line, in itself, is not too important any more. Quite often a reporter, just out of journalism school and on his first job, will get a by-line when sent out to write up the late developments at the Y.M.C.A. This is not to say that this stuff is not important. It is as necessary as the morning headline, but many men who really are the kings of a news room seldom see their names in print. These are the rewritemen and deskmen. The young reporter will go out to interview a celebrity at the airport. He writes the stuff in his little book; drinks a Coca-Cola; revises what he has written; walks over to the library to look up a word or a quotation; tears it all up; chats with a couple of friends about this and that; gets over to the office and writes the story; looks it over; corrects it; maybe writes it over again; and finally turns it in. The job of the deskman is a little more intense. The phone rings about ten minutes before the paper goes to press. On the other end of the line is a sheriff, or a policeman, or a part-time correspondent of the newspaper. In great excitement, the caller says that there's been an accident on the highway; above the din of passing traffic, ambulance and police sirens, the caller pours out names, places, circumstances, and other details; a click in the ear, and the deskman rolls a piece of paper into his typewriter; he has to record the names of the occupants of the car; who was driving; who was hurt; which hospital the injured were taken to; the first officer on the scene; arrests, if any; home addresses of the occupants; where they were going; any other car involved; who was driving that one; and on; and on; and in three or four minutes the story has to be in the hands of the printer, with the proper heading in perfect shape; and everything had better be accurate right down to the middle initial.

Reporters and deskmen, however, share one distinction. They never "have it made." You can be the Ace for years, but *one* item, a carelessly checked story, and nothing that has gone before means a thing. There are no erasures once the edition hits the streets, and there are very few second chances. I guess that is one of the reasons the business is so fascinating. There is no challenge like it. It is probably the most valuable occupation known to our society. And this fascination, inconsistent with the remuneration involved, has been transferred to the general public. Hardly a man alive with common sense and red blood hasn't seen himself at one time or another as a reporter.

If I were managing editor of a metropolitan daily newspaper, the first thing I would do would be to throw out at least 50 per cent of the syndicated junk. To fill this valuable space I would use my own staff of young men and women. I would turn them loose in the state, county, and city in search of the Big Story. As a case in point, there are at least ten newspapermen here in Charlotte who not only can write better than Robert Ruark and Constantine Brown, but who have more education and far more intelligence.

And I say this as a member of the fraternity of syndicated columnists, myself.

The trouble is, most of the columnists lose sight of the Big Story.

I sold newspapers as a boy on a busy corner (Norfolk and Delancey) of New York. The days were filled with great events: "Archduke Ferdinand Assassinated"; "Russia Mobilized"; "England Warns Kaiser"; "Germany Invades Belgium"; "Hindenburg Smashes Russians at Tannenberg"; "Von Kluck Reaches Suburbs of Paris."

The reader grabbed the newspaper out of your hands before you had a chance to fold it properly. But these were not the real banner days. Not by a long shot. On the days you had to go back two or three times to get more papers the headlines were "Society Girl Found Dead in Opium Den"; "Another Murder in Hell's Kitchen"; "Police Lieutenant Becker Electrocuted."

And, by far the biggest day of all was when Leo Frank was lynched down in Georgia. I remember that the Yiddish papers that day had front page streamers in red ink, which I had never seen before.

The *Manchester Guardian* recently concluded that newspaper readers are interested in the same type of story on both sides of the Atlantic; and that the most stimulating newsbill (equivalent of our tabloid headline) is the announcement of a story concerned with any one of these interesting subjects—murder, sex, dope, kidnaping, or children.

James Gordon Bennett grasped the idea when, as editor of *The New York Herald,* he decided to cover a murder story. A prostitute was found dead in a sleazy rooming house. In accordance with the custom of the 1850's, this should have been a one-line item among seventy other reports on an inside page. But Bennett put a screaming headline on his paper, "Prostitute Found Slain," and ordered his artist to draw a pciture of the body showing a naked leg dangling over the side of the bed. That headline and the dangling leg ushered in a new era in American journalism.

If you were asked to list the great American news stories, you would think of the Lindbergh kidnaping; Leopold and Loeb; the disappearance of Charlie Ross; the disappearance of Dorothy Arnold; did Nan Patterson kill Caesar Young in the hansom cab in Central Park? the Girl in the Red Velvet Swing; and a great many others, including the marriage of Grace Kelly and Prince Rainier.

The news and photo coverage of this last-named wholesome event is worthy of a study by an expert psychologist.

One of the greatest story plots of all time, in all history, in all languages, in all religions, in all cultures is the Cinderella theme. In every play, novel, story, movie, article, and speech, humankind is forever trying to seek out the wonderful story of the one who comes upon the good things in life—suddenly—as if by magic.

And, of course, the Rainier-Kelly wedding was Cinderella come to life, and among the greatest stories ever told.

What interested me particularly was that so many people, in their complete absorption, cried out, as if in desperation: "I am sick and tired of reading so much about Grace Kelly."

It is only when a story completely overwhelms you (you are afraid that you are actually losing contact with reality) that you resort to this protest, often stopping strangers on the street in order to keep a firm grip on yourself: "I am terribly sick of reading so much about Grace Kelly"; the implication being that you are eager to get back to the speeches of Everett Dirksen. But the symptoms are well known and the protesters cannot hope to fool the news and wire services, the experienced reporters and managing editors.

The New York Times is the most consistently excellent newspaper in the world. It is also one of the finest American institutions, along with Harvard, the New York Yankees, and the Supreme Court. The *Times* has an unvarnished integrity. It maintains correspondents in every nook and cranny of the globe. It will report the price of hemp on the Bombay exchange.

The *Times* lists the names and titles of every diplomat, statesman, ruler, potentate, president, or cabinet member who comes to New York each day, records at what hotel he registered and what ship brought him. When a thief is arrested the *Times* always gives the name of the arresting officer. If Kenyon beats Oberlin, the *Times* explains what a surprising upset this is. Yet the real proof that the *Times* understands the real news is that it has never failed to include the full Sunday section of brides. Often it runs into extra pages. The entire section is devoted to pictures of girls in wedding gowns and each one of these stories is as freshly written as the next. In fact, to read through this section is to take a deep breath of fresh air. The *Times* knows this. The human story still is a bride.

Or a murder . . .

I remember how my second son, Harry, Jr., dug into murders some years ago when he was police reporter for *The Charlotte Observer*.

Harry's most interesting murder story involved a respected businessman held for the murder of his wife. One morning at 7:30, Richard Russell called the police and told them he'd found his wife murdered. The police found Mrs. Russell in the basement, scantily clad, with her head beaten to a pulp. The coroner established that the woman had died some five hours earlier. In their investigation police found a pair of trousers belonging to Russell which had been cut up into strips and flushed down the toilet. Further investigation revealed that the woman had been killed in the bedroom she shared with her husband and dragged feet-first downstairs. The police, in arresting Mr. Russell, alleged that he had spent those five hours between the time of the killing and his call to the police "cleaning up" the place. But, the police claimed, he forgot to clean the blood spots on the ceiling of the bedroom. The man's stenographer was also taken into custody when the police discovered a stack of love letters. But hours of questioning failed to shake Russell's story that his wife had been killed downstairs while he was sleeping upstairs. All this time everyone was waiting patiently for the "confession."

In Charlotte we have two big daily papers—*The Charlotte Observer,* the morning paper, and *The Charlotte News* in the afternoon, and naturally there is the usual rivalry between the two news rooms. All through these days of the Russell questioning, Harry, Jr., was praying that Russell would confess on "his" (Harry's) time (4:00 P.M. to midnight) instead of on *The News'* time (6:00 A.M. to 4:00 P.M.). But actually I doubt whether good reporters really want the fellow to confess. If he confesses the story is over. On the other hand, without a confession, they can keep writing good stories, and Harry, Jr., went to town. He described the color of the wallpaper in the bedroom where the murder had taken place, the pictures on the wall, the clothes in the closet, the quality of the mattress, etc. Those are the things people want to read, and those are the things that make the newspaperman.

(The fellow finally copped a plea at his trial, but by that time Harry was busy covering a grand jury investigation of the police department, and his colleague, Kays Gary, covered the trial.)

My own selection of the all-time American news story would be the one that concerned Miss Elizabeth Borden, the New England marm with the thin lips, who was accused and tried for murder of her father and stepmother. The story has been told a million times and has been made into drama, comedy, opera, and even a ballet *(The Fall River Legend).* And for the first decade of this century the teachers found it difficult to teach "Twinkle, twinkle, little star . . . " because most of the kids were filled with jingles such as:

Lizzie Borden took an ax
And gave her mother forty whacks;
When she saw what she had done,
She gave her father forty-one.

All of these stories are part of the human drama and there is nothing to be ashamed of because they absorb our interest.

Recently a convention of news editors voted for the all-time big story and first on the list was the "Discovery of America by Christopher

Columbus." Leaving out matters of faith and religion, it would be hard to dispute that choice—but only in perspective. The newsboys of Europe did not shout, "Extra! Columbus Discovers a New World." Only a few people were interested, and the only question they asked was, "What did he find there?" The great mass of the people took the news just about as we took the news that Admiral Byrd had discovered Little America near the South Pole. If Europe had a William Allen White at the time the Columbus story broke, I am sure he was getting all the attention with an article on "How Old Should a Child Be Before He May Be Whipped?"

As a boy, I kept a scrapbook of the leading news story of each day from July 1, 1914, to November 11, 1918. I used those old-fashioned notebooks and when it was all over I had about fifteen of them.

In later years, I discovered that the Big Story in every instance was on the other side of my important clipping.

On the other side of the clipping which told of the loss of Lord Kitchener on the H.M.S. *Hampshire* was an announcement by the Borden Milk Company that it would put up milk in sanitary bottles, no more dipping out of the can at the grocery.

On the back of the photo showing the Kaiser Wilhelm and his five younger sons on parade, I found an advertisement of John Wanamaker calling attention to boys' "going-back-to-school" wool suits at $7.95.

Here is a photo of General Joffre in conference with David Lloyd George and on the other side a box score of a game between Cleveland and the Red Sox. The score was 4 to 1. Ernie Shore was the pitcher for Boston, Bagby pitched for Cleveland, and Hooper hit a home run.

There are photos of the Belgian Ambassador Emanuel Havenith arriving in New York; the Irish nationalist John E. Redmond appearing before Parliament; the story of the death of "Austria's Aged Emperor," and a photo of the German submarine commander who had sailed across the Atlantic.

And behind each of these world-shaking events was the more important story; a fire on Twenty-third Street and Tenth Avenue—twenty people were dispossessed by the flames but they found refuge next door at the public baths.

And a statement by Carrie Smith, regional president of the W.C.T.U.: "If there were no drinking, there would be no war."

Behind the news story of a new offensive in the Meuse-Argonne, I read that Father Francis Joseph O'Brien, a recent graduate of the Iona Seminary in New Rochelle, had been appointed to his first parish on 116th Street.

This was the real news of those war years. Because this was the every-
day life of the people.

Thirty-five years from now, despite the Khrushchev pronouncements, the twirling sputniks, and artificial planets, the Big Story will still be about people who struggle to pay the rent and get up the tuition for a girl in college.

The story is about people who lose jobs and find better ones. How they go off to hear a first sermon of the new priest, and how they raise their families, and how they die.

And the moral is, don't paste up your scrapbooks with that old-fashioned white school paste. It is a terrible problem trying to unpaste them without tearing the clippings. And thirty years from now you'll be interested only in "what was on the other side."

On his way to and from the Globe Theatre, William Shakespeare could see the tall sails of the *Golden Hind* in which Sir Francis Drake had circumnavigated the globe.

The poet was beginning to reach toward his creative powers when the Spanish Armada was destroyed and the first Elizabeth ushered in Britain's age of Gloriana.

Yet Mr. Shakespeare, who "held a mirror up to life," never mentioned a single one of these events.

Instead, he was busy with the Big Story, the human drama: the story of good children and unkind children; the story of noble men and of cowards; and the story of the mother who upsets her son by remarrying too soon after the father's death.

Think of the many empires that have been won and lost since that afternoon when Cleopatra sailed down the Nile, draped in a cloth of Venus, under a canopy of gold, to meet her lover, Mark Antony:

> Age cannot wither her, nor custom stale
> Her infinite variety. . . .

Shakespeare meant, of course, that "age cannot wither" the Cleopatra story. He knew then what all good reporters know now, that the Big Story is not of our technological wonders, nor of the enchantment of unknown lands.

The Big Story is rather of the mysteries of the human heart.

Richard L. Neuberger
NEWS AT THE LEGISLATURE

How informed is the public about its government? Discussing this question, Richard L. Neuberger, a famed journalist before he entered the Oregon state legislature and the United States Senate, finds that people are often more knowledgeable about national politics than about their own state politics.

STATE legislatures are the lawmaking bodies closest to the American people. How good is the news coverage of the average legislature in the United States? Do the folks at home really know what goes on under the marble dome of the state capitol?

After having participated desultorily in the coverage of legislative sessions in at least half a dozen Western states, I look at the problem today from the other side of the mahogany rail. I am a member of the Oregon State Senate. My constituency is the 13th district, which comprises the city of Portland. I was elected last November to a four-year term.

The two dominant papers in the state are the *Oregonian* and the *Journal.* Both are published in Portland, the only large city. Each has three men covering the session. These include the capital correspondent of each paper, the political editor, and one other member of the general news staff. They file to the two papers a grand total of approximately 7,000 words every legislative day.

Although both the *Oregonian* and the *Journal* have profound editorial biases, the coverage by their correspondents is factual and untinged by opinion. The two papers are conservative in policy—both urged the election of Dewey—but this policy rarely creeps into the news stories about the legislature. Controversial issues such as fair employment practices, workmen's compensation, and Columbia Valley Authority are handled as they occur, with no slant given.

129

In addition to the coverage of the legislature in considerable detail by the two Portland dailies, the Associated Press and United Press each has two staff men in the Senate and House chambers. The session also is followed closely by the pair of dailies published in Salem, the state capital. These are the *Statesman* and the *Capital-Journal.*

Here, again, the coverage is factual, truthful and unbiased, although the editorials of the *Capital-Journal* are too far from reality to communicate with it by smoke signals. To be candid, the only "policy" material I have noticed emanating from the legislature is that which some senators and representatives send back to their home-town papers. This plays up the local lawmaker as quite a hero. And, because the members from the smaller communities and rural areas are almost invariably conservative, the columns mailed by them to the country press tend to portray the liberals from Portland as a pretty shabby lot.

Of course, this is not serious, for it reaches only a small proportion of the voters. The *Oregonian* and the *Journal* blanket Oregon. One or the other of these big dailies reaches into every remote upland and mountain valley. I have been a guest at ranch houses so isolated that the nearest schoolhouse was too far away for the children of the family to come home except for Christmas. But when the mail arrived, these people got the *Oregonian* or the *Journal.*

Yet despite this blanketing of the state by the big dailies—and in spite of the basically truthful coverage of the legislature by those papers— I find many people uninformed on what is taking place in the carpeted chambers of their capitol building.

As chairman of the Senate Committee on Municipal Affairs, I talked a few days ago with the mayor of a city of 25,000 people. He knew nothing at all about bills in our committee which vitally affected his community. Perhaps I was even more chagrined that he did not know the identity of the committee chairman!

Yet, in general conversation, I found this man fully acquainted with the progress of the Congressional debate on repeal of the Taft-Hartley Law. He knew who was sponsoring the Columbia Valley Authority bill in Washington, D.C., but not who was sponsoring a memorial backing the bill in Salem, Oregon.

I have wondered a good deal about this, and I have asked quite a few questions. As a result, I have come to the conclusion that, because of one particular reason, many Americans know a lot more about what takes place in the capital of the nation than in the comparatively nearby capital of their state.

That reason is the columnists.

The big Portland dailies are well buttressed with columnists from Washington, D.C., and the East. The *Journal* prints Pearson, Stokes,

Sokolsky, Lawrence, and Pegler. The *Oregonian's* repertoire includes Childs, Lippmann, Fleeson, Thompson, Alexander, and Lyons. Thus both papers encompass a fairly wide circle of opinion from national sources.

Yet neither paper publishes a column from Salem, the capital of Oregon. This, in my opinion, is why people in our state often know more about what goes on in the legislative halls 3,000 miles away than in halls a mere 50 miles distant.

The real story is often the inside story. Pearson specializes in revealing the story behind the headlines. Men like Childs, Stokes, and Lawrence specialize in analyzing it from varying viewpoints.

There is no counterpart of this in the coverage of our state government in Oregon. Each of the two big dailies has a whole stable of Washington columnists, but none at the legislature.

Frequently, the very rectitude of the men covering the capital keeps them from going behind the scenes. Some years ago the *Oregonian* and the *Journal* heavily tilted their news columns. Political items inevitably were weighted. But as older staff men were retired, as people became more conscious of journalistic ethics, a new generation of writers was told to "play it straight." The facts were allowed to speak for themselves.

The men covering our legislative session will tell you what takes place, but they have strict orders against opinionated news stories. They need a "news peg" before they can allege that a former governor is lobbying for gamblers or that state school timber has been sold for a fraction of its value. The columnist is held back by no such rules. He can flail out at corruption and chicanery, news peg or no news peg. In some instances, this may be bad *per se,* but it does afford easy access to the "inside story."

Newspapers occasionally shy away from the story close at hand. They are notoriously braver about the skullduggery of the Russians than that of the local real estate board. This may pertain somewhat to the analogy of Washington, D.C., and the state capital. It may be easier to run the comments of a hard-hitting political columnist who operates 3,000 miles away than one whose writings concern people within walking distance of the editor's office.

If we are to give vitality to state government, I am convinced we must cover our state capitals as thoroughly, as intimately, and as revealingly as Washington, D.C., is covered. It does not make sense for each of our big Portland papers to print four or five editorial-page columns from the capital of the nation but no counterpart of these from the capital of Oregon. Nor are potential authors lacking. I am sure the chief political writers of the *Oregonian* and the *Journal* could produce legislative columns with as much vitality as the so-called "inside story" which those papers buy from afar.

The hold of columnists is one of the phenomena of our time. From the gossip in the senatorial lounge over coffee and sandwiches each noon, it is obvious that even many of the politicians acquire much of their knowledge of politics through reading the columnists. The appeal of a straight news dispatch cannot compete with a column which supposedly divulges the "intimate" story. Unquestionably this is not too salutary a circumstance, but it exists and must be recognized.

Most of our newspapers plead for state sovereignty vis-à-vis the octopus of the federal government. But state's rights also must be accompanied by state's responsibilities. One way to begin would be to cover the 48 legislatures with as bright a spotlight as that the press focuses on Capitol Hill.

Newspapers rail against federal dominance, but it is obvious that they themselves have not been immune to it.

Yet whatever shortcomings newspapers may have, they are far superior to radio as a means of political coverage. This was demonstrated to us early in the legislative session, when a pressman's strike closed both Portland dailies. People suddenly were reliant exclusively on radio for reports of the legislature. We found our constituents completely uninformed. The torrent of mail on pending issues dwindled to a trickle. Interest in the legislature all but vanished. A resolution was even introduced in the Senate suggesting that the legislature adjourn until the presses of the *Oregonian* and *Journal* should roll again.

Topics considered under the dome of a state capitol, whether they involve school bonds or the comparative merits of using a river for salmon or water power, often are too complicated for the staccato of radio. Furthermore, labor leaders and League of Women Voters officials said that a roll-call read over the air made scant impression on listeners. Only in type on the printed pages, where it could be studied and analyzed, did the tally of *yeas* and *nays* acquire any real significance.

John Deedy
PRESIDENTIAL CANDIDATES AND THE BACKING OF THE PRESS

Adlai Stevenson called ours a "one-party press in a two-party country." How serious a problem is this? What effect, in reality, does the press have upon how we vote? In the following selection, John Deedy looks at some recent presidential elections and the degree of press support various candidates have received.

Editor & Publisher furnishes the tally: daily newspapers lined up 634 for Nixon, 146 for Humphrey, and 12 for Wallace.

Which once again gave the Republican presidential candidate the backing of roughly 80 percent of the daily press, an invariable, it is apparent, which is upset only when a blatant disaster is on the ticket. A Barry Goldwater.

Lyndon Johnson received 440–359 newspaper support over Goldwater, with 237 papers uncommitted. But Democratic presidential candidates generally don't fare that well. Quite the opposite.

Kennedy received only 20 percent support from the press when he ran against Nixon in 1960, and that's all Adlai Stevenson gained the two times he ran against Eisenhower.

Stevenson reflected on the situation after his experience. Ours is a "one-party press in a two-party country," he commented, borrowing a phrase from Richard Strout of the *Christian Science Monitor* (TRB of *The New Republic*).

Well, a third party might one day alter part of that proposition, but the "one-party press" notion seems destined to stand so long as property rights invest publishers with unilateral decision over vital points of policy. Publishers, by and large, are card-carrying Republicans.

Sometimes, like this year, the publishers' man wins. But even when he does, popular vote percentages come nowhere near corresponding to the percentage of the publishers' support. This is a point which bothered A.J. Liebling. "A situation in which 80 percent of the press consistently takes a position in which it is followed by only about 50 percent of the people must be an unhealthy one," he wrote after the Nixon-Kennedy campaign.

However, Liebling was hopeful. He saw television's influence on the '60 campaign as the introduction into presidential campaign politics of a new force that would act as a control "on misrepresentation of the candidates' qualifications and ideas by a press that in many regions is a partisan monopoly."

Liebling was optimistic. "To regain public confidence, newspapers from now on will have to work up some difference of opinion among themselves," he wrote. He seemed sure they would.

Well, they haven't yet, and, if *Editor & Publisher's* '68 figures mean anything, the day when they will is not exactly around the corner.

Irving Rosenthal
WHO WRITES THE "LETTERS TO THE EDITOR"?

Measuring the effect of a newspaper on its readers is often difficult. One tangible measurement exists, however—"Letters to the Editor." In the following article, Irving Rosenthal, Professor of English at City College of New York, examines "Letters to the Editor" and the people who write them.

TO SOME eight million Americans who write letters to the editors of newspapers and magazines each year, "access to the press," a phrase being bandied about increasingly in academic journalistic circles, is far from a reality. No one knows exactly what percentage of the letters mailed to newspapers around the country reaches publication, but the odds are decidedly against the letter writer. At *The New York Times* they're around twenty to one.

Most of those who write to newspapers, according to a recent survey in *Journalism Quarterly*, are elderly or middle-aged ("a refuge of the retired"), male by a ratio of three to one, predominantly well educated, well read, well informed, and ego-centered or "community motivated." These characteristics apply to most authors of the 40,000 letters that will have been mailed to the editor of *The New York Times* by the end of this year. But as one of the country's major and influential forums, the *Times* draws more letters from leaders and opinion-makers than does any other U.S. publication.

Letters to newspapers are no novelty. The *Times* ran its first one five days after its first issue appeared on September 18, 1851, and letters continued to appear frequently and in varying numbers, dropped as space-fillers wherever there was an opening on the editorial page. It wasn't until 1896, when Adolph Ochs took control of the paper, that letters began to work their way up to the important position they now occupy not only in the *Times* but in newspapers all over the country.

"A paper with principles and ideals has a bounden public duty to present every side of a question," Ochs told a Columbia journalism student writing a master's thesis about him in 1931. "Only in this way can a constructive, worthwhile public opinion be formed." He put himself on record that "no other newspaper stands as ready to open its columns to free and impartial hearings as does the *Times.* The only restriction is that these opponents have something worthwhile to say."

For years letters continued to be printed in random fashion, and when there weren't enough of them, the editorial page was filled out with news stories. It wasn't until April 23, 1931, that they were brought together, as they are now run, in a designated space on the right side of the page under a standing head, LETTERS TO THE EDITOR. "I take the letters column of our newspaper seriously," said John B. Oakes, the editorial page editor, in a speech of "The Critical Responsibility of the Press" at the University of California a couple of years ago, "and I consider the letters to the editor as a vital counterpoint—or perhaps antidote is a better word—to the editorials themselves."

Winnowing the 6 per cent chosen for publication requires the full-time services of a six-person staff in the *Times* letters department. After going through a carefully worked out system of selection, the chosen letters are given a key position on the editorial page daily or the op. ed. page on Sundays. Seventy-five to 200 letters come in each day on the average. The volume has a high correlation with the intensity of the week's news, and a single event—such as President Kennedy's assassination, which drew the largest number of letters (and more than 2,000 poems) for any one event—can bring a thousand in a day.

The first step is to weed out the small quota every publication receives from kooks, obscenity-slingers, publicity seekers, and self-serving do-gooders. Like Congressmen, the *Times* is frequently the object of letter-writing campaigns; these are easily detectable and generally are given little heed. Not always detectable, however, is the authenticity of the letter writer, although care is always taken to check it. One hoax did manage to get through—a letter criticizing General LeMay's candidacy last year from one Grant Hall, who described himself as a cadet at West Point. The letter appeared in the first edition, and was pulled after an alert copyreader pointed out that Grant Hall is a dormitory at the academy. The *Times* maintained its balance, though; it slugged in a letter captioned "Wallace's Choice" from a correspondent in Shreveport, Louisiana.

All letters received are analyzed statistically according to subject, pro or con, and the information is passed on to *Times* executives and editorial writers to let them know what their readers are thinking. The letters then go through the mill, with readings by Kalman Seigel, the letters editor; Mildred Liebowitz, his assistant editor; and Ralph Chodes, assistant to the letters editor, to make the final selection of the anywhere from four to six letters printed on what is referred to as "short days," seven to nine on "long days," and thirteen to fifteen on Sundays. Mondays and Saturdays, when only one signed column is run in the upper right-hand corner of the editorial page, are the long days; the other midweek days are short. The space is rigidly assigned, down to a fraction of an inch. Poems, for years a daily feature, are now printed only on long days and Sundays. To round out the selection, they are chosen, more for fit than any other reason, from a bank of verse purchased by Tom Lask, the poetry editor, and set in type.

After the final selection, the letters are edited, mainly for grammar and style—no major or substantive changes are made without consulting the writer (not infrequently precipitating a confrontation with "pride of authorship")—and every detail in the letters is checked for accuracy by a researcher. They are then sent down to the composing room and submitted to Oakes in page proof form late in the afternoon. He generally goes along with Seigel's judgment.

Oakes won't soon forget what he refers to as a "bitter experience" when he did assert his editorial prerogative on one occasion in May 1963 by cutting a paragraph out of a long letter from Bertrand Russell. A month before, Russell had written another letter protesting this country's Vietnam policy and accusing it of various atrocities. The *Times*, no hawk itself, had published the letter and on the same day had printed an editorial criticizing Russell for "unthinking receptivity to the most transparent Communist propaganda" and characterizing one of his statements as "arrant nonsense."

In his reply to the editorial Russell attempted to offer evidence for his charges and included one long paragraph detailing chemical warfare allegations made by the "South Vietnam Liberation Red Cross." Oakes cut out this paragraph, both for reasons of space and a question about the reliability of the group. The deletion touched off a hot exchange of transatlantic cables and letters (with a threat by the British philosopher to "consult my solicitor") that will no doubt show up some day in a printed collection of Russell's letters. The *Times* has published two letters from him since then.

Seigel, who has headed the department since May of last year after thirty years on the *Times* staff as a prize-winning reporter and assistant metropolitan editor, makes it a point to read every letter that comes in. What he and his staff look for, he says, are letters that tie in with current news and are written by people who know their subject and present it clearly. They pass up vituperative or anonymous letters or those signed with a pseudonym, although on rare occasions they'll permit the use of initials if there's a good reason. They tend to shun "professional" letter writers, insist on exclusive publication, limit the length of a letter to a maximum of 400 to 450 words, and generally follow a policy of not printing more than two letters a year from a single contributor.

Seigel is particularly on the lookout for letters disagreeing with editorial positions taken by the *Times*. "The letters column," Oakes says, almost in the words of his uncle, Adolph Ochs, "is one place where the reading public can make itself heard. We consider it a major responsibility to give space to representative letters, especially those taking a point of view in conflict with our own."

On important controversial issues, during an election campaign or after some electrifying news break, when the letters sometimes run into the hundreds and even thousands, an effort is made to reflect the proportion of pro and con mail received and to give a cross section of views expressed. When the news and the volume of mail justify it, the *Times* devotes an entire letters section to a roundup on a single subject.

All letters that come in—they are never solicited or, of course, paid for—are filed away for a least six months; printed letters are kept for five years, and the writers received mounted copies. The contents of the letters as the courts have ruled, belong to the writers, but the letters themselves become the property of the *Times*.

Without question, the single issue that has elicited the largest mail in the 118-year history of the paper is the Vietnam war. Since January 1, 1966, some 20,000 letters have been received, with a ratio of 7 to 1, against the war. The 6 per cent of the letters printed reflected the preponderance of reader opposition to the war, but in view of the paper's strong editorial stand against the war, the proportion has been somewhat weighted to give the "other side" more of a voice.

In the year from June 1, 1968, to May 31, 1969, according to an analysis of letters on issues that drew the greatest amount of mail, the opposition to the war, as reflected in letters, has become even more intense—10.68 per cent pro and 89.32 per cent con. Other major issues that drew large volumes of mail during the year were the student rebellion (42.19 per cent pro, 57.81 per cent con), black militancy (34.77 and 65.23), the anti-ballistic missile (17.98 and 82.02), poverty programs (80.28 and 19.72), "law and order" (23.82

and 76.18), draft reform (98.53 and 1.47), abortion (68.80 and 31.20), the space program (82.40 and 17.60), U.S. aid to Biafra (88.55 and 11.45), and school decentralization (38.57 and 61.43).

Although scientific validity is limited, the information gleaned from a study of the letters that pour in provide what Dr. James N. Rosenau, a Rutgers political scientist, refers to as "hard" data on the views of the "attentive public" that makes up the bulk of the *Times* readership. Rosenau, who has been conducting a continuing survey of the public's influence on our foreign policy, makes periodic visits to the *Times* to pore through letters and statistics.

Although the principal function of the letters department, located a few doors down the hall from Oakes's office on the tenth floor of the Times Building, is to screen letters for publication, it also acts as a clearinghouse for mail that it passes on to other departments and individuals. Some letters are printed in the drama, sports, or other sections, and some have even served as springboards for news and feature stories. For example, a flurry of suggestions, with drawings, of shapes for the conference table at the Paris talks produced a sprightly feature for the news columns last year. Criticisms of news handling are routed to the news department for investigation and reply by George Palmer, a former foreign correspondent. Oakes dictates replies to three or four letters a day.

Seigel, like his predecessor, Louise Polk Huger, who ran the department for twenty-two years, acknowledges every letter. He uses a set of forms graded from simple, anonymous "thank you" cards to signed letters expressing regret over "space limitations." What the formula is he'd rather not disclose, but he obviously has a system to determine who deserves what.

By signing his name to most of the notes, he is fair game for every disappointed letter writer, and he gets a sizable flow of personal mail —besides telephone calls and even visits from delegations if they can get through—to complain, argue, threaten, invoke their friendship with the publisher, or drop the names of anyone else they may know. One University of Wisconsin instructor up for promotion tried to wheedle publication of his letter by pleading that it was important to him for his "publish or perish" vita. Another man attached a note to his letter saying that he'd love to see at least one of his letters published "before I die."

On highly charged issues Seigel is generally in the hot seat, with proponents of both sides often accusing him of unfairness. Part of his job is being diplomatic with Jews and Arabs, union teachers and community supporters, Biafrans and Nigerians. When he gets it from both sides, he knows he hasn't been all wrong.

One disgruntled writer, Robert Yoakum, described his travail in an article in the Winter 1966–67 issue of the *Columbia Journalism Review* captioned, "How I tried to write a letter to the *Times* and found myself cut to the quick." In 1964, it appears, the *Times* had endorsed a candidate for a Congressional seat from Connecticut. Yoakum took exception and wrote a letter that did not appear, but Oakes responded with a friendly note explaining the reason for the endorsement. Two years later, Yoakum wrote again when the *Times* re-endorsed the same candidate in opposition to his own. This time he got a call from Miss Liebowitz to inform him that the letter would be run, but it had to be cut. He agreed it was too long and called back with a shorter version. She called later to say it was still too long and asked him to cut it to 300 words, explaining that the pre-election pressure of letters was enormous. He cut it to 340 words. The next day Miss Huger telephoned to ask him to boil it down further to a couple of paragraphs, "on instructions from Mr. Oakes." Yoakum felt his letter would have no meaning then, but he couldn't budge Miss Huger.

Oakes replied in the following issue of the *Review:*

I am really surprised that your esteemed publication saw fit to give as much space as it did to that silly piece by Mr. Yoakum. His letter was not published —as he well knows—because of its length.

In essence, Mr. Yoakum's complaint, similar to that of many hundreds of other Letters-to-the-Editor writers, is that the *Times* did not give him the space he thought was due. We have to make a judgment on letters space and subject matter every single day, and we try to exercise that judgment fairly. Mr. Yoakum's special pleading should be viewed in light of the fact that his letter would have been run if he had not been so incredibly stubborn in refusing to cut it to what we considered a reasonable length. Our own editorial comment on the Congressional race to which he took exception occupied not more than three or four lines.

Prompted no doubt by a conditioned reflex that springs whenever he thinks of letters space, Oakes then added a third paragraph suggesting that "you can use this letter in whole or in part if you wish. I'd suggest the second paragraph above would be all that's necessary, but you can use the whole thing if you care to." The *Review,* not similarly afflicted, used the whole thing.

With the increasing number of letters coming to the *Times* each year and the fact that the death of the *Herald Tribune* has put added responsibility on the paper to give the "other side" a voice, the tightness of space for letters is a problem. Oakes is trying to do something about it. Last spring three-fourths of the op. ed. page on Sundays was turned over to letters (during the less turbulent days of the Twenties and Thirties letters were given a whole page on Sundays), and although the 40,000 letters expected this year will be higher than the record

37,719 received in 1968, the percentage published will probably rise to over 7 per cent.

Oakes is sensitive about charges that preference is given to big names. Although the *Times* has published many letters from the mighty, and likes to add a couple of lines in italics explaining who they are, most letters come from "average readers." Some names that have graced the letters column in recent years include three men who later became President: Kennedy, Johnson, and Nixon; also Hubert Humphrey, Dean Acheson, Robert Kennedy, John Kenneth Galbraith, Felix Frankfurter, Prince Sihanouk of Cambodia, Jean-Paul Sartre, Martin Luther King, Helen Keller, William Faulkner, and a number of others Seigel doesn't have to look up in the *Who's Who* at his elbow. He won't mention names, but some well-known people have also been turned down, either because of lack of merit in what they said or because they have used up their two-a-year quota. Arthur Hays Sulzberger, former publisher and father of the paper's present publisher, once complained semi-petulantly, "Can't I get a letter into my own paper?" He managed to get eight of them published, under a pseudonym.

The most prolific, and persistent, writer of letters to the *Times* is a Brooklyn Tech economics teacher, Martin Wolfson. He has been keeping up a steady stream of five or six letters a week, sometimes on three or four subjects a day, with frequent notes of criticism or suggestions to various editors thrown in, for over twenty years. He also writes regularly to a dozen other papers, and estimates that he has had 2,000 letters published since his first one in *New Republic* in 1927. "I think the country is on the way down and out," he said. "Even if much of what I write is not used, I think editors and others learn something from it. I have seen some of my ideas and phrases in *Times* editorials, in the mouths of statesmen and union heads. I want to contribute to the salvation of our country, and I feel it is my duty to save it for a better life." Since 1946, when the *Times* started its card file, he has had fifty-three letters published.

But he has a long way to go to catch up to Charles Hooper, who described himself as "the world's leading newspaper letter writer," a title that will probably never be challenged. Hooper, a native of New York, left the city in 1913 to go West. He settled in Coeur d'Arlene, Idaho, and living on a private income, spent the rest of his life until his death in 1941 as, he stated, "probably the only man who day in and day out, year in and year out, spends all his time in writing letters." His purpose, he added, was "to expose error, correct abuses, and reform evils, especially in the fields of religion and morality." He never quite realized his ambition to have a letter published in every newspaper in America (he also wrote to papers in England, France, Germany, Italy, and Spain—in their own languages), but he produced "an output beyond calculation—my feeble guess is hundreds of thousands." In 1936, before the two-a-year limit was imposed, he had sixteen letters published in the *Times.*

Two years earlier the *Times* had paid tribute to him as "Letter writer to the World," and said in an editorial:

Letters to the editor are a valued part of every newspaper. Their variety of topic is endless. They correct—and make—errors. They reflect a multitude of views and moods. They abound in curious information. They constitute a debating society that never adjourns, in which everything knowable is discovered. A sodality of voluntary correspondents, approving, wrathful, critical, philosophical, humorous, full of admonition, reproof, instruction, miscellaneous knowledge, has succeeded the long-winded Publicolas and Catos of our long suffering ancestors.

A recent critic has said that the daily column of little letters to the London *Times* is an evidence and index of a high civilization. Apart from persons with axes to grind, the mass of newspaper letter writers must be amateurs. So it is a happiness, to discover in Idaho a professional letter writer who is also an amateur in the sense that he asks no pay.

That last sentence is not quite accurate. It is true that Hooper asked no pay, but he estimated that he had received something like $70 for his letters through the years, from a handful of newspapers that used to pay a dollar or two for each letter published.

That may have been one way to make a buck—and little more—in the old days. But more than that, letter writing has obviously always provided a lot of people with all kinds of satisfaction, be it from an opportunity to engage in a form of individual public service, to enlarge one's ego—or simply to get something off one's chest.

from THE KINGDOM AND THE POWER

A newspaper's effect on the individual reader is one thing, its effect on the government, quite another. Perhaps no newspaper in history has had the influence of the New York Times *on government policy. Gay Talese, a former* Times *reporter, discusses this influence in the following selection from* The Kingdom and the Power, *his study of the* New York Times.

The Times' editorial page had been critical of the war in Vietnam for years, and the dispatches from *Times* reporters on the scene had repeatedly angered or embarrassed President Johnson and President Kennedy, the latter once even suggesting to Punch Sulzberger that the paper replace its man in Vietnam, David Halberstam. *The Times* refused, and Halberstam's reporting won a Pulitzer in 1964.

This did not mean, however, that there was not disharmony within the *Times* building on the subject of Vietnam. There existed, in fact, a wide variety of hawks and doves—there were hawks in the News department, in the Advertising department, and in the Advertising Acceptability department (which refused, for "legal reasons," a protest ad from a group of artists, writers, and editors, including a *Times* editor on the Sunday *Magazine*, Gerald Walker, who had organized the protest that advocated nonpayment of a portion of the Federal income tax). And there was a preponderance of doves among the younger reporters, the copyreaders, and particularly the copyboys and campus correspondents. One young man, hoping to employ the influence of the bullpen in the peace movement, scrawled in red indelible ink on the walls of the private elevator that carries the bullpen editors up to the composing room each night to make up page one: "Mr. Bernstein, Please Stop the War!"

Punch Sulzberger, a Marine veteran of Korea, had sanctioned *The Times'* antiwar editorial policy on Vietnam, but this policy more approximately reflected the strong dovish attitude of Sulzberger's cousin, John Oakes. The *Times* editor most appalled by Oakes's viewpoint was the tall, lean, gray-haired Hanson W. Baldwin, the paper's military specialist since 1937, and an individual who in 1960 could barely conceal his displeasure over the failure of the captured U-2 pilot, Gary Powers, to kill himself after being shot down by the Russians. (". . . why did the pilot survive? This is a question that only Mr. Powers can answer," Baldwin wrote in *The Times,* "and he may spend the rest of his life trying to answer it satisfactorily. . . .")

Lined up behind Oakes or Baldwin, or taking positions between the two extremes, were other editors and editorial writers whose views on Vietnam occasionally fluctuated, being more emotional on some days than on other days; and one result was that *The Times'* tone on Vietnam was never entirely predictable. There was even an example in November of 1966 when an editorial on Vietnam changed its tone between the first and second editions. In the first edition, the lead editorial, commenting on the absurdity of a Christmas truce in Vietnam that lasted only for a few hours, began:

Kill and maim as many as you can up to 6 o'clock in the morning of December 24 and start killing again on the morning of December 26. Do your damnedest until 6 a.m. December 31 and again after January 1, 1967, when it will be all right to slay, to bomb, to burn, to destroy crops and houses and the works of man until 6 o'clock on the morning of December 24, 1967.

"Glory to God in the highest, and on earth peace, good will toward men . . ."

When Punch Sulzberger received his *Times* early edition at home that night and read the editorial, which had been written by Herbert L. Matthews, he called Oakes at home and said that he felt it should be killed. Sulzberger felt that the editorial was too emotional. Oakes, who had been off that day, it being Sunday—his place being taken by his deputy, A.H. Raskin, the former labor specialist—read the editorial, agreed that it was too emotional, but thought that killing it would be too obvious. Oakes convinced Sulzberger that it should be merely toned down, and Oakes did the editing himself in time for the second edition that night, eliminating Herbert Matthews' opening paragraph and starting the editorial with Matthews' second paragraph:

By all means, let there be peace in Vietnam for a few hours or a few days over Christmas and the New Year. It is not much, but it is that much better than uninterruped war . . .

The emotional version drew a great number of approving letters from readers around the country, while the second version received a few;

but hardly anyone outside the *Times* organization noticed these changes that morning, the meshing of minds, the soul-searching, the treatment of touchy subjects being matters that usually stay within the walls of the *Times* building—usually, but not always. For within a month of the Matthews editorial there would be edited within the *Times* building a story so big and controversial that it would cause conflict and reappraisal not only among *Times* editors but through the nation and the world.

The hint of something unusual began in Washington on December 14, 1966, when, after Hanoi radio broadcasts charged for the second straight day that American planes had bombed residential areas of North Vietnam's capital, the United States admitted for the first time that it had raided military targets in Hanoi; and reporters in Washington now wondered if these raids had also killed civilians.

The next morning a cable from Hanoi arrived at the *Times* building for Harrison Salisbury. The newly appointed foreign-news editor, Seymour Topping, received it first, read it, and walked over to Salisbury's desk, asking, "Does this say what I think it does?" Salisbury studied it. "Yes," he said finally, the language of the cable not being entirely clear. "I think it does."

"You're in," Topping said.

Salisbury's visa into North Vietnam was awaiting him in Paris. To make sure he was interpreting it correctly, Salisbury sent a return cable asking the North Vietnamese for a confirmation of this message; the next day the confirmation was received. He was to fly to Paris to pick up his visa, then fly on the International Control Commission plane into Hanoi.

Salisbury's older son, the one who had been three years old when Salisbury had gone off to London in 1942, was going to be married in New York at the end of December. Salisbury telephoned his son now and told him he would be unable to attend the wedding, that he would be out of the country. But he did not say where or why, and the young man did not ask.

Salisbury's departure was a well-kept secret. Daniel, Topping, and Catledge knew of it, of course, but they discussed it with no one—not even John Oakes, who was later piqued by their failure to keep him informed. The reporters and copyreaders in the newsroom soon became aware of Salisbury's absence from his desk, but they imagined that he was on one of his out-of-town speaking tours—in Siberia, perhaps, for they now thought of Salisbury as a man doomed to some exiled spot within the executive suite of *The New York Times*. In a matter of days, the rumor went, Rosenthal's elevation to assistant managing editor, and Salisbury's departure from the newsroom, would be announced.

Harrison Salisbury's stories from North Vietnam began to appear in *The Times* during the last week of December, and they landed like bombs on Washington. In his first, after inspecting the damage in Hanoi and talking to the people, Salisbury reported:

> Contrary to the impression given by United States communiqués, on-the-spot inspection indicates that American bombing has been inflicting considerable civilian casualties in Hanoi and its environs for some time past. . . . It is fair to say that, based on evidence of their own eyes, Hanoi residents do not find much credibility in United States bombing communiques . . .

Two days later, in describing the devastation done to the North Vietnamese city of Namdinh, Salisbury wrote:

> Whatever the explanation, one can see that United States planes are dropping an enormous weight of explosives on purely civilian targets. Whatever else there may be or might have been in Namdinh, it is the civilians who have taken the punishment.

Now in Washington, for the first time, American officials conceded to the press that American pilots had accidentally struck civilian areas in North Vietnam while attempting to bomb military targets. And a quiet bitterness and even an open hostility began to develop between some government officials and *Times*men in the Washington bureau.

"Here come the men from the Hanoi *Times*," said one official to two *Times* reporters from Wicker's bureau, one of whom liked Salisbury no more than the government spokesman. Secretary of State Dean Rusk, in a television appearance at the CBS studio, became aggressive with another Washington bureauman after the show; drinking his third Scotch, Rusk looked hard into the *Times*man's eyes and asked, "Why don't you tell your editors to ask Mr. Salisbury to go down and visit the North Vietnamese in *South* Vietnam?"

A few nights before, as Punch Sulzberger slept in his apartment on Fifth Avenue, he was awakened by a telephone call from Washington. It was Secretary Rusk. It was around 10 p.m., and though not fully awake, Sulzberger thought he heard Dean Rusk saying apologetically, "I hope I haven't taken you away from the dinner table."

Sulzberger, forty-one years old, was too embarrassed to admit that he had gone to bed so early. But he was alert enough to know that Rusk was surely calling about Salisbury.

"What were his instructions?" Rusk asked Sulzberger.

"He had no instructions," Sulzberger said.

"When is he coming out?"

"I guess I'll have to amend that, sir—he did have instructions to stay as long as he could with the proviso that he not become the resident correspondent of *The Times* in Hanoi."

"Is Mr. Salisbury asking the right questions?"

"I hope so," Sulzberger said.

There was no hardness in Rusk's voice—none of the tension that Sulzberger remembered of his talk with John Kennedy when the President wished to have *The Times* replace Halberstam in Vietnam. After Rusk had hung up, Sulzerger called Clifton Daniel and asked him to call the Secretary of State back and get from him any questions that Rusk might wish to have Salisbury ask the North Vietnamese. Daniel did, but Rusk had no questions.

Other people had questions, however, many of them, and they re-echoed much of the old criticism of Harrison Salisbury as a newspaperman—he was politically naive, he was being taken in by the Communists, he did not properly attribute his sources in North Vietnam. The *Washington Post* charged that Salisbury's casualty figures in the Namdinh raid were identical to those given in Communist propaganda pamphlets—to which Clifton Daniel replied in a statement, "It was apparent in Mr. Salisbury's first dispatch—and he so stated in a subsequent dispatch—that the casualty figures came from North Vietnamese officials. Where else would he get such figures in Hanoi?"

Within *The Times*, too, there was criticism of Salisbury's reporting, particularly from Hanson Baldwin, who was overheard muttering unpleasantries about Salisbury through the halls. Other *Times*men sincerely believed that Salisbury's lack of exactness in identifying his sources in his early dispatches had needlessly dragged *The Times* into another controversy. Still others, partisans of the desk wars in the newsroom, found new excuses for attacking Salisbury, with one *Times*man saying, "If Hanoi keeps Salisbury, we'll stop the bombing."

But Walter Lippmann wrote:

Mr. Salisbury's offense, we are being told, is that in reporting the war as seen from Hanoi, he has made himself a tool of enemy propaganda. We must remember that in time of war what is said on the enemy's side of the front is always propaganda, and what is said on our side of the front is truth and righteousness, the cause of humanity and a crusade for peace. Is it necessary for us at the height of our power to stoop to such self-deceiving nonsense?

Harrison Salisbury returned to the United States in January, 1967, tired but exhilarated, ducking platoons of photographers and reporters at the San Francisco airport to take a different route to his plane to New York; and then, later in the morning, his taxicab pulled up outside the *Times* building, he hopped out, and walked through the marble-floored lobby toward the open door of an elevator. The first *Times*man he saw in the elevator was Hanson Baldwin. Salisbury greeted Baldwin with a wide grin. Baldwin nodded stiffly.

At the third floor, Salisbury stepped out and entered the newsroom. Had he been riding a chariot behind three white horses, his entrance would not have been more conspicuous. *The Times'* editors behind their desks stood. They walked over to shake his hand. His stories had gotten a fantastic reaction around the nation and the world, and the criticism of his reporting, so very trivial in view of the achievement, was now forgotten within *The Times*. Although it would take historians to evaluate the impact of Salisbury's reporting on the peace movement in America in 1967, the growing disenchantment with the Johnson administration, and the general public's disbelief and disillusionment with the men who were running the government, the Salisbury stories were considered by *The Times'* editors to be worthy of a Pulitzer, and thus he was nominated.

He would not, however, receive the prize for international reporting in 1967. While the Pulitzer jury had recommended him to the Pulitzer advisory board, the latter would reject the recommendation in a six-to-five vote, a decision that would be widely protested in editorials around the nation, but to no avail. Harrison Salisbury's stories, as Senator Mike Mansfield of Montana later conceded, had provoked a "sort of vendetta," or as a past president of the American Society of Newspaper Editors said, Salisbury failed to get the prize because he had "embarrassed the hawks in and out of the United States Government," and the hawkish members of the Pulitzer advisory board had gotten even. But Salisbury himself, after the disappointing announcement had been made, said that he did not care so much about the dissenting votes of the advisory board; he was more gratified by the vote of confidence that he had received from his fellow editors on *The Times*.

As Salisbury had arrived in the newsroom on that January day from North Vietnam, there was hanging on the bulletin board a memo to the staff from Clifton Daniel. It read:

The rumors are true.

A. M. Rosenthal is being promoted to assistant managing editor . . .

What was not said, however, was that Salisbury was *not* being kicked upstairs. He would also remain an assistant managing editor. Rosenthal would assume many duties as Daniel's deputy, and Salisbury would be answerable to Daniel for special stories: he had a dream assignment, one in which he would have the rank to travel and write as he wished. He would begin by planning the coverage of the fiftieth anniversary of the Bolshevik revolution, an assignment that would take him back to Russia for a few weeks. He would continue to write his books, his articles, his speeches. Salisbury's victory abroad, it seemed, had fortified his position at home.

And so on the day following his arrival home, Salisbury began a series of guest appearances and speeches around the country—he stood before a large crowd of journalism students and others in a crowded auditorium at Columbia University. Salisbury stood very tall in front, looking around the room through his sturdy steelrimmed glasses for a moment waiting for the audience to settle itself before beginning his speech. Seated in the back was a twenty-year-old boy that Salisbury knew, a student with very long blondish hair that fell over his ears. The hair was too long, but Salisbury knew that the boy would not cut it. He had worked as a *Times* copyboy the summer before in Punch Sulzberger's office, Salisbury knew, and *Sulzberger* had dropped hints, but the boy had reappeared each day with the long blond hair over his ears. The boy was Salisbury's younger son, Stephen.

Stephen listened quietly with the rest, now, as his father spoke about the adventure behind the enemy lines in North Vietnam. After Salisbury had finished, there was great applause. Then the students raised their hands to ask many, many questions about Vietnam, and China, and Russia.

Then one student, not Stephen but another young man with very long hair, stood and asked Harrison Salisbury if he did not find it irritating sometimes to be criticized so much. Salisbury shook his head.

Then, pausing just a moment, Salisbury added, "I have a little distrust for a newspaper man who gets too many bouquets. He must be missing part of the story."

W. A. Swanberg
THERE IS NO OTHER NEWS

*"Hearst's war," it was called and there was much truth to the charge. The
Spanish-American War of 1898 was an unnecessary war, a war created to a
great extent by the public fury which William Randolph Hearst's* New York
Journal *had aroused. In this selection from his biography* Citizen Hearst,
*W. A. Swanberg recreates the frenzy of that week in February, 1898, when
Hearst declared war and millions cheered.*

HEARST'S coverage of the *Maine* disaster still stands as the orgasmic
acme of ruthless, truthless newspaper jingoism. As always, when he
wanted anything he wanted it with passionate intensity. The *Maine*
represented the fulfillment not of one want but two—war with Spain
and more circulation to beat Pulitzer. He fought for these ends with
such abandonment of honesty and incitement of hatred that the stigma
of it never quite left him even though he still had fifty-three years to
live.

Intelligent Americans realized the preposterousness of the idea that
Spain had blown up the *Maine*. Proud Spain had swallowed insult
to avoid a war she knew she would lose. Her forbearance had borne
fruit until the explosion in Havana caused journalistic insanity in New
York. The disaster was the worst blow Spain could have suffered. The
Maine might have been wrecked by an accidental explosion of her
own magazines. If she was sunk by plotters, it was most reasonable
to suspect those who stood to gain from the crime—the Cuban rebels,
whose cause was flagging and would be lost unless the United States
could be dragged into the struggle. There was one other possibility:
that a group of Spaniards or Cuban loyalists, working off their hatred
unknown to the Spanish government, were responsible.[1]

Lundberg, in his antagonistic *Imperial Hearst*, 81, suggests that Hearst may have had some
connection with the explosion!

Even the *Journal* admitted disbelief that Spain had officially ordered the explosion.[2] But this was tucked away in small type and later disavowed. The big type, the headlines, the diagrams, the cartoons, the editorials, laid the blame inferentially or flatly on Spain. For a week afterward, the *Journal* devoted a daily average of eight and one-half pages to the *Maine* and war. In the face of Sigsbee's wise suggestion that "public opinion be suspended," the *Journal* lashed public opinion day after day.

Some idea of the *Journal's* enormities, though an inadequate one, is given by a day-by-day recapitulation of its headlines and stories.

February 16: "CRUISER MAINE BLOWN UP IN HAVANA HARBOR." This was simple truth, written before the propaganda machine got into motion. It was the last truthful front-page headline for almost two weeks.

February 17: "THE WARSHIP MAINE WAS SPLIT IN TWO BY AN ENEMY'S SECRET INFERNAL MACHINE." The cause, of course, was unknown. This issue had a seven-column drawing of the ship anchored over mines, and a diagram showing wires leading from the mines to a Spanish fortress on shore—a flight of fancy which many readers doubtless took as fact. The hatred of Spaniards for Americans was mentioned. The caption read, "If this [plot] can be proven, the brutal nature of the Spaniards will be shown in that they waited to spring the mine until after all men had retired for the night." The *Journal* said, "Captain Sigsbee Practically Declares that His Ship was Blown Up by a Mine or Torpedo." Sigsbee said no such thing. He later wrote, "A Spanish officer of high rank . . . showed me a New York paper of February 17 in which was pictured the *Maine* anchored over a mine. On another page was a plan showing wires leading from the *Maine* to shore. The officer asked me what I thought of that. It was explained that we had no censorship in the United States . . . Apparently the Spanish officer could not grasp the idea."[3]

February 18: "THE WHOLE COUNTRY THRILLS WITH THE WAR FEVER." This came at a time when Spanish and Cuban military, civil and ecclesiastical leaders were giving the victims a solemn state funeral in Havana, with every mark of respect, dedicating the plots used at Colon Cemetery to the United States in perpetuity. On this day, for the first time, the combined circulation of the morning and evening *Journal* passed a million.

February 20 (over a drawing): "HOW THE MAINE ACTUALLY LOOKS AS IT LIES, WRECKED BY SPANISH TREACHERY, IN HAVANA BAY."

2 Feb. 21, 1898, issue.
3 Sigsbee, *The Maine*, 125.

February 21: "HAVANA POPULACE INSULTS THE MEMORY OF THE MAINE VICTIMS." This was over a story alleging that Spanish officers had been overheard to boast that any other American ship visiting Havana would "follow the *Maine*."

February 23: "THE MAINE WAS DESTROYED BY TREACHERY."

Although the *Journal* knew all along who sank the ship, it offered $50,000 reward for the solution of the mystery. It also began a drive for a memorial to be erected to those lost in the explosion. Hearst donating the first $1000. It began as usual by soliciting famous men whose participation could be exploited, among them ex-President Cleveland. Cleveland won some measure of immortality by replying, "I decline to allow my sorrow for those who died on the *Maine* to be perverted to an advertising scheme for the New York *Journal*."[4] Other "big names" were less percipient, General Nelson Miles, Levi Morton, Chauncey Depew and O. H. P. Belmont being among the many who lent their prestige to the drive.

On February 18, at this most inopportune of times, the Spanish cruiser *Vizcaya* arrived in New York harbor from Cartagena on her "courtesy call." Her commander, Captain Antonio Eulate, shocked when informed of the *Maine* tragedy, ordered his colors half-masted and said he would take no part in any festivities planned in his honor. In view of the public hysteria, the police and naval authorities took strenuous measures to protect the *Vizcaya*, surrounding her with a cordon of patrol boats. The *World*, almost as frenetic in its Hispanophobia as the *Journal*, warned that the *Vizcaya* might have treacherous intentions, saying, "While lying off the Battery, her shells will explode on the Harlem River and in the suburbs of Brooklyn."[5] However, the *Vizcaya* did not fire a shot.

The Spanish authorities, incensed by the *Journal's* warmongering, retaliated. *Journal* men were forbidden to board the *Vizcaya*. More important, the *Journal* was denied further use of the cables from Havana. It took cognizance of this with an announcement headed, "SPANISH COURTESIES TO AN AMERICAN NEWSPAPER," and boxed on the front page with a flowing American flag. It read:

The *Journal* takes great pride in announcing that on account of its too decided Americanism and its work for the patriots of Cuba this newspaper and its reporters have been forbidden entrance on board the Spanish warship *Vizcaya*; its dispatches are refused transmission over the Government cables from Havana.

These Spanish acts, of course, do not prevent the *Journal* from getting all the news. . . . The *Journal* is flattered by these delicate attentions from Spain . . .

4 N.Y. *Evening Post*, Mar. 28, 1898.
5 N.Y. *World*, Feb. 16, 1898.

It expects to merit still more attention when the United States decides to end Spanish misrule and horrors in America.[6]

The *Journal* also presented its readers with a newly-devised "Game of War With Spain," to be played by four persons with cards. Two contestants would portray the crew of the United States battleship *Texas*, doing their best to "sink" the other two, who manned the *Vizcaya*.[7]

Hearst had rounded up a carefully-selected group of jingoistic legislators who were not averse to a free trip to Cuba. Senators Hernando Money of Mississippi, John W. Thurston of Nebraska and J. H. Gallinger of New Hampshire, and Representatives William Alden Smith of Michigan and Amos Cummings of New York, embarked from Fort Monroe on the Hearst yacht *Anita* as *"Journal* Commissioners" to make a survey of conditions on the island and to write reports for the *Journal*, their expenses being paid by Hearst. Representatives Smith and Cummings were members of the House Foreign Affairs and Naval Affairs committees respectively. The *Journal* meanwhile appealed to its readers to write their Congressmen, and said it had so far relayed 15,000 such letters demanding war.[8]

The *Journal* raged at Senator Mark Hanna for deprecating the war talk. It referred to him frequently as "President Hanna," to indicate how completely McKinley was his puppet. The cowardly peace policy of the administration was dictated by a base desire for profits in Wall Street, which could be depressed by war. "President Hanna . . . announced that there will be no war," said the *Journal*. ". . . This attitude is fairly representative of the eminently respectable porcine citizens who—for dollars in the money-grubbing sty, support 'conservative' newspapers and consider the starvation of . . . inoffensive men, women and children, and the murder of 250 [*sic*] American sailors . . . of less importance than the fall of two points in a price of stock."[9]

Anyone advocating peace was a traitor or a Wall Street profiteer, probably both. When Navy Secretary Long dared to say that "Spanish official responsibility for the *Maine* explosion might be considered eliminated," Long joined the *Journal*'s list of officials who had sold out the nation's honor to Wall Street. This was all part of a money-making coup engineered by Hanna, said the *Journal*, with Long as his pawn, for Hanna had advised his friends before the announcement to buy stocks which rose several points as a result of Long's words and netted them $20,000,000.[10]

6 *Journal*, Feb. 21, 1898.
7 *Journal*, Feb. 20, 1898.
8 Feb. 26, 1898.
9 Feb. 24 issue.
10 *Journal*, Mar. 4, 1898.

The treasonous President McKinley had already publicly stated his opinion that the *Maine* was wrecked by an accidental explosion of her own magazines. The perfidious Secretary of the Navy had defended Spain. In Havana at the time was sitting a United States naval board of inquiry, sending down divers to examine the *Maine*'s hull and taking testimony from survivors in an effort to determine the cause of the disaster. Spain had asked, and been promised, that no American newspaper correspondents would take part in the investigation. The *Journal*, with the *World* and *Sun* close behind, was whipping public fury to a point where all these official efforts were rendered useless, a trivial shadow play unheard behind the din of the headlines.

Martin Mayer

HITTING THEM WHERE THEY LIVE

*How important is newspaper advertising? How effective is it? In this selection
from his book* Madison Avenue, U.S.A., *Martin Mayer provides some answers
to these and other questions about advertising and the press.*

"Radio is about the only way you can reach some markets. Take teenagers. They don't watch television, everybody knows that, it's been
proved over and over again. They certainly don't read. But they listen
about three hours a day."

Spokesman, Radio Advertising Bureau

■   ■   ■

"When a sales manager really gets in trouble in a market, they have
a meeting and somebody from the advertising department will say,
'Let's merchandise our TV show.' But in the end it's always, 'Oh, hell,
let's go into the newspapers and knock the town loose.'"

Spokesman, Hearst Advertising Service

■   ■   ■

"We do research studies, match up markets with television viewing
habits. The food companies wanted to know about people who buy
frozen foods; we found that the heavy purchasers of frozen foods are
also the heavy viewers of television. Gasoline and oil manufacturers—
we found that the heavy drivers are the heavy viewers. The heavy
cigarette smokers—the two-pack-a-day people—are heavy viewers,
but you get them mostly late at night. Don't talk to me about over-

commercialization on television. Just open your god-damned newspaper: it's seventy per cent ads."

Spokesman, Television Bureau of Advertising

THE local advertising medium is, of course, the newspaper. Newspapers are the oldest advertising media, and they are still, in grand total, by far the biggest. Though they receive only 27 cents out of the manufacturer's media dollar, they take nearly 78 cents of every dollar spent by retailers and grocery stores to advertise themselves and the wares they sell. (Some of this money comes from manufacturers, too, via "co-operative advertising programs," by which the retailer advertises that the manufacturer's products are for sale in his store and the manufacturer pays part or all of the advertising bill—usually all, whether he planned it that way or not.)

Advertising space in newspapers is sold at so much per agate line per column (there are fourteen agate lines to an inch, roughly 22 inches of type, usually eight columns wide, on a standard-size newspaper page; a full page runs 2,400 to 2,500 agate lines). Sometimes the line rate is "flat," and will not change however much space an advertiser buys; sometimes it is subject to quantity discounts, which may range up to 25 per cent for the advertiser who takes the equivalent of forty or so pages a year (a considerable requirement: forty pages of national advertising in the Chicago *Tribune,* for example, costs $162,489.60 at full discount).

The basic line rate applies to an ad placed "r-o-p," for run-of-paper, meaning that it can appear anywhere at all, on any page, at the top or the bottom of a column, buried in among other ads or next to reading matter, as the luck falls. A good agency space buyer ought to be able to protect his client against a really evil fate, but if the advertiser wishes a complete guarantee, he may order specific pages or positions, at an extra charge. Thus, the basic national rate of the daily *New York Times* is $2.05 per agate line ($4,920 a page) before discounts; an advertiser who wants to guarantee a position at the top of a column and next to reading matter must, however, pay an additional 85 cents per line; an advertiser who insists that he must be on the society page pays an extra 25 cents a line; an advertiser who demands a specified position on page 2 or page 3 pays an extra $1.50 a line. In practice, these charges are at "publisher's option," and apply only if the advertiser insists on his position. If his agency merely asks for it nicely, and he is a regular customer, he will likely get what he wants at no extra charge.

Many national advertisers feel that they are already paying an extra charge—indeed, that they are being held up on the highway—because the newspaper's line rate is always far lower for the local retail store than it is for the manufacturer. On the average, the retailer pays less than half what the newspaper will charge a national advertiser for the same space. This argument is quite old now, and to all practical purposes it was settled in St. Louis in the 1930's, when the newspapers cut their national rate to bring it level with their retail rate and gained virtually no additional national advertising for their pains (which were considerable: the first reaction was a howl of rage from retailers, who wanted corresponding cuts in *their* rates).

The national advertiser's complaint was never entirely legitimate anyway, since a considerable rate differential is clearly justified by the facts. The newspaper keeps every penny of the retail rate, while 15 per cent of the national rate must go to an advertising agency. Newspapers do not need to maintain large sales staffs to convince the local retailer that he needs them, while the national advertiser and his agency must usually be wheedled and wangled, wined and dined, and sold. Local ads are a positive asset to the paper in the eyes of its readers, who look for retailers' announcements of sales, bargains and specials, while the national ad is just something on the page. Finally, the local merchant advertises week in, week out, at all seasons, while the national advertiser usually schedules his appearance only in the heavy buying seasons of spring and fall. "The retailer signs up for a year," says Herbert Moloney of Moloney, Regan & Schmitt, which represents such papers as the Denver *Post*, the Cincinnati *Enquirer*, the Portland *Oregonian*, the Houston *Post* and the Toledo *Blade*. "If the copy for his ad doesn't arrive on time, the paper simply puts a box around his space and writes, 'Compliments of John Smith's Store.' A national advertiser who comes in and goes out can't expect the same rate. I live in Rye. When I take the train to and from Rye, I pay a commutation rate; if you want to visit me once in a while you pay much more for your trip. That's fair, too." Often, however, newspapers which give considerably reduced "commutation rates" to the heavy local advertiser will refuse to give any quantity discount whatever to the national advertiser, even if he runs his ad every day, all year long; and then the national advertiser's gripe carries conviction.

Media reps like Moloney, Regan & Schmitt sell the great bulk of newspaper space which is bought by national advertisers, and are ordinarily the advertiser's and the agency's only regular contact with the newspaper. (Somebody from the paper will usually come to town once a year, and the rep sets up a cocktail party for him; and he may sell too.) New York newspapers handle their own national advertising sales to Madison Avenue agencies, and a few out-of-town papers maintain their own national sales offices in New York. Usually, however, a salesman representing a number of papers can do a better job for less (the newspaper rep's commission customarily though not always runs around 10 per cent), and the paper relies on its rep. Though reps solicit each other's papers once in a while, the relationship between newspaper and national representative is a highly stable one, and shifts occur very rarely.

The rep's job is threefold: to sell newspapers as a medium, to sell the markets in which his papers are published, and to sell his specific newspaper against competing journals in the same market. Even in big cities, the second part of the job may be the whole battle, because there is only one paper in the market—in three of the nation's twenty-five largest cities, Kansas City, Atlanta and Providence, the newspaper business is a monopoly. "But sometimes it's more difficult to sell a single-paper market," says Leonard Marshall of Cresmer & Woodward, the firm handling, among others, the Los Angeles *Times,* which carries more advertising linage than any other newspaper in America. "You're the only one shouting, 'Tucson! Tucson!' When there are two of you shouting, you seem more important."

Selling a market to an advertiser whose sales in the market are low is usually a hopeless task, but the reps will try it if their papers give them sufficient statistical material to make a good case. Some markets, for example, are expanding rapidly by the stimulus of new industry; the rep offers the advertiser a chance to win a dominant position "in the fastest-growing market in North Carolina." Often a brand which is important nationally sells poorly in a given city; the rep for a newspaper in that city (arriving with a study of brand sales in the market, ordered by the newspaper) urges the advertiser not to let his competition run away with this "A" market, but to push forward via newspapers to his rightful place. At the same time, the rep is selling the competition on the need to advertise more heavily, to hold a leading brand position. Some newspapers have gone to considerable trouble to organize their medium-sized cities as good "test markets" for new products or new packages, arranging with retailers for inexpensive store audits and supplying certain research services at low fees or without charge. The Springfield (Mass.) *Union-News-Republican* advertises the slogan, "Test Effectively, Test Efficiently, Test Springfield." For the convenience of manufacturers who want to try something out in several medium-sized cities scattered through the country, there is a special organization, the Burgoyne Test-City Group, which advises on proper balancing and on technical aspects of the test.

Competitive selling in a market often involves a good deal of infighting. Paper A may have a larger circulation than paper B, or a lower cost-per-thousand; or it may reach a section of the community which is more desirable from the advertiser's point of view. "Suppose we're

running a grocery ad, and the budget gives us only one paper in
Cleveland," says J. Walter Thompson's Art Porter. "The Cleveland *Press* has the big, family circulation. But if we have an ad for the New York Central or for F.I. du Pont [a stock-brokerage house], we want to reach men readers, we'll put it in the morning *Plain Dealer*, get the commuters." Often, two newspapers make completely conflicting claims: page 607 of a recent issue of *Newspaper Rates and Data* contains a full-page ad announcing that "Dallas *News* readers have MORE . . . spend MORE . . . and there are MORE of them!"; on page 608 the Dallas *Times Herald* claims that it "Reaches More People with More Money to Spend!" The explanation is that the *Times Herald* has a larger circulation in the Dallas metropolitan area ("where 57.9 per cent of the families have 68.8 per cent of the buying power in the whole Dallas Retail Trading Zone"), while the Dallas *News* has a large circulation in the surrounding countryside ("Out-of-town customers are responsible for 35.2 per cent of Dallas retail sales volume!").

Newspapers, capitalizing on their important position in the community, sell an advertiser more than just space: they also sell "merchandising help," offering to broaden a manufacturer's distribution in local stores and convince local retailers that they should put their best efforts behind a brand advertised in the local paper. Representatives from the newspaper will work with the manufacturer's sales staff in analyzing the local market, and may even go along with the salesmen to pep up a presentation to local buyers. The case is stated most simply by Jim Gediman, a lean, traditionally cynical, dedicated newspaperman who is executive vice-president of the Hearst Advertising Service, which acts as a national rep for nearly all the Hearst papers' "Nobody will ever know a market like a newspaperman; it's a relationship like a parish. Even if he's a dope he can't help being an expert, better than an Einstein if Einstein's perspective is the Biltmore bar and the Westchester route. A rabbit, to put the matter crudely, knows more about warrens than an eagle."

Newspapers love to publish case histories of what their merchandising staffs have done for advertisers, without charge. One big booklet, called *The Big Plus* in honor of what newspapers give advertisers, described half a dozen such cases—among them a set of seven mailings sent to all salesmen at local appliance stores by the Indianapolis *Star* and *News*, to back up a Frigidaire campaign; a free carton of cigarettes and a free silent butler (somewhat gaudy, this) sent to the *wives* of executives and buyers at major local tobacco outlets, distributed by the Toledo *Blade* in honor of a Philip Morris campaign announcing a new package; a set of Squibb "Open House Specials" displays physically set up in drugstore windows by members of the Seattle *Times* advertising department. (The displays, of course, were provided by Squibb, and bold as brass on each of them appears the common box, "as advertised in LIFE.")

It is general practice among newspapers in medium-sized and smaller cities to send a weekly newsletter to all drugstores and grocery stores, notifying proprietors that certain brands will be advertised by their makers in the newspaper during the coming week. Often, for a larger campaign, special mailings will be sent, including some gimmick to remind the retailer that he ought to stock up now, to be ready for the big demand that will follow the newspaper ads. (If the retailer stocks up, the manufacturer has already won the battle: "inventory pressure" always moves merchandise.) And, of course, the newspaper's retail advertising staff will suggest "tie-in" ads to the retail stores, to accompany the big national campaign; this activity, while useful to the manufacturer, cannot be counted as a favor to him by the paper.

In their efforts to help the manufacturer while helping themselves, some newspapers make great expenditures on market and consumer research. The Chicago *Tribune* runs a Consumer Purchase Panel similar on a local scale to J. Walter Thompson's national operation. The Los Angeles *Times* and the Cleveland *Press* conduct home inventories, sending members of their staff to a selected sample of households to check personally on the contents of the pantry shelves; they also look around to see if a newspaper is in the house. Other papers, among them the New York *World-Telegram,* the Cincinnati *Post,* the Boston *Herald-Traveler* and the St. Louis *Globe-Democrat,* conduct regular store audits in a carefully selected sample of local stores, to determine the effective distribution of nationally advertised products in the local market.

The most elaborate such program, by far, is run by the Hearst Advertising Service, which supplies national advertisers with "an operating sales control" for each of the twelve markets in which there is a Hearst newspaper. These "control" plans include complete detail maps of each city and its suburbs, subdivided into sales districts according to traffic flow, with the different kinds of stores clearly marked on the maps. Pittsburgh, for example, has 20 sales divisions; Baltimore has 27. Experience has taught the Hearst people that by keeping an eye on a few of these districts a manufacturer can predict what will happen throughout the entire city; if desired (for a small fee), the Hearst merchandising staff will watch these districts for him. When a Hearst merchandising man, checking through a retail store, finds that an advertiser's product is out of stock, he will kindly call the distributor; if he finds the advertiser's point-of-sale posters and display cartons reposing quietly in their shipping box, he will (bullying the retailer if required) put them up himself. Little things like that can make a great difference.

Not every newspaper likes the idea of merchandising support to advertisers. "Many papers feel," says a spokesman for the Bureau of Advertising, the central promotion agency of the industry, "that they're selling white space, plus the prestige of the paper, and that's enough." The *New York Times*, for example, does not believe that the advertiser is entitled to merchandising just because he buys space—or that merchandising help is worth much, anyway. "What does the paper really do?" says Irvin Taubkin, head of the *Times* promotion department. "It takes some kid fresh out of school, or still in school, a part-time junior in the ad department, and he trots around to grocery stores with proofs of the ad. Well, here you have a manufacturer, spending millions of dollars on advertising, but neglecting the final job with the grocer, leaving that to some kid from the newspaper; it doesn't make sense." Nevertheless, the *Times* will support its advertisers, "when there is a mutual advantage"—that is, it will send letters to the trade, informing people that national ads are to break in the *Times*. "I sit up here," says Taubkin somewhat gloomily, "trying to think of ways not to say NO."

And not every advertiser is sold on the value of the newspaper's merchandising support: as some clients would rather dispense with fancy agency services and pay less than 15 per cent commission, agencies would often like to eliminate the merchandising help and pay a lower line rate. "These guys," says one media buyer, "put more money into preparing the reports of what they've done than they put into actual work on the job." Others feel that a distinction must be made between work done by the newspaper on its own initiative, in a disorganized way, and work carefully planned by the paper, the agency and the advertiser in conference to determine what this brand really wants in this locality and what this newspaper merchandising staff can really do to help it.

There is another problem about newspaper merchandising support, too, which most people in the business would rather not discuss — the question of when the nice offer to help the advertiser becomes a nasty threat to hurt the company which does not advertise or (worst of all) withdraws its advertising from the paper. In *National Advertising in Newspapers*, a book published in 1946, Neil Borden reported on the pressure which newspaper publishers have brought to bear on reluctant advertisers and their agencies—floods of inspired mail from local retailers and distributors, queries from local bankers, planted questions at board of directors meetings, even letters from congressmen. Borden's book was too pessimistic about the future of newspapers as national media. He did his research in wartime, and used as his reference figure the newspapers' 28-cent share of the national advertiser's dollar in 1941, the last prewar year. With television on the horizon and magazines showing spectacular circulation gains over 1941, Borden clearly felt that the newspapers would be unlikely to hold on to their 28 per cent share; in fact, however, despite the emergence of television, newspapers in 1957 had held even, at 27 per cent. But Borden's contention that many advertisers are reluctant to buy into newspapers, for fear that they will have terrible trouble buying out, still held true eleven years after his book was published.

McCandlish Phillips
THE STORY BEHIND THE JEWISH KLANSMAN

When does an individual's right to privacy end? Do an individual's current public actions automatically make the facts of his past life fair game? The case of Daniel Burros, New York head of the Ku Klux Klan, emphasized these age-old questions in a dramatic way. The unchallenged facts of McCandlish Phillips' story in the New York Times *brought an unexpected result. Here is the story behind the story.*

ON OCT. 19 the House Committee on Un-American Activities identified Daniel Burros, 28 years old, of Queens, as the New York head of the Ku Klux Klan. The committee said it was trying to find him. The Times found him first. My boss, A. M. Rosenthal, the metropolitan editor, had also learned that Burros, former second-in-command of the American Nazi party, was Jewish. He put me on it.

It was Friday, Oct. 22, when Abe Rosenthal walked over to my desk, sat down in the green chair next to me and told me what he knew. I had not planned to work that day. I had a lot of days off accumulated and I had decided to take a four-day weekend.

I was at home, praying, a few days before, and the impression came through, loud and clear, that I was to work on *both* of my regular days. So I changed my plans, though I couldn't see why. That's why I was at my desk that morning.

"Look," Abe said, "here's the head of the K.K.K. for New York, and he's a Jew. Let's take a look at it. Get hold of this guy and see if you can find what makes a Jewish kid from Queens grow up to be a Nazi. It could make a terrific story."

I made a couple of quick phone calls and filled out leads that had come to Abe from a friend in a Jewish agency, enough to put together a typed list of nine places where we might try for information. I told Abe that, if we struck like lightning at all nine places, we might be able to bring in the whole story that night. He quickly assigned two of his youngest reporters, Ralph Blumenthal and Steve Roberts, to check schools and employers, and agreed to ask the Washington bureau to check two Washington angles.

This left me clear to look for Burros, described as a "knowledgeable and virulent Nazi" who was out of jail pending appeal on a two-year term for rioting and possessing a switchblade knife. If everything had clicked, we might have had our story that night. As it turned out, almost nothing clicked.

Burros had no phone. We had two possible addresses, so I suggested that a photographer and I go out to Queens to try for a quick interview and picture. I asked for a man built along Pat Burns's lines, who might throw a sense of due caution into Burros, who had a rather nasty record of convictions for street disturbances at Nazi rallies. Pat was out, but Carl Gossett, who is at least tall, came down, and we headed for South Ozone Park.

We found the first of Burros's supposed addresses over some small shops on Lefferts Boulevard. The man in the pizzeria said there was no one with that name in the flats upstairs. But, outside, two kids recognized Burros' name and pointed us to a brick apartment house about two blocks away.

Lefferts Boulevard and Linden Boulevard is a heavily trafficked corner, with a cop and a stoplight, and a big Bohack supermarket half a block away. A defaced Army recruiting poster swings in a metal frame right where the Q10 bus stops. A globe light over the entrance to the building was busted. There were six steps and an iron railing up to a glass door with a shade, half drawn.

The door was unlocked. In the tiny tiled vestibule we found four nicked and brown-stained old brass mailboxes—one marked Burros. We rang the bell. No answer. Other bells. No answers.

I asked the traffic cop if he knew anybody named Burros. Sure, he said, the old man had walked down the street an hour ago and would probably be back. He did not know the son.

It was a waiting job. I began talking to everyone who stopped near the building. "Oh, yeah, the boy," a middle-aged man said. "He's short and stocky-like, with glasses. I don't know what he does. He's in and out all the time, all hours of the day."

Somebody else said he was blond, so we had a fairly good idea of the size and shape we were looking for. It began to drizzle at dusk. Carl waited until it was too late to catch the first edition. Then he pulled his raincoat, a Burberry with a half-dozen inexplicable flaps, out of the car trunk and wrapped me in it for mist-proofing. He called his desk and was told to go home for the night.

Story matter can be phoned in right up to deadline, so I stayed. A plumpish woman came home with some groceries. "He's a very good boy, never destructive or anything," she said. It became clear that the King Kleagle's neighbors knew little of his political activities.

It grew dark and raw. I was a bit chilled by the prospect of meeting Burros, and the dull yellow lights that glowed behind window blinds looked inviting.

At about 7:30 a bus pulled in and an old man stepped off. He went straight for the building door, head down.

"Mr. Burros?" I asked.

His face turned up inquiringly to mine, catching the mist. "Yes," he said.

He was a stocky, thick-necked, square-headed man with a round, pale and lumpish face. There was a bulbous nose and somewhat pouted cheeks. There was a kind of deadness to his face. He had a slightly frayed, very thick coat. He was not well dressed.

"I need to reach Dan," I said.

"Who are you?"

I gave him my name and waited. He just stared, so I told him: "I'm with the *New York Times*. We have a story about Dan, and I need to talk to him." He turned.

"I got nothin' to say," he said, hurrying into the house.

By now the chances of making the first edition were gone. Because of that and the chill, and partly because I vaguely did not wish to encounter Burros that night, I walked over to a bar and called the city desk. Sheldon Binn, assistant metropolitan editor, said to come back in.

I went back to Burros's house for one parting try. I thought the best way to reach him would be to leave a note, so I wrote it on news-print copy paper and took it into the vestibule.

An old woman opened her door right into the vestibule. I told her who I was and what I was after. "They're a very quiet family," she said slowly. "The mother works, the father is sick. You don't hear much from them." I tried to stuff my note through the brass mail slot on Burros's box, but it wouldn't fit. I began to hook one edge in and leave the rest sticking out of the little slit.

"I wouldn't do that," she said in a kindly tone. "We've got a nut living upstairs and she's liable to take it."

She admitted me past the inner door. I went up a narrow, rubber-lined flight of steps and found a neat, very plain hall with a single bulb overhead. I slipped the note under Burros's door, came down and went for Times Square by the IND line.

At the office I checked my mailbox. Steve Roberts had picked up some good stuff from a high school yearbook, The Clipper. Ralph Blumenthal had been to the Anti-Defamation League to check a confidential file on Burros, but the man who had the file was understandably a little cozy with it. He passed on some oral notes only. Ralph got a Manhattan address for Burros, a little mailing office in Times Square; a list of his arrests in Washington and other items. There was also a one-line message from the Washington bureau: "Nothing so far on New York's grand dragon." I felt a little downhearted. We had spread a wide net that day and had caught minnows. I called Abe at home to tell him where we stood, and he said to come back at it on Monday, alone. He suggested that I send a telegram to back up my note to Burros. As soon as I got back in Monday, I found a yellow slip in my box: "Your telegram undelivered . . . no such number." I made up another one and dispatched it, but none of these drew an answer. I learned later that Burros was out of state.

In retrospect, I am glad that I did not see Burros sooner. I had four full days to search every possible avenue of discovery and to trace his life. If I had seen him earlier, all the rest of the work on the story would have been under the darkening cloud of his threats to kill me. The paper would never have allowed me to go out and get the rest of it.

I have a friend who sometimes speaks of God's timing and how it is usually slower than ours—but perfect. The timing here proved to be supremely good from several standpoints.

If there is an abrupt transition here, it is because I am dropping 11 full pages of the complete story of the episode. What it boils down to is that all a reporter can do is grab at every clue, no matter how slender, and throw it into his bag. Every once in a while he spills them all out and finds that he has a lot of little pieces, like a jigsaw puzzle, which he must try to assemble. None of the pieces by themselves seem to mean very much. Life is pretty miserable until that happy moment when you find you have enough pieces to see how they fit together.

Thursday was a day of sweet triumph. I had many pieces on Burros's life and behavior, but not much that would explain the man. I knew what, but not why.

I got in touch with a Fascist who knew Burros well and was quite willing to talk. As he did, Burros, the incomprehensible Jewish Nazi, a man with an I.Q. of 154, began to come clear.

I had seen Burros's publication, The Free American—the Battle Organ of Racial Fascism, with its frequently repeated slogans, "PERISH JUDAH" and "HITLER WAS RIGHT." I learned that when young people, with no record of Fascist association, would come to Burros and ask about getting into Fascism or Odinism (the white-supremacy cult Burros embraced), he would advise them not to go overboard and mess up their lives as he had his.

When Thursday, my fifth day on the story, ended, I thought I had everything I needed except the interview. I tapped out a five-page memo to Abe, reporting that Burros would make a "fascinating, absorbing study," and ended it with a proposal that I get up very early the next morning and plant myself outside his door, on the chance that he was there and would come out. Abe was out of town at a conference, but his assistant, Arthur Gelb, took over. His generalship in the next few trying hours was superb—even, as I later saw, when I disagreed with it.

Having reached the point of acute and immediate need of meeting Burros, I got up at 5:15, and took the IRT, switching at 59th Street and heading for Ozone Park via Brooklyn—a process that took a frustratingly long time.

At the last stop I walked down the long flight from the elevated platform and turned onto Lefferts Boulevard.

The instant I made that turn I caught a fleeting glimpse of Daniel Burros turning into a barber shop. He had turned maybe half a step before I had, so I saw him, but he did not see me. The timing was split-second, utterly perfect. If I had come down to that last step and had turned literally two seconds later, I would have missed him, and I am quite sure I would have gone straight to his home without looking into the barber shop. I might have met him there later, but as it turned out it was far better that I meet him in a public place.

I had never seen Burros, but I had seen photographs, and the recognition that morning was sure. It was 8:02 A.M. There was a big clock on a roof advertising sign on the opposite corner. When he came out he turned and came toward me. I stepped toward him and told him my name. Had he received my note or telegrams? He said he had, but had been out of state. He told me he was relieved to find that I wasn't a Federal officer.

"Well, I need to talk to you," I said. He said, "Okay."

He did not seem sinister, but fairly polite and civil. He said the Imperial Wizard had forbidden him to engage in any press conferences, but he agreed to sit down for a few minutes and go over some of the facts I had. Actually, he went a good deal beyond that and offered some revealing amplifications. He suggested we find a place where we could sit. We walked six or seven blocks until we came to a place that was open—a dim luncheonette with three or four narrow booths and maybe eight stools at a counter, and it was in the shadow of the elevated structure. We had passed an open bar, but neither of us drank.

I don't know why we chose the booth that backed right up against the entrance vestibule, but I am glad we did. He sat opposite me— a round, short, sallow young man who looked a little like a small heap of misery. He kept his eyes tucked way down tight at a corner of the table flashing only an occasional direct glance at me. It seemed to me that he was profoundly embarrassed about himself.

He ordered a Coke and I had scrambled eggs. The waitress gave us both knives and forks and napkins. His tone was pleasant enough, and when he saw that I was not treating him like a D.A. he relaxed and talked more freely.

As we talked he saw that we had a very strong line on him. He said, "Gee, fantastic," several times at the details, and I think he may have been a little pleased. He showed me his Klan identification and gave me the matchbook-size picture, showing him in a white hood, that ran in the paper.

I had a pathetic image of a man who was "hooked" on Fascist extremism; of a man who was so far into the web that he saw no escape.

We came to the central question of the interview. "There's one thing about you that just does not fit into the picture, and I can't figure it out," I said. He had glanced at his watch several times and said he wanted to catch a 1 P.M. bus for Pennsylvania.

"Your parents were married by the Rev. Bernard Kallenberg in a Jewish ceremony in the Bronx," I told him.

"Are you going to print that?" he asked.

It was a matter of obtainable public record, on file in the Bronx Supreme Court House, and I said I did not have the authority not to print it.

Here was a rabid anti-Semite, committed to a program of genocide. Here was also a Jew. Surely, this was the ultimate contradiction. Though it had long been successfully hidden, it now bent back upon him with stunning force, like a giant spring long held down but suddenly released.

It may have been that at that moment the whole impossible structure of his adult life collapsed in ruin. He became a desperate man. He said he had worked for years to keep that from being known. Now I wanted to print it in the paper. He told me he was going to have to kill me before he left the luncheonette.

The whole atmosphere of that luncheonette changed. It was not the place I had walked into. There was blackness in it, blackness crowding around me, and perplexity within—and fear. All that came with a few short words, but there seemed to be a power of evil in them. I did not panic, though I may have been near the edge. Outwardly, I was calm.

He said he had a vial of acid. He had one hand under his coat. I would have to promise not to print his Jewish origin, the deepest secret of his life. I tended to discount the acid. (I did not articulate it in my mind, but I thought later that it was unlikely that anyone would take a vial of acid to a barber shop at 8 in the morning.) But I was worried about the knife and fork he had at his fingertips. I knew I could not move quickly in the narrow booth.

Burros spoke with a matter-of-fact intensity. He did not raise his voice. To a man who deals habitually in fantasies of genocide, the threatening of a single life hardly demands an angry outburst.

He said he would kill me unless I promised. I pledged I would not print it until I had talked to him one more time, and I gave him my number and told him to call me by phone that evening. I think I hoped this would take some of the immediacy off the kill-Phillips question.

Burros was deeply entangled in Fascist extremism and saw no escape. I believed I had a responsibility to try to talk to him, but there was the pressing distraction of his threats.

"If you publish that, I'll come and get you and I'll kill you; I don't care what happens to me. I'll be ruined. This is all I've got to live for."

A few moments later he said: "If you print that, I will be ruined. All my friends, all my associations, everything I've lived for for the last seven years will be gone."

I wanted to get out of the luncheonette and out on the sidewalk. There, I thought, I would at least be maneuverable. I could run or duck. I took a dollar out of my wallet and put it down on the check. "Let's go outside." I said, and walked out. Most of the fear seemed to drain away. I knew, too, I had everything I needed from the interview.

Now I had before me a desperately needy person, a man who needed God with awful urgency, and right away. "I'm through talking to you as reporter to subject," I said. "The interview is over. Now I want to talk to you as one human being to another."

The sidewalks were nearly empty, or maybe I did not notice other people. We seemed to be alone as we walked slowly along under the elevated. There were many words about death. I reminded him of what the Bible says: "It is appointed unto men once to die, but after this the judgment."

"I'll take my chances on that when it comes," he said.

The question of his entrapment came up. He said he was trapped by the threat of what I would print. "No," I said. "You're trapped by who you are, by everything you've got mixed into."

At the very end, for perhaps two minutes, he listened. I spoke very carefully, trying to reach him.

"If any man be in Christ," I said, quoting the New Testament, "he is a new creature. Old things are passed away; behold all things are become new." I knew the "any man" of that promise was wide enough to take in even Daniel Burros.

"You're trying to con me," he said.

I said I was not. "What you have to do to break the grip Fascism has on you is to call upon the name of Jesus Christ," I said. "If you do that, He will take care of the rest." We shook hands and parted. He went off toward his home. I went up the elevated steps.

Before I left he had threatened my life six times. It was not until Monday, when Homer Bigart reported it, that I learned that he had pretty much demolished a bedstead with vicious karate kicks. If I had known of that skill I might not have felt as relatively comfortable as I had walking with him.

When I reached the office, Burros had already called once. He called three more times. Once he asked if he could trade me some other story for the one about his Jewish origin. I said I couldn't make a trade. In the last call, at 3:50 P.M. Friday, it was clear that he knew I was going to write the story. This time there was finality in his words.

"I know I can't stop that story," he said. "But I'm going to go out in a blaze of glory," he said he wouldn't say just how or when, but he would put on a show in the *Times* building. He said he knew he would "catch some lead" in the process. It sounded like a threat to come in and shoot the place up.

I typed out a quick six-page memo on the confrontation. ("I met our man Burros this morning. He told me repeatedly he will kill me . . ."). Art Gelb was at a publisher's luncheon upstairs. "I came down and the first thing I was greeted with was your memo," he said later. "I was kind of stunned by the threat. I thought we should notify the police. Clif Daniel said by all means, and we should also alert our own security guards."

Art called Deputy Police Commissioner Joseph Martin, and Eugene Zaccor, Times security chief, swung into action. He asked for the photo, and soon had copies of the Burros picture in the hands of all his men. Joe Martin offered a police bodyguard to take me to and from the office.

Jim Goodale, head of the paper's legal department, was called in to take charge of the affair. I wrote the story, being careful to check just about everyone who came in the news department door. "Don't go home tonight," a reporter cracked, "without leaving your advance obit and a glossy photo. We may need it."

I felt that there was virtually no danger until *after* we ran the story. I also thought that I would be a lot more comfortable if we could drop the shoe and see what happened. I wanted the story to run that night, for the Saturday, Oct. 30, paper. I went to Arthur a couple of times and pressed him on it. I lost. He was right. But he was open to my entreaty to try to get it in the Sunday paper. I didn't want to prolong the uncertainty.

As it turned out, I needed extra time. I worked on the story until close to midnight. I had five columns.

Two detectives drove me home that night. I ignored orders and came in alone the next morning, and later found that I had set off a small security crisis. Mr. Daniel and Jim Goodale apparently decided I was a bad security risk, and put a 24-hour bodyguard on me when I left the office. Since Burros had threatened the whole staff, plant security was made as tight as possible. Incoming visitors were scanned with care.

On Friday night Art Gelb came over to my desk about 7 o'clock. He asked about Burros's Jewishness. I had evidence (photostats of documents and his own admission), but not absolute, court-testable proof. Gelb asked if Burros had a bar mitzvah. I did not know. Since I knew for a dead fact that Burros was Jewish, I was for going ahead on that basis. But Arthur decided to send somebody out to Queens to check every synagogue within two miles of the Burros home.

He chose Irving Spiegel, partly because Pat is our Jewish-affairs specialist, partly because he is a skilled police reporter and partly because he speaks Yiddish. It was an inspired choice. The next day Pat and Ralph Blumenthal began very early and toured three synagogues, hitting two that had solid facts and entering one where they were welcomed with unusual affection because they made up the necessary 10-man quorum for the service. Without them, it could not have been held, but they got enmeshed in the service and Ralph was summoned to the platform to hold the Torah, while Pat, wrapped in a prayer shawl, tried to combine a proper piety with an almost mad desire to get the facts for our first Sunday editions.

Art Gelb was at home. He had left instructions that the story be held pending the result of Pat's synagogue search. Now the clock was running out. Art was about to order the story held over another day.

At 1:20 P.M, at the last screaming moment, the phone rang. Pat almost shouted to Bill Luce, who was running the metropolitan desk that day, "I got it, Bill." To get it he had to say at one point to a resistant rabbi, using his Yiddish, "The Germans had a Hitler, and the Jews have a Hitler, too."

George Barrett was on the phone with Art. Bill Luce broke in to tell him. Art gave the order to run the story. Pat called me with the bar mitzvah and a few beautiful color details.

That night I was practically ordered by the editors to get out of town at *Times* expense, but I wanted to be close to my church, which meets in a living room in the building in which I live, so I stayed at home. For the next four days I had as my house guests a series of *Times* security guards, whose quality very much impressed me. At one point small raps came on the door and tiny voices mumbled something about "Trick or treat." My bodyguard got up, went over to the door, and called through it, with altogether chilling authority: "ALL RIGHT, NOW—YOU GET AWAY FROM THAT DOOR!" It was no question; it was pure command, and it must have scattered the tots like dandelion seed. I suspect I have an unearned reputation as an ogre among the neighborhood's 9-year-olds.

Arthur Gelb called me at 1 P.M. Sunday. He had news for me, he said. There was unconfirmed word from Pennsylvania that Daniel Burros had shot himself to death. Homer Bigart's story the next day told it all—his rage at seeing the *Times* story, his wild tantrum, the two shots that he put into his chest and his head. I reflected on how, on the day I had met Burros, he had already made firm plans to go to Pennsylvania, removing himself from the city.

Arthur was worried about how the news would affect me. The previous evening, when I had got home, Mrs. Hannah Lowe, a missionary friend, said to me, "Read the Third Psalm." It seemed appropriate that night, and when I talked to Arthur Gelb I suggested that he read it. He said a few days later that he had, and appreciated what it said.

When he called that Sunday afternoon, he tried to tell me the news gently, slowly. I felt sad. I knew that Dan Burros had been caught in a net of evil that had pulled him down to death at 28. I said: "What I think we've seen here, Arthur, is the God of Israel acting in judgment."

CRIME AND THE PRESS:
THREE VIEWS

The American trial-by-jury system is one of our most hallowed concepts. A man is innocent until proved guilty, we proclaim. Yet, what happens to a man's rights when he is, in effect, tried by the press? To what extent do the newspapers affect the pursuit of justice and condition our beliefs about crime and criminals? The following three articles deal with these vital questions. Irwin Ross, the author of "Trial by Newspaper" is a former reporter for the New York Post *and author of* The Image Merchants. *Robert M. Cipes, the author of "Controlling Crime News: Sense or Censorship?" is a lawyer and writer now living in California. Terry Ann Knopf, the author of "Media Myths on Violence" is a research associate at the Lemberg Center for the Study of Violence, Brandeis University.*

Irwin Ross
TRIAL BY NEWSPAPER

ON APRIL 24, 1964, police in Brooklyn, New York, picked up a semi-literate nineteen-year-old Negro named George Whitmore, Jr., on suspicion of attempted rape. The next day, after Whitmore had been continuously questioned for twenty-two hours, the police announced that he had confessed to three crimes—the attempted rape, the murder of a charwoman in Brooklyn, and the killing of Janice Wylie and Emily Hoffert, young career girls who had been brutally stabbed to death in their Manhattan apartment eight months before. The gruesome Wylie-Hoffert case had shocked New Yorkers as few crimes of violence do; the police, under great pressure to solve the murder, had floundered helplessly. Now their professional honor was vindicated.

The newspapers hailed the coup. The *World-Telegram's* headline, "Wylie Murder Solved: Drifter Admits Killing 2," was typical. All the papers set forth details of Whitmore's confession, as authoritatively furnished by Chief of Detectives Lawrence J. McKearney—how Whitmore had been wandering around New York that summer morning, how he had casually entered the girls' apartment when he found the door unlocked, how he had been surprised by one of the girls while "rummaging around" in the kitchen, and how he had successively murdered each of them. The *Journal-American* interviewed the father of one of the victims, its story beginning with his characterization of Whitmore: "An animal . . . obviously deranged . . . a horror . . . should be imprisoned with no chance of parole."

At his arraignment, however, Whitmore repudiated his confession, his court-appointed lawyer arguing that it had been exacted under duress. The newspapers were unimpressed, and in rebuttal published further details of the confession, endorsing the police contention that Whitmore had such intimate knowledge of the crime that he had to be the murderer. Reading all this, the average citizen could only agree with Chief McKearney that "we got the right guy. No question about it."

A great many questions subsequently arose, however, as well as evidence that Whitmore had been 120 miles away on the day of the crime. Nine months after his arrest, District Attorney Frank S. Hogan cleared Whitmore of the Wylie-Hoffert murder charge. Another suspect was arrested for the crime. The delayed exoneration was welcome, but Whitmore had meanwhile suffered grievous damage, for he had been tried, convicted, and damned in the newspapers long before he had his day in court.

In the intervening period, he had also stood trial in Brooklyn on the lesser charge of attempted rape and had been convicted, partly on the basis of the same contested serial confession. But it soon became clear that he had not received a fair trial, owing to the prejudicial atmosphere created by the press. In March, Brooklyn District Attorney Aaron E. Koota joined the defense in asking that the verdict be set aside and a new trial scheduled. The court agreed.

Trial by newspaper is not a new phenomenon in the United States. Recently, renewed debate on the subject has been stimulated by the Warren Commission's criticism of the way the press covered the initial police investigation of President Kennedy's assassination. The Commission put most of the blame on the Dallas police department for its amazing lack of restraint in releasing information; item after item of evidence against Lee Harvey Oswald, as well as hearsay and unverified leads, were announced to the world at a series of frantic impromptu press conferences. As for the news media, they were criticized for badgering the police beyond the call of normal journalistic diligence.

"A fundamental objection to the news policy pursued by the Dallas police," the Commission wrote, "is the extent to which it endangered Oswald's constitutional right to a trial by an impartial jury. . . . The disclosure of evidence encouraged the public, from which a jury would ultimately be impaneled, to prejudge the very questions that would be raised at trial."

Partly as a consequence of the events in Dallas, the American Bar Association launched an intensive study of how the requirements of fair trial can be reconciled with the demands of a free press. Committees of the American Society of Newspaper Editors and the American Society of Newspaper Publishers went to work on the same question. The Justice Department, after months of deliberation, issued a policy directive limiting the kinds of information to be released to the press by the FBI and U.S. attorneys. Late last December, the Philadelphia Bar Association got in ahead of the crowd with a set of guidelines that would drastically restrain police, prosecutors, defense counsel, and the news media. For its pains, the Bar Association found itself denounced by the Philadelphia press for trying to subvert the First Amendment.

In law, the accused is presumed innocent until proved guilty. The press pays formal obeisance to this principle but frequently betrays it in practice. In a variety of ways, news stories tend to convey a presumption of guilt. If the police announce that the accused has confessed, the press usually accepts the assertion as proof of guilt, even though the confession may later turn out to be false. If no confession is mentioned but the police provide a lengthy chronicle of what the accused is supposed to have done, the newspaper account usually reads like a statement of fact rather than merely an elaboration of the charge. The occasional qualifying phrase "as the police allege" or "the police charge that" is likely to be lost on the average reader.

Moreover, the news media often report incriminating evidence which the judge may rule to be inadmissible at the trial. And inevitably, prominent attention is given to the defendant's prior criminal record, if he has one, which cannot be mentioned in court unless the accused takes the stand in his own defense.

The endless elaboration of detail about what the accused supposedly did or confessed or was previously convicted of readily creates an impression of guilt. Moreover, even the rhetorical devices of journalism favor acceptance of an accusation as a fact. Thus, "Malcolm X Assassin Charged" is a more effective, though far less accurate, headline than "2nd Muslim Seized in Malcolm Killing." It is a commonplace when an unprepossessing suspect is arrested for him to be referred to as "hoodlum," "thug," or even "killer."

In routine criminal cases, especially in large cities, prejudicial pretrial publicity may not matter: by the time the defendant goes on trial, weeks after the crime, prospective jurymen will have forgotten the half-column news story, if indeed they ever read it. But in sensational crimes, which agitate the entire community, memories are longer, and the cascade of one-sided news accounts usually begins again on the eve of trial. Only an illiterate shut-in who does not listen to radio or watch television could avoid any acquaintance with the case.

In *The Innocents,* a recent book about celebrated miscarriages of justice, Edward D. Radin tells of the weird case of James Foster, a hapless itinerant worker whose unfavorable press notices almost led him to the electric chair. Late in the spring of 1956, a burglar shot a prominent merchant, Charles Drake, in the living room of his home in Jefferson, Georgia. Mrs. Drake, who had been hurt, was able to give the police a description of the intruder. Some days later, detectives found a likely suspect in Foster—then in jail in Gainesville, Georgia, on a traffic violation—for he vaguely fitted the killer's description.

Foster was brought to Jefferson and identified by Mrs. Drake in a confrontation in her home. Colorful newspaper accounts described the bereaved widow as demanding "Why did you kill my husband?" The newspapers also pointed out that Foster had previously served time in Florida for armed robbery. Unmentioned was the fact that his complicity was meager and the judge had let him off with a light sentence.

Soon afterward, the newspapers presented even more conclusive "evidence." Foster's cell mate in jail stated that he had spoken of murdering a man in Jefferson. The newspapers now had a "confession" with which to hang Foster; they did not ask whether the cell mate was telling the truth or merely trying to curry favor.

When Foster went on trial for murder a few weeks later, his lawyers asked for a change of venue because of the pervasive atmosphere of prejudice in the community. It is a standard motion when a trial by newspaper seems to preclude a fair trial by jury. The judge denied the motion. The case against Foster consisted of Mrs. Drake's identification and the "confession" related by his former jail mate. Foster's defense, supported by several witnesses, was that he had been with Gainesville friends throughout the entire evening when the murder took place in Jefferson. He was convicted and sentenced to death.

Then a strange thing happened. A group of townspeople who had been convinced by his defense raised money for an appeal, and while it was making its way through the higher courts—a period which lasted for two years and resulted in successive defeats for Foster—the true killer was found and confessed. Foster was freed.

Even where pretrial publicity does not result in a conviction, its inequity can be painful. A few years ago in a park in San Francisco, a young nurse and her escort were assaulted by a knife-wielding maniac. The escort was bound and gagged, after which the nurse was raped, beaten, burned with a cigarette, and shorn of her hair. The girl got a good look at the rapist, whose most prominent feature was buckteeth, which led to the headline tag "Fang Fiend."

A few days later, the police picked up a twenty-three-year-old ex-convict on suspicion of the assault. He had no buckteeth, and he kept protesting his innocence, but the distraught girl identified him in her hospital room. "That's Him!" the headlines quoted her, and the papers went on to detail the suspicious evidence which the police found in his quarters: surgical tape, scissors, rubbing alcohol, and vaseline. "These common items took on added significance," one newspaper noted, "since the park rapist used surgical tape to bind his victims and he carried a kit of various medical supplies."

The papers made great play with the suspect's prior criminal record, including "two sex arrests." These were actually less damning than they sounded, for in one instance, the youth, then seventeen, had been convicted of statutory rape (intercourse with a girl below the age of eighteen), and in the other the police had dropped the charge as "unfounded." Even the suspect's alibi—that on the night of the crime he was at home tape-recording some of his writing—was used against him, with the press quoting a police inspector as commenting that the tapes revealed him to be a "sexual psychopath and sadist." The inspector went on to suggest that the poet-sadist had become so intoxicated with his own words that he had rushed from his apartment to turn fantasy into horrible fact.

By the time the papers were finished with the "park rapist," it would have been difficult to find a prospective juror in San Francisco who was unacquainted with the case against him. Then, unexpectedly, the police arrested another man for the crime and released the poet. He had been as innocent as he claimed, and on examination, his verse showed no evidence of sadism or sexual psychopathy.

In recent years, the federal courts have taken a stern view of prejudicial reporting. In *Marshall v. United States,* one Howard R. Marshall was convicted of illegally dispensing pep pills. At his trial, the prosecutor had tried to introduce evidence that Marshall had previously practiced medicine without a license. The judge cut off this approach, saying that "it would be just like offering evidence that he picked pockets or was a petty thief . . . and I think would be prejudicial to the defendant."

Thereafter, two newspapers published the inadmissible evidence while the trial was still on. The judge questioned each of the jurors privately and discovered that seven of them had read one or both articles, but they all assured the judge that their impartiality had not been damaged, and he allowed the trial to proceed. In 1959, the Supreme Court reversed Marshall's conviction, stating, "The prejudice to the defendant is almost certain to be as great when the evidence reaches the jury through news accounts as when it is a part of the prosecution's evidence. It may indeed be greater for it is then not tempered by protective procedures."

A 1961 Supreme Court decision, *Irvin v. Dowd,* vividly documented the impact of pretrial publicity on jury attitudes. Six murders had been committed in the vicinity of Evansville, Indiana, in a four-month period.

After the suspect was arrested, both prosecutor and police officials issued press releases saying that he had confessed to all six killings, though he was subsequently brought to trial for only one.

As Justice Tom Clark summarized the press campaign: "A barrage of newspaper headlines, articles, cartoons and pictures was unleashed against him during the six or seven months preceding his trial. . . . These stories revealed the details of his background, including a reference to crimes committed when a juvenile, his convictions for arson 20 years previously, for burglary. . . . The headlines announced his police line-up identification, that he faced a lie dectector test, had been placed at the scene of the crime. . . . Finally, they announced his confession. . . ." Before the trial, a roving reporter even solicited man-in-the-street opinions about the accused's guilt and appropriate punishment, and broadcast these interviews over local radio.

The defendant's lawyers initially won a change of venue from Vanderburgh County, where Evansville is located, to adjoining Gibson County. They then tried to get a second change of venue, on the grounds that public prejudice was as great in Gibson County, but it was refused. Of the 430 people on the jury panel, 370 stated on examination that they thought the accused was guilty, their opinions ranging from suspicion to outright certainty. Of the twelve jurors finally selected, eight admitted that they believed the defendant to be guilty but claimed that they would be fair and impartial. The Supreme Court was unwilling to take them at their word, stating, "With his life at stake, it is not requiring too much that petitioner be tried in an atmosphere undisturbed by so huge a wave of public passion." It reversed the conviction and ordered a new trial.

Crime-reporting that is heavily weighted against the defendant is a difficult problem to eradicate because the police, the prosecutor's office, and the press all have a stake in the present system. The police have an understandable desire to show they are doing an effective job. More than vulgar headline-grabbing, though there is a good deal of that, can be involved here. As Police Chief W. H. Parker of Los Angeles has rather ponderously put it, "The commission of heinous or serious crimes in a community invariably results in the public demand for an enumeration of police efforts directed toward a solution. . . . This includes, of course, the apprehension of suspects and an explanation of the basis for such arrests." In the absence of effective restraints, explaining the basis of arrests often involves trying the suspects in the public prints.

The District Attorney's office faces similar pressures. Rarely is a prosecutor in the position of New York's Frank S. Hogan, who has held office for over two decades, invariably being elected with major all-party support. Hogan could take a principled position eleven years ago that he would no longer release confessions by defendants, but most D.A.'s have to fight for their political lives at every election and continually face the temptation to sacrifice a bit of the punctilio of due process in order to burnish their public image.

The press is under compulsions of its own. There is, first of all, its purely commercial interest in purveying crime news; few stories sell papers as well as a sensational murder does. But tendentious crime-reporting can also be the consequence of a crusading zeal that is genuinely disinterested: in an effort to bring criminals to book or to prevent a political "fix," it is all too easy to prejudge the guilt of defendants against whom the weight of evidence seems overwhelming.

The British arrange things much better. When a suspect is arrested, almost nothing can be published except his name, age, address, occupation, and the charge against him. If he has made any admissions to the police, they cannot be alluded to in print; nor can the press indicate how he is supposed to have committed the crime; publication of any evidence is forbidden, as is prior criminal record or any expression of belief in his guilt or innocence. Even the defendant's photograph cannot be printed if there is any likelihood that the question of identification will be a relevant point at the trial. These restrictions are enforced by the contempt powers of the British courts. Infractions result in fines and even jail sentences imposed on the offending journalists.

While the British press occasionally grumbles, it hardly suffers from the court-imposed restraints. Once a case comes to trial, newspapers are free to publish everything that transpires in the courtroom; if anything, the popular press plays up crime news even more sensationally than in the United States. All that happens is that the commercial exploitation of crime is postponed from the arrest to the trial stage. Nor does the British system produce public relations problems for the police; after the case is over, there is plenty of occasion for the police to take their bows. On the other hand, in Britain there is no problem about politically ambitious district attorneys, for full-time prosecutors are not employed. One week a barrister will be retained as a prosecutor, the next as defense counsel.

In this country, the results of the British system are more admired than its methods; few reformers propose adopting them here. For one thing, the Supreme Court has shown extreme reluctance to uphold contempt proceedings against the press, on grounds of infringing the First Amendment. That problem aside, it is felt that it would be unwise to allow so vast an expansion of a judge's contempt powers. We have too many political hacks and incompetents on the bench; the possible caprice and vindictiveness of judges, suddenly capable of fining and imprisoning editors, are rightly feared. "We know that judges as well as editors can be tyrants," Mr. Justice Douglas has tartly observed.

On the other hand, our present methods of dealing with prejudical publicity are clearly inadequate. Adjournments sometimes provide time for passions to die down, but not in celebrated cases, where press attention resumes as the trial date approaches. A change of venue can be useful only when a case is of purely local interest. Reversals of conviction in general provide an ineffective remedy; if the defendant is innocent, he may have been victimized by a long stay in jail; if he is guilty, society may be victimized, for after the long lapse of time it may be difficult to secure a conviction in a new trial.

As a consequence, various proposals have been made to curb publicity before a defendant's rights have been prejudiced. The most moderate approach is cooperative self-restraint; in Oregon and in Massachusetts, representatives of the news media and the bar have adopted voluntary codes of good behavior. Since Oregon's "Statement of Principles" was adopted in 1962, no substantial complaints of press excesses have occurred, but Oregon does not have an especially sensational press. The "Massachusetts Guide for the Bar and News Media," now two years old, has been adopted by twenty-six daily and thirty-one weekly papers, but except for the *Christian Science Monitor,* all Boston papers have rejected it. The problem with voluntary codes, it is clear, is simply their voluntarism.

Legal authorities have made a number of proposals for compulsory restrictions. In a speech before the American Bar Association last year, Dean Erwin N. Griswold of the Harvard Law School suggested that the bar's canon of ethics be amended to prohibit both prosecutors and defense counsel from releasing a wide range of prejudicial information. The restrictions would be clearly spelled out; infractions could then be dealt with by the grievance committees of the local bar associations and by disbarment proceedings in the courts. "Until we take this step," Griswold said, "we cannot really criticize the news media very severely if they publish the information which lawyers give them."

As for enforcing more restrained behavior on the police, Griswold proposed that it be done through the rule-making and contempt powers of the courts. Imposing comtempt penalties on garrulous cops, he argued, did not involve the same constitutional problems as punishing a newspaper for contempt. Federal legislation along these lines has been proposed by Senator Wayne Morse. Morse's bill would levy fines of up to $1000 on any federal investigator or prosecutor, as well as defendant or counsel in the federal courts, who released for publication information that was not part of the court record "which might affect the outcome of any pending criminal litigation."

A more far-reaching proposal by New York Supreme Court Justice Bernard S. Meyer has aroused considerable interest. Meyer advocates passage of a law which would prohibit both the release and the publication of prejudicial material; thus the press as well as police and lawyers could be punished. The restrictions would apply only to jury trials, for judges in any event have to be exposed to prejudicial material when they rule on the admissibility of evidence.

In Meyer's proposed statute, certain matters would be specifically prohibited, such as publication of prior criminal record, or of a confession, or of the offer of a settlement in a civil case, or of opinions about the credibility of a witness or the guilt of the accused. In addition, there would be a second category of material which might or might not be prejudicial, such as interviews with the victims of a crime, statements about the expected testimony of a witness, publication of the addresses of jurors. Whether the printing of such matters substantially endangered a fair trial would have to be determined by a jury, evaluating all the circumstances of the case.

The press, understandably, is apprehensive about all such proposals. Any suggestion of court-enforced restraints raises fears of full-blown censorship. Many journalists, though by no means all, also oppose restricting the utterances of the police and the D.A.'s office, on the grounds that the public's "right to know" would be infringed. While the right to know, unlike the right to print, has no constitutional sanction, it is clearly in the public interest that the police, prosecutors, and courts be subject to continual journalistic scrutiny. This goal can be achieved, however, without the press's inquisitiveness being satisfied at so premature a stage in a criminal proceeding as to victimize a defendant. The right to know is not an absolute, in the police station any more than in the Pentagon or the State Department. While unnecessary secrecy in any area of government is to be avoided, the press can hardly demand instant candor.

On the other hand, proposals like Meyer's, Morse's, and Griswold's, while pointing in the right direction, all share a common defect: they admit of no exceptions. To ensure that a jury is uncontaminated by extraneous impressions, they would prohibit virtually all statements to the press, before and during a trial, by both defense counsel and prosecutors.

Such a sweeping approach assumes that justice is always done in the courtroom, that throughout the fifty states we always enjoy an equitable and efficient judicial system. The truth is that on occasion pretrial publicity serves the ends of justice; instead of damaging the case of an innocent defendant, it may ensure fair treatment. It has not been unknown in some parts of this country for trade-union organizers occasionally to be run in on trumped-up criminal charges; what would be gained if defense lawyers were prevented from saying that the real crime was organizing a union? Similarly, during the civil rights upsurge in the South, the ostensible charge on which arrests are made is usually far removed from the real offense—an assertion of constitutional rights which the local authorities regard as intolerable. It would certainly be a perversion of justice if defense attorneys (and newspapers, under Justice Meyer's proposed statute) were to be punished for stating that their clients were being unfairly harassed.

Some of the most celebrated civil liberties cases of the past could never have been effectively fought if Dean Griswold's or Justice Meyer's proposals had been in effect. In the Scottsboro case, back in 1931, nine Negro youths who had been riding a boxcar through Alabama were falsely charged with rape by two white girls (one of whom later recanted) who were on the same train. Eight of the boys were convicted and sentenced to death in a judicial atmosphere that would have dismayed an English court. The case remained a *cause célèbre* throughout the thirties. There were endless trips to the appellate courts, two reversals by the U.S. Supreme Court, and several jury trials in Alabama; in the end, most of the youths were released. But had some of the restraints currently proposed been operative, the campaign for the Scottsboro nine would have had to halt every time a new trial was pending. It is difficult to see how such restrictions would have furthered justice, and they would certainly have made it more difficult to raise money for the defense.

The George Whitmore case, with which this article began, ironically illustrates not only the inequities of the present system but also how the engines of mass publicity can aid a hapless defendant. On the basis of false information from the police, the New York press initially damned Whitmore beyond the point where he could get a fair trial. On the other hand, long before District Attorney Hogan exonerated him of the Wylie-Hoffert killings, a number of newspapermen became suspicious of the charges and launched a press campaign in his behalf. It is true that an assistant district attorney had also begun to doubt the validity of Whitmore's confession, and in the end (partly aided by journalistic investigators), turned up the crucial evidence that cleared him. But no one who has followed the case doubts that relentless newspaper attention has had much to do with the scrupulous concern for Whitmore's constitutional rights now manifested by all the authorities.

What would have happened to Whitmore if the British rules or Dean Griswold's rules had been in effect? At the outset, his false confession would not have been published; he would unquestionably have been tried on the initial charge, that of attempted rape, by as close to an impartial jury as one can get in a sensational case. Once the press began to doubt his guilt, the papers would either have been prevented from saying anything in print or would have at least been denied access

187
Robert M. Cipes
CONTROLLING
CRIME NEWS:
SENSE OR
CENSORSHIP?

to Whitmore's lawyers while the two additional trials were pending. Whitmore has clearly gained by the present arrangements.

Obviously, some balance must be struck between total lack of restraint and restrictions so severe as to defeat, under some circumstances, the very ends they seek to secure. As a practical matter, it is unlikely that any legislation could pass that would penalize the press for derelictions in crime-reporting. The only approach that has a chance to work is one that would stop the flow of prejudicial material at its source: the police department and the prosecutor's office, which routinely furnish the press with the bulk of information about confessions, incriminating evidence, "bombshell" witnesses.

As a general rule, the defense counsel should be put under the same restraints, for it is clearly as unfair for one side as for the other to try its case in the newspapers. But one escape clause should be provided, wide enough to accommodate the exceptional case like the Whitmore affair or the Scottsboro boys—defendant's option. The defendant already has the option in criminal trials of deciding whether to testify. Under the present proposal, the defendant who thought he was being framed could take his case to the press; his lawyer could talk. In that event, of course, the prosecutor would have the right to respond. One would anticipate that only under unusual circumstances would the defendant exercise the publicity option; in most cases he would be better off avoiding all but the most neutral press comment.

This may not be a perfect solution, but it is one which is likely to prevent the excesses of trial by newspaper without relinquishing the safeguards of a crusading press. In the vast majority of cases, it would sweep away the fog of prejudice that frequently clouds the jury's vision. It would, in short, return the trial to the courtroom.

Robert M. Cipes
CONTROLLING CRIME NEWS:
SENSE OR CENSORSHIP?

FOUR days after the assassination of President Kennedy, the New York *Times* published a letter from its own managing editor, Turner Catledge. Catledge wrote that a *Times* news report had erred when it referred to Lee Harvey Oswald as "President Kennedy's assassin." Said Catledge: "Although Oswald was accused of the assassination and the Dallas police thought they had an airtight case against him, he was never tried and convicted. Under the American system of

justice, he is innocent until proved guilty. Future articles and headlines will reflect that fact."

While such posthumous regard for Oswald's rights is overdone, it
reflects growing concern with standards of crime reporting. There
are surely more significant issues of public affairs, yet because the
prerogatives of the press are involved, there are few which have generated so much newspaper space and such heated debate. In response
to the Warren Commission Report, and with tensions heightened by
a recent spate of sensational trials, the legal and journalistic professions are groping for standards which will bridge the uneasy gap between the constitutional rights of the press and those of the accused.
An American Bar Association committee has drafted a tentative code
to regulate crime publicity, which has met with almost uniform condemnation by newspaper publishers and editors. This month the code
will be hotly debated at the ABA's annual meeting in Hawaii; later it
will be voted on by members. As the battle between the press and bar
seems headed for its final round, a close look at the controversial proposals is in order.

The publicizing of sensational crime is as old as crime itself. In America,
with its dual institutions of trial by jury and assertive journalism, the
key issue is the influence of publicity on the minds of jurors. One critic
posed it this way: "In the case of a particularly audacious crime that
has been widely discussed, it is utterly impossible that any man of
common intelligence, and not wholly secluded from society, should
be found who had not formed an opinion." This was in 1846. During
the newspaper circulation wars at the turn of the century, Arthur
Train called yellow journalism the "most vicious factor in the administration of criminal justice." Train damned the newspapers for creating
false sympathy for defendants, rather than bias against them. This
does not change the issue, of course; it simply illustrates a difference
in environment.

Each decade has had its *causes célèbres,* and each *cause célèbre* has
produced a wave of revulsion and talk of curbing excessive publicity.
But it has remained just that—talk—with no tangible reforms. This
time *may* be different. One result of the Warren Report was the ap-
pointment of the ABA committee to study publicity. It is known as
the Reardon Committee, after its chairman, Justice Paul Reardon of
the Massachusetts Supreme Court. Last October, after two years of
work, the committee released its recommendations. It found that
most prejudicial material is not the result of independent news reporting but originates with law enforcement officers and lawyers
(both prosecution and defense). Hence the committee recommends
strong controls over all participants in a criminal case. Its theory is
that by drying up the source, most offensive material will not find

its way into the newspapers. The committee would not entirely immunize the press. It could be punished for contempt of court but only for flagrant abuses which affect the jury's verdict.

189
Robert M. Cipes
CONTROLLING
CRIME NEWS:
SENSE OR
CENSORSHIP?

Despite the modest nature of its proposals, the Reardon Report has outraged the journalistic community. For example, the president of the American Society of Newspaper Editors has called it "detrimental to society," "selection of news, suppression of news, censorship of news," leading to "abuse and confusion," encouraging "the police tendency towards secrecy," "misguided, quixotic, unnecessary and harmful to our democratic system." Strongest criticism is reserved for proposed controls over news sources. Columbia Law professor Telford Taylor touched the crucial point when he said: "What first appeared to be an issue of whether or not restrictions should be applied to the press has now emerged as a question of whether or not the press will permit the bar to restrict itself."

Consistent with a resolve to clean its own house, the ABA committee begins by proposing a change in the canons of legal ethics. This would prevent lawyers from releasing any information or opinion about a criminal case with which they are associated "if there is a reasonable likelihood that such dissemination will interfere with a fair trial or otherwise prejudice the due administration of justice." The committee feels that the existing canon on publicity (adopted sixty years ago) is too general, and it has rarely been enforced. The new canon would bar lawyers' statements about the following: a defendant's prior criminal record or information as to his character or reputation; the existence or contents of any confession; the performance of any examination or tests or the defendant's refusal to submit to such an examination; the testimony of prospective witnesses; the possibility that the defendant will plead guilty; and any opinion as to the defendant's guilt or innocence, although a defense attorney may state that his client denies the charges.

During the trial itself, no lawyer can release or authorize any statement relating to the case, except that he may quote from or refer without comment to public records in the case. Lawyers who violated the canon would be subject to disciplinary action, which could mean suspension or disbarment. The restrictions are similar to those laid down by the Justice Department two years ago for federal prosecutions. It is in state courts, however, that most crimes of violence are tried and that the worst publicity abuses occur.

The Reardon Committee originally proposed to restrict the release of crime information by court personnel and police officers along the same lines as its restrictions on lawyers. Again, no legislation would be necessary; control would depend on the court's inherent power to enforce its own rules. In the case of the police, however, this raises a serious question of "separation of powers"—whether the judicial branch of government has power to discipline employees of the executive branch. The Reardon Committee thinks that it does, but in a spirit of compromise has modified its original proposal. It now recommends that the police adopt voluntary controls and that court rules be resorted to only in the event that such controls prove ineffective.

The Reardon Committee assumes that since most offensive publicity comes from the mouths of the trial participants, controlling them will indirectly cure abuses by the press. But what happens when the press acts on its own, when an editor personally initiates a prosecution? This was pretty much the situation in the Sheppard case. Federal District Judge Weinman, in reversing Dr. Sheppard's conviction in 1964, sized it up accurately in these words:

"If ever there was a trial by newspaper, this is a perfect example. And the most insidious violator was the Cleveland *Press.* For some reason that paper took upon itself the role of accuser, judge, and jury. The journalistic value of its front page editorials, the screaming, slanted headlines and the nonobjective reporting was nil, but they were calculated to inflame and prejudice the public. Such a complete disregard for propriety results in a grave injustice not only to the individual involved but to the community in general. . . . If ever a newspaper did a disservice to its profession; if ever the cause of freedom of the press was set back, this was it."

But if the identity of the villain was clear to Judge Weinman, it was not to the Supreme Court. Its forty-page opinion does not so much as mention the Cleveland *Press* or its editor, Louis Seltzer, the man responsible for the Sheppard vendetta. Instead, the villain in the eyes of the Court is the trial judge, Edward Blythin (since deceased). It was Blythin's "failure to insulate the proceedings from prejudicial publicity and disruptive influence [of newsmen in the courtroom] which deprived Sheppard of the chance to receive a fair hearing." How Blythin, who did not enter the case until months after the press had done its damage, could have insulated the proceedings is a problem in metaphysics which the Court does not resolve.

The Sheppard opinion found it unnecessary to consider "what sanctions might be available against a recalcitrant press." In its anxiety to evade this issue, the Court scrambled for a precedent, some authoritative guide that would get it off the hook. The most authoritative thing available was the Chief Justice's own Warren Commission report. Not bothered by dissimilarity in the cases, the Court proceeded to build the flimsy Sheppard structure on the Warren foundation. It is obvious from reading the opinion that Justice Clark, its author, not only had the Warren Report at his elbow as he wrote; he also literally tore some pages from the report and called them the Sheppard case:

191
Robert M. Cipes
CONTROLLING
CRIME NEWS:
SENSE OR
CENSORSHIP?

"Neither the press nor the public had the right to be contemporaneously informed by the police or prosecuting authorities of the details of the evidence being accumulated against Oswald [Sheppard]." And again: "Bedlam reigned at the courthouse [read "police station"] during the trial and newsmen took over practically the entire courtroom, hounding most of the participants, especially Sheppard." Clark does not tell us that the entire courtroom consisted of four rows, so it was impossible for newsmen not to take it over.

Bending over backward to avoid offending the press, the Court virtually sat on the trial judge. Rarely has appellate hindsight mustered such a catalogue of "should-have-dones." The judge should have considered locking up the jury during the trial, though Sheppard's counsel advisedly refrained from requesting it. He should have granted the defense motion to change the place of trial, though as one Justice indicated during the oral argument, no county in Ohio was free from the poisonous publicity. The judge should have postponed the trial until after local elections in which he was running to succeed himself. But the election actually took place during jury selection and before the trial began, so the purpose of a short postponement is unclear. Finally, the Court condemned the trial judge for "requesting," rather than "warning," the jury not to read newspapers during the trial.

Without specifically referring to the Sheppard opinion, the Reardon Committee doubted the efficacy of these remedies. "None of these techniques," it said, "can at the same time (1) assure a fair trial in the face of prejudicial disclosures that saturate the jurisdiction and (2) preserve other rights of the defendant and the right of the people to see that the guilty are properly punished." The committee illustrated its point with the following examples: "A continuance, if it is to be long enough to dissipate the effects of the potentially prejudicial publicity, may require the defendant to sacrifice his right to a speedy trial. And its purpose will be defeated if the publicity is renewed when the case finally comes up. A change of venue may also require the sacrifice of state or federal constitutional rights (as will waiver of jury trial) and will undoubtedly be ineffective if the case is one of wide notoriety. Voir dire [examination of prospective jurors] . . . cannot fully cope with a juror's failure to be candid or with influences that occur below the level of consciousness. Sequestration [locking up the jury during the trial] does not remedy the effects of pretrial publicity and may itself prejudice the defendant because of the inconvenience and annoyance to the jurors. Admonitions to the jury have often proved ineffective [as conceded by almost half the judges responding to the committee's poll]."

If the Supreme Court thought the restricted scope of the Sheppard opinion would be understood or its professional courtesy to the press reciprocated, it was due for disappointment. The president of the

American Society of Newspaper Editors said the opinion would "hide from public knowledge virtually all of the facts of law enforcement and the administration of justice." He called it a step in the direction of the English rule where the contempt power is invoked freely against journalists. Misunderstanding of the Sheppard case reached crisis proportions when a famed constitutional law professor told a conference of state trial judges (meeting in Canada) that the opinion invited them to use the contempt power against the press. Although Justices are not accustomed to publicly interpreting their opinions, the professor's statement was too much for Justice Clark. Addressing the same conference the next day, Clark protested. It's all a mistake, the Justice declared. We didn't say anything about the contempt power, or set standards for the press. Perish the thought. The Justice even denied that the Court intended to prescribe rules for judges: "We laid guidelines the court *might* follow, not guidelines they *must* follow."

Even this unusual effort at clarification did not dispel the misunderstanding. Some judges continued to read the Sheppard opinion literally. At Sheppard's own retrial, for instance, the new judge (having read what Clark said about "bedlam") refused to give seats in the courtroom to any but local newsmen or wire-service representatives. Reporters from such national publications as *Life* and the New York *Times* had to wait in line daily beginning at 7:30 A.M. in order to compete with curious housewives for the few vacancies in the courtroom. Those who left their seats to meet a deadline did so at the risk of losing them. Some days these reporters did not get in at all.

Only a month after the Sheppard case was decided by the Supreme Court, an event occurred which was to throw an already fuzzy subject into a state of confusion. On July 14, 1966, eight Chicago student nurses were slain in their dormitory. Effective police investigation quickly produced a suspect, Richard F. Speck, whose fingerprints were found in the dormitory and who was identified from a photograph by the lone survivor. Speck's photo was plastered on every front page as a massive manhunt began. As a result of this publicity he was soon recognized, by a physician treating him after a suicide attempt.

In April, Speck was convicted of the eight murders and sentenced to death. Since prejudicial publicity is bound to be an argument on appeal, it is worth examining what that publicity was. The first question is the propriety of news disclosures before Speck's arrest. Taking the Reardon Report as a guideline, it specifically permits the police to release any information necessary to aid in the defendant's apprehension or to warn the public of any dangers he may present. Clearly there is a public interest in stopping a dangerous criminal before he commits further violence. Thus the Chicago police acted properly in publishing Speck's picture and conducting the manhunt. It was not necessary, however, to announce positively and repeatedly that Speck

193
Robert M. Cipes
CONTROLLING
CRIME NEWS:
SENSE OR
CENSORSHIP?

was "the killer," nor to disclose all the damaging evidence against him, especially the fingerprint evidence (the accuracy of which became a key issue at the trial). Even if disclosures were necessary to aid in Speck's apprehension, public interest in the disclosures ends when the suspect is arrested. Here, however, the police superintendent compounded earlier injury by adding even stronger public assurances of Speck's guilt.

As the trial date approached, the judge granted a change of venue from Chicago to Peoria. Though any difference in the degree of news coverage was doubtful, the prosecuting attorney did not oppose the motion. Like the judge, he would do everything possible to preserve the conviction that would almost certainly be obtained.

Shortly before trial, the judge issued a fourteen-point order regulating reporters. It covered everything from sketching in the courtroom (prohibited) to the consequence of visiting the men's room during trial (loss of one's place). More seriously, reporters were allowed to print only what occurred in open court (a ban going far beyond anything recommended by the Reardon Report). To make this worse, they were forbidden to purchase transcripts—a strange way to ensure the accuracy of their reports. These restrictions were all the more arbitrary in view of the jurors' sequestration, meaning they would never have access to newspaper reports. As the trial approached, and the judge was subjected to unanimous condemnation from the press, as well as a lawsuit, he retreated one by one from many of his fourteen points. It was still necessary, however, for the state's highest court to rule, in a suit by the Chicago *Tribune*, that reporters could buy official transcripts anytime they wanted to.

The formal purpose of the trial judge was of course to protect the rights of defendant Speck. The actual purpose was to protect the state's conviction against reversal, and his own judicial rectitude. Without clear guidelines, the tendency of any trial judge, particularly in this era of close appellate oversight, is to err on the side of caution. Had the Reardon proposals been in effect in the Illinois courts during the Speck trial, the fourteen-point fiasco would never have occurred. All of which suggests that uniform standards in the end may be the press's best protection against arbitrary censorship.

It took six weeks to pick a jury in the Speck case, longer than it took to try the case. Partly this was because of the enormity of the crime; one murder gives each side 20 peremptory challenges, eight murders required 160. A "peremptory" challenge is exercised without stating any reason. If differs from a challenge "for cause" which the court exercises; there were also many of these in the Speck case, on grounds of opposition to capital punishment or an acknowledged belief in Speck's guilt.

For a crime like the Chicago massacre this six-week ritual is perhaps inevitable; the Reardon proposals would not avoid it. Indeed, by setting higher standards for jury selection they might actually aggravate the *voir dire* process. A juror who has formed an opinion about the defendant's guilt will be challenged for cause "unless the examination shows unequivocally that he can be impartial." And any juror who remembers any significant prejudicial information will be challenged "without regard to his testimony as to his state of mind."

The committee's conclusions about juror prejudice jibe with the results of a University of Chicago study. It found that pretrial examination is "grossly ineffective" to screen out bias; jurors often lie in a desire to be chosen, feeling that rejection reflects on their good faith. But existing rules, while irrational in assuming that court instructions can cure bias, at least have the pragmatic virtue of getting a jury selected. The *voir dire* examination in the Speck case might still be going on were the Reardon proposals in effect. Perhaps this only emphasizes the need to concentrate on the early stages of a case, before publicity has done its damage. Yet even here it would be visionary to expect perfect control. "There are some crimes so terrible," as the late Mark DeWolfe Howe said of the Speck case, "that you can't expect either the police or the press to observe the normal rules."

Another Reardon recommendation deals with preliminary hearings. The defense may exclude the public from any pretrial hearing where evidence is heard which could not be admitted at the trial. (A record would be kept and be made public after the trial.) Without such a restriction a preliminary hearing could be used to publicize inflammatory material. This has been the English experience, about which I shall have more to say presently.

I have described the committee's indirect controls over publicity. How about controls placed directly on the press? Can a court legally hold a newspaper editor or publisher in contempt, as is commonly done under English rules? The Reardon Committee is convinced that the contempt power may be used, providing that it is limited to narrow and clearly defined situations. The committee attributes infrequent use of the power not so much to lack of authority as to the fact that courts have placed so few restraints on the press in the first place; in other words, there has been no occasion for enforcement. The Supreme Court has never passed upon use of the contempt power in a criminal *jury* trial, though it has reversed contempt convictions in several nonjury cases.

Under the committee's code there are two types of cases in which contempt may be appropriate. One is where a person, going beyond public records, makes a statement willfully designed to affect the outcome of a trial and which seriously threatens to have that effect.

This applies, however, only when a jury trial is in progress, and thus may be criticized as too narrow. The type of pretrial poisoning which took place in the Sheppard case, for example, would not even be punishable under this clause. The committee has taken pains to come within the "clear and present danger" test which the Supreme Court created for First Amendment restrictions. No new legislation would be necessary to authorize this use of contempt, says the committee, except in a few states and in the federal courts.

195
Robert M. Cipes
CONTROLLING
CRIME NEWS:
SENSE OR
CENSORSHIP?

The second type of case permits contempt action against anyone (including a reporter) who violates a judge's order not to release information produced in a hearing closed to the public. This means that a judge cannot control disclosures (for example, of an inadmissible confession) unless he engages in the rather drastic procedure of closing his courtroom. If he follows the common practice of holding a hearing outside the jury's presence, he cannot prevent a reporter from disclosing what went on in the hearing. He can only request the reporter's cooperation. This is the present practice, and the Reardon Committee would not change it.

A recent case suggests that the practice can be made to work. In March, after the bank-robbery conviction of an alleged Mafia member, Federal Judge Jacob Mishler praised reporters for not printing allegations about the defendant's past which were not admissible at the trial. "The coverage of this trial," Judge Mishler said, "may be the most forceful argument against imposing restrictions on the press."

The reception for the Reardon Report among the working press, as I have indicated, has been less than cordial. Most of its proposals have been rejected by the American Society of Newspaper Editors and the American Newspaper Publishers Association. One tactic of these groups is to deny the existence of a problem, claiming a failure to show any real damage from crime publicity. Actually the Reardon Committee based its recommendations on a study of hundreds of reported decisions, on extensive interviews with trial participants, and on its own content analysis of crime-news coverage in more than twenty cities during a one-year period (1965). While the committee concedes that the *percentage* of cases with a serious publicity question is small, it shows that the *number* of such cases is substantial, far greater than has been generally believed. Nevertheless, in April the ANPA raised $150,000 for an empirical study of the problem, which is sure to provide an excuse for further delay.

The Newspaper Publishers' report is more defensive than the Editors'. Starting with the premise that "the American Press has demonstrated its devotion to the cause of fair trial," the report predictably concludes that no controls of any kind are necessary. In fact, its only recommendation is that "the press stand ready at any time to discuss these problems with appropriate individuals or groups." This is not even as strong as the Editors' 1965 suggestion for "energetic, frequent, and continuing conversations among those concerned" with the problem.

The chief author of the Editors' 1965 report (other reports were issued in 1966 and 1967 to respond to Reardon) was Alfred Friendly, then managing editor of the Washington *Post*. Friendly apparently took his own suggestion to heart and began engaging in continuing conversations with a Washington attorney, Ronald Goldfarb, an expert on the contempt power. The result of the conversations was collaboration in a book, *Crime and Publicity*, published May 15 by the Twentieth Century Fund. The book is undoubtedly a welcome ally for the Reardon Committee, agreeing with its essential recommendations.

Unfortunately, Friendly's value as an ally may be weakened by the inconsistent positions that he has been taking elsewhere. In 1964, when the Supreme Court of New Jersey laid down publicity guidelines less sweeping than Reardon's, Friendly was quoted as being "flabbergasted" by the court's opinion. Inconsistencies persisted after publication of the Reardon Report. In a bulletin to the Editors' group, Friendly chided his colleagues for overreacting to the bar report. One of his criticisms: "To argue, as almost every critic of the report has, that the proposed restrictions against what *should not* be released will invite secrecy about what *should* be made public is somehow not convincing." Yet Friendly himself, in a contemporaneous piece in the Washington *Post*, wrote that the dangers of the Reardon proposals lie "in the excuse they may give to the police for suppressing what should not be suppressed and what the Reardon group is perfectly willing to have released."

The impact of the Reardon proposals on Southern civil rights cases is a specter often raised in opposition to the report. Railroading of Negro suspects and cover-up of white murderers are what the report is charged with abetting. The truth is that the report is largely irrelevant in these cases. If the Reardon proposals are not available, the redneck sheriff will find some other excuse for secrecy, or he will simply dismiss reporters without any reason.

On the other hand, sanction against flagrant press abuses may never be imposed in the South, since contempt punishment must come from the local judiciary. Take the newspaper in Lynchburg, Virginia, which wrote almost daily that a Negro defendant's Northern lawyer was "linked with Communist-front organizations." These reports may be enough to get the defendant's conviction reversed, but the reversal will not deter the newspaper, as the threat of contempt might.

197
Robert M. Cipes
CONTROLLING
CRIME NEWS:
SENSE OR
CENSORSHIP?

In trying to rally liberal opinion, the news media do not make a convincing case for their impact on civil rights cases. The failure of a district attorney to prosecute or a jury to convict, and official resort to secret detention and star-chamber trials—these are not simply signs that the criminal process has broken down and is in need of reform. Their real meaning is that government itself has become corrupt. Unfortunately, this is not a condition that will be cured by exposés in Northern newspapers.

Last February, another in the series of press-bar reports came out. This one was by a committee of the Bar Association of the City of New York, chaired by seventy-eight-year-old Judge Harold R. Medina of the federal court of appeals. The Medina Report differs from the Reardon Report in denying power to hold news media in contempt and power to impose judicial controls on police. It is stronger than Reardon, however, in the restrictions it would place on lawyers, such as the duty to pressure clients and witnesses not to make out-of-court statements.

Judge Medina concluded his report "with a feeling of optimism," but unfortunately it proved to be misplaced. The judge was sure that the reluctance shown by news media was due to a threat to their independence and their constitutional rights. "Once it becomes firmly established that these fundamental rights are not in jeopardy and that their contribution to the purification of the judicial process is a voluntary one . . . their cooperation will be more generously forthcoming." Judge Medina, like Justice Tom Clark before him, was unprepared for the press's ungenerous treatment. "A code of silence," a "policy of secrecy in law enforcement," said the American Society of Newspaper Editors. "Frankly, I think those people don't realize who their friends are," Medina lamented.

The Editors' group believes that "putting prior restraint on news sources is equivalent to putting prior restraint on the press." What the drying up of "live" sources really means, however, is that the laborious task of digging out the facts must be done independently. Independent reporting of crime news is now largely a myth, according to a leading trail lawyer, Milton R. Wessel. He writes, "A large number of criminal indictments themselves would go completely unnoticed if not highlighted by a tip from the police or the district attorney, and sometimes by the defense counsel." Getting crime news without assistance between indictment and trial is even more difficult. "Absent an official tip of some kind, the reporter has no way of knowing what applications or motions will be heard." And covering the trial, says Wessel, is the most difficult, time-consuming job of all. "The press can't afford to assign full-time reporters . . . to any but the most exceptional cases. Stenographic transcripts are much too expensive, usually not available in time, frequently incomprehensible without exhibits and long study."

Recognizing that without help publicity will be limited, participants in a trial often point out to the press significant matters in the record, advise them when an "interesting" witness will testify. These officials, says Wessel, adopt "the fiction that they are merely reciting what is public, ignoring that it is not otherwise available and in any event they are editorializing by selecting episodes that they consider favorable. These comments . . . actually serve to create partisan news and prejudicial comment, which for practical reasons would never otherwise exist."

This is not mere theory. Wessel's point was proven in a long criminal trial in which both he and this author participated. At Wessel's request, the trial judge directed all participants to withhold any comment concerning the case until its conclusion. No restriction was placed upon the press itself, but it was arranged that "off the record" tips, summaries, and digests would not be given to reporters, nor would anyone furnish free copies of transcripts to them. Despite the obvious public interest in the case, writes Wessel, and trial disclosures of relatively sensational matter, "the amazing result was that there was absolutely no public comment anywhere about it for over a month following the beginning of trial." When one reporter finally did come upon the case, it was so difficult for him to follow that he ended up writing his articles on the theme "No Publicity in Fraud Trial." Wessel does not suggest that drying up present sources will foreclose press coverage; he believes that it will encourage the press to select and concentrate on those cases which are truly newsworthy.

Despite scary predictions that we are moving toward the British system of strict press controls, there is little in the proposed codes that is remotely suggestive of the British system. For one thing, besides marked differences in social and political conditions, the legal conditions for the contempt power in England make sanctions possible that would never be dreamt of here. There is no constitutional guarantee of free press, and reporters and editors may be punished without having threatened any "clear and present danger" to justice. In fact, they may be punished simply for outraging the dignity of the court, regardless of any prejudice to litigants.

The British themselves have been showing signs of discontent with the way in which press controls have been operating. Insulation of criminal trials from prejudicial publicity—in notorious cases like that of Stephen Ward or Dr. John Bodkin Adams—has been more theoretical than real. The press may report anything which takes place at a preliminary hearing, a pretrial inquest to decide if there is enough evidence to hold a defendant for trial. Much of this testimony may be inadmissible at the trial, but the press is free to report it anyway. In the case of Dr. Adams, who was ultimately tried for poisoning an elderly patient, charges of similar murders had been aired at the preliminary hearing and widely publicized before trial. Currently there is a bill in Parliament which would practically do away with the preliminary hearing, in part because of its abuse for publicity purposes.

199
Robert M. Cipes
CONTROLLiNG
CRIME NEWS:
SENSE OR
CENSORSHIP?

British concern about the excesses of their yellow journals, which often seem to outdo ours, has been matched by doubts in the other direction—as to the failure of the responsible press to oversee critically the administration of justice. A joint committee of British jurists and journalists recently found that the press was suffering from excessive caution, probably owing to fear of the contempt power. A relaxation of some features of the law was sought. Not only must the British press contend with contempt laws; it must also live with strict libel laws which clearly operate in favor of plaintiffs, in sharp contrast to our libel laws.

To state the British law only underlines how truly free the American press is from legal restrictions. What is it, then, that the editors and publishers are so agitated about? Joseph Kraft has referred to the human tendency to trivialize, to focus on issues symbolically related to what bothers us, but simpler to understand. The American press does have cause for alarm, but not by reason of a narrowly defined code governing a narrow and not terribly vital area of public affairs.

The press says it is fighting for "the public's right to know." To know what? That Sam Sheppard slept with his lab technician, or that young Dr. Coppolino had an affair with Mrs. Farber? The very pettiness of most crime news, the poverty of examples of important exposures both suggest that somehow this whole press-bar fight has been inflated. Newsmen boast of their "watchdog" function and cry about being "muzzled," but has anyone gotten down to examining the dog to see if it can really bite?

To understand the malaise of the American press I think we must look beyond the courtroom and the police station. The press was given its privileged status in order to question and, if necessary, counteract the exercise of government power. In that function it is defaulting. Writing in the *New York Review of Books*, Andrew Kopkind has described the real sources of news suppression: "In ways which journalists themselves perceive only dimly or not at all, they are bought, or compromised, or manipulated into confirming the official lies: not the little ones, which they delight in exposing, but the big ones, which they do not normally think of as lies at all, and which they cannot distinguish from the truth."

The press has been tilting at windmills in this noisy debate about crime news, dissipating energies which might be better spent in a larger struggle, already deferred too long. The press is off fighting brushfires while its own house is burning down.

Terry Ann Knopf
MEDIA MYTHS ON VIOLENCE

SEVERAL years ago a resident of a small Northern town kept insisting to a local newspaper reporter that a policeman had been shot and killed during a racial disturbance there. The reporter checked and rechecked but was unable to substantiate the story. In fact a policeman had been killed, but in another city. The man simply had heard a garbled version of the story—not an unusual occurrence in the confusion that prevails during crises.

Crisis situations increase the need for news. During most serious disturbances, news media are bombarded with calls from anxious citizens wanting information, clarification, verification of what they have heard. So important is the flow of news through established channels that its continued absence can help precipitate a crisis. In 1968 in Detroit the absence of newspapers during a protracted strike helped create a panic: there were rumors in the white community that blacks were planning to blow up freeways, kill suburban white children, and destroy public buildings; in the black community, that white vigilantes were coming into the area to attack the residents. Gun clubs sprang up in the suburbs; black leaders urged preparation of survival kits. On March 7—nearly four months after the strike began —Mayor Cavanagh had to go on TV to plead for calm.

As racial disorders have become a familiar part of the national scene the media have demonstrated a growing awareness of their responsibilities and a healthy willingness to experiment with new policies and procedures. Technical improvements also have been made. The City of Detroit, for example, has built a press room large enough for 150 people, with independent telephone lines. Operational techniques have been modernized—the Pittsburgh police, among others, have on occasion provided a helicopter for the press. And central headquarters or "press centrals" have been established to help eliminate conflicting reports. Moreover, a number of cities have adopted or revised guidelines for reporting. These guidelines—sometimes formal, sometimes informal—urge that unnecessary interpretation be minimized, rumors be eliminated, unverified statements be avoided, and superlatives and adjectives in "scare" headlines be excluded. One set of guidelines put the matter simply: "Honest and dispassionate reporting is the best reporting."

In accordance with these guidelines, newspapers have tended to move away from the "shotgun" approach—the front-page buildup, complete with splashy pictures and boxscores of the latest "riot" news. Dramatic but meaningless predictions have also largely disappeared. In May, 1967, *U.S. News & World Report* declared that Newark was "not expecting trouble," while Cleveland was voted the city "most likely to explode—again." Cleveland failed to erupt in 1967, but Newark experienced one of the most massive outbursts in our country's history. This kind of journalism is much less common today.

There is also evidence of greater sympathy and sensitivity toward blacks. How far have we come? Consider the following comment from the New York *Times* on July 23, 1919, concerning the violent disorder in Washington, D.C.:

The majority of the negroes (sic) in Washington before the great war were well behaved. . . . More of them admitted the superiority of the white race, and troubles between the two races were undreamed of. Now and then a negro intent on enforcing a civil rights law would force his way into a saloon or a theatre and demand to be treated the same as whites were, but if the manager objected he usually gave in without more than a protest.

These changes represent considerable improvement. But serious problems remain. Glaring instances of inaccuracy, exaggeration, distortion, misinterpretation, and bias have continued at every level— in newspapers and newsmagazines large and small, Northern and Southern, liberal and conservative.

The wire services are probably the most underexamined segment of the media, although as much as 90 per cent of the news in some newspapers on a given day may come from the wires. One error in a wire service report from one city may be repeated in hundreds of newspapers and newscasts. In York, Pa., in mid-July, 1968, for instance, incidents of rock- and bottle-throwing were reported. Toward the end of the disturbance UPI in Harrisburg asked a stringer to get something on the situation. A photographer took a picture of a motorcyclist with an ammunition belt around his waist and a rifle strapped across his back. A small object dangled from the rifle. On July 18, the picture reached the nation's press. The Washington *Post* said:

Armed Rider—Unidentified motorcyclist drives through heart of York, Pa., Negro district, which was quiet for the first time in six days of sporadic disorders.

The Baltimore *Sun* used the same picture and a similar caption:

Quiet, But . . . An unidentified motorcycle rider, armed with a rifle and carrying a belt of ammunition, was among those in the heart of York, Pa., Negro district last night. The area was quiet for the first time in six days.

The implication of this photograph was clear: The "armed rider" was a sniper. But since when do snipers travel openly in daylight completely armed? Also, isn't there something incongruous about photographing a sniper, presumably "on his way to work," when according to the caption the city "was quiet"? Actually the "armed rider" was a sixteen-year-old boy who happened to be fond of hunting groundhogs—a skill he had learned as a small boy from his father. On July 16, as was his custom, the young man had put on his ammo belt and strapped a rifle across his back, letting a hunting license dangle so that all would know he was hunting animals, not people. Off he went on his motorcycle headed for the woods, the fields, the groundhogs—and the place reserved for him in the nation's press.

More recently, an AP man in Dallas filed a story on a student takeover at Southern Methodist University. The Fort Worth *Star-Telegram* in its evening edition last May 2 put the story on the front page and gave it a banner headline:

BLACKS SEIZE OFFICE OF

S.M.U.'S PRESIDENT

Police Are Called to Stand By

DALLAS (AP)—Black students with some support from whites took over the office of the president of Southern Methodist University today and swore to remain until their demands are met. . . .

Reports from the scene said from thirty to thirty-five students were in control of [President] Tate's office.

The takeover occurred during a meeting of Tate and a campus organization, the Black League of Afro-American and African College Students.

The story had one major flaw—it wasn't true. While about thirty-five students had met with the university president, they were not "in control" of his office; nor had they "swore to remain" until their demands were met. No such "takeover" had occurred. Glen Dromgoole, a staff writer for the *Star-Telegram,* later reported what really happened. The black students had met with the president for more than five hours discussing recent demands. The talks were more friendly than hostile. (At one point hamburgers were brought in.) By the end of the meeting, agreement had been reached on most of the issues. Apparently the wire service reporter had accepted the many rumors of a student takeover.

Martin Hayden of the Detroit *News* has suggested "an almost mathematical relationship between the level of exaggeration and the distance of news transmission." Edwin Guthman of the Los Angeles *Times* maintains that the early wire service report "is at the crux of the news media's problem." However, it is more likely that instances of misreporting remain a problem at *every* media level. The Lemberg Center for the Study of Violence, in investigating twenty-five incidents in which the news media had alleged sniping, found that, along with the wire services, local and nationally known newspapers bore a heavy responsibility for imprecise, distorted, and inaccurate reporting.

While treatment of racial disorders is generally more restrained today, the news media continue to overplay the more violent or sensational aspects of a story. The central media concern during the disorder at Cornell University last April, for example, was the emergence of the blacks from the student union. A picture of the students carrying rifles and shotguns, splashed across the nation, had a distorting effect on public opinion. The New York *Times* put the picture on page 1, and *Newsweek* used it on its cover the following week. Certain facts were largely ignored: prior to the disorder a cross had been burned in front of a black women's dormitory; the students had heard radio reports that carloads of armed whites were moving toward the campus; when the students emerged from the building their guns weren't loaded. What was basically a defensive response by a group of frightened students came across in the media as a terrorist act by student guerrillas.

Aspects of the disorders are dramatic and do merit extensive coverage. But the media still tend to equate bad news with big news and to confuse the obvious with the relevant. Thus when sixty-five students at Brandeis University took over a building last year it rated a story on the front page of the New York *Times*—despite the fact that there was no violence, that classes continued, and that the university suffered only minor inconvenience. I was on campus then. My only recollection of anything unusual was that on the first day or two an attendant asked to see my identification, and for the next week and a half I noticed large numbers of reporters, press cars, cameras, and other equipment. I sometimes wondered if there weren't more reporters outside than students inside the building.

The *Times,* along with most newspapers, missed the unusual climax at Brandeis. In a war of nerves with the students, President Morris Abram showed consummate skill in handling the situation, remaining flexible on the issues, mobilizing the support of the student body and faculty, and, above all, refusing to call in police. Eleven days after the crisis had begun the students quietly left the building—a dramatic victory for the Brandeis community, a dramatic example of how to handle a university crisis in contrast to fiascoes at Columbia and San Francisco State. Yet the students' departure merely merited a *Times* story about three inches long, well off the front page.

Disparities between the headlines and news stories are another problem. Often much less occurs in the story than the headline would indicate. Last year, for example, some concerned parents in Jacksonville, Fla., removed their children from Kirby Smith Junior High School after a local radio station had broadcast an exaggerated report of a fight between black and white students. The school principal later indicated that "classes continued and there was no panic." Nevertheless the Miami *Herald* headlined its story last April 25: MOMS MOB SCHOOL AFTER RIOT 'NEWS.' Sometimes no violence occurs in the story, dramatic headlines to the contrary. A story appearing in the Boston *Globe* last May 10 told of a peaceful rally by a small group of students at a local theological seminary. According to the *Globe,* the rally was "brief and orderly," But the headline above the story read NEWTON CAMPUS ERUPTS.

The use of the word "riot" presents another problem because it has no precise meaning in terms of current disorders. *Webster's* defines a "riot" as a "tumultuous disturbance of the public peace by three or more persons assembled together and acting with a common intent." The difficulty is that "riots" have become so frequent and come in so many sizes and shapes as to render the word meaningless. There is something ludicrous about lumping together as "riots" Detroit, with forty-three deaths, 7,000 arrests, and $45 million in property damage, and an incident in which three people break a few store windows. Yet this is precisely what the news media still do. The continued media use of the term contributes to an emotionally charged climate in which the public tends to view every event as an "incident," every incident as a "disturbance," and every disturbance as a "riot." Journalists would do well to drop the word from their vocabulary altogether.

No law says the media have to interpret and not simply report the news, but having assumed this responsibility they have an obligation to make reasonable judgments based on careful analysis. Unfortunately, journalistic attempts in the direction of social science research have been rather amateurish, particularly where new trends and patterns are concerned. The case of the Cleveland "shoot-out" is a good example. On July 23, 1968, an intense gun battle broke out between the police and a group of black nationalists led by Ahmed Evans. Before the disorder was over 16,400 National Guardsmen had been mobilized, nine persons had been killed, and there was property damage estimated at $2.6 million. The Cleveland *Press* on July 24, 1968, compared the violence to guerrilla activity in Vietnam:

. . . it didn't seem to be a Watts, or a Detroit, or a Newark. Or even a Hough of two years ago. No, this tragic night seemed to be part of a plan.

A reporter writing in the New York *Times* of July 28, 1968, stated:

It marks perhaps the first documented case in recent history of black, armed, and organized violence against the police.

More recent reports have revealed that the "shoot-out" was something less than a planned uprising and that the situation was considerably more complicated than indicated initially. Unfortunately, following the events in Cleveland, disorders in which shots may have been fired were immediately suspected by the press of being part of a "wave." A series of errors involving a handful of cities became the basis of a myth—that the pattern of violence in 1968 had changed from spontaneous to premeditated outbreaks. Few of the nationally known newspapers and newsmagazines attempted to verify sniping reports coming out of the cities and over the wire services; few were willing to undertake independent investigations; and far too many were overly zealous in their assertions of a new "trend" based on limited and unconfirmed evidence. Unwittingly or not, the national media had constructed a scenario on armed uprisings.

Although having more time to check and verify reports than daily newspapers, the newsmagazines were even more vocal in their assertions of a "new pattern." On September 13, 1968, *Time* took note of an "ominous trend" and declared that the violence "appears to be changing from spontaneous combustion of a mob to the premeditated shootouts of a far-out few." The story went on to indicate that "many battles" had begun with "well planned sniping at police." Nearly a year later, on June 27, 1969—long after investigation by a task force of the National Commission on the Causes and Prevention of Violence, by the Lemberg Center, and by the New York *Times* (which reversed itself on the Cleveland question) had cast serious doubt about premeditated outbreaks in Cleveland and elsewhere—*Time* still was talking about the possibilities of a "guerrilla summer" and reminding its readers of the time in Cleveland when "police were lured into an ambush." Once started, myths are difficult to extinguish.

The most recent myth created by the media involves an alleged "shift" in racial disturbances from large to small cities. Last July 25 a syndicated reporter for the News Enterprise Association (NEA) noted:

The socially sizzling summer has begun—but unlike recent history, it seems to be the minor, not the major, cities which are sweltering.

In an article entitled "Riots, 1969 Style," *Newsweek* declared on August 11:

. . . the traditional riot scenario is still being played out this summer—with one major difference. This season the stage has shifted from the major population centers to such small and disparate communities as Kokomo, Ind., Santa Ana, Calif., Cairo, Ill., Middletown, Conn., and Farrell, Pa.

Last September 9 the New York *Times* captioned a picture:

New Riot Pattern: Rioting in Hartford, Conn., last week . . . underscored the fact that smaller cities this summer have had more racial trouble than the big ones.

Similar stories appeared about the same time in scores of other newspapers, including the *Wall Street Journal,* the Baltimore *News American,* the Woburn, Mass., *Times,* and the Pittsburgh *Press.*

In fact, racial disorders occurring over the past few years—not just this past summer—have been concentrated in smaller cities. About 75 per cent of all outbreaks recorded in 1968 by the Lemberg Center's Civil Disorder Clearinghouse occurred outside the 100 largest cities. For the first six months of 1969 and also for the summer no appreciable change in the percentage was noted. Furthermore, many of the cities cited as prototypes of this latest "new pattern"—Hartford and Middletown, Conn., Cairo, Ill.—have had disorders in previous years. The difference is that such outbreaks were completely overshadowed by a few enormous outbreaks in large cities such as Newark and Detroit.

Discovering the origin of these and other myths would be useful—a faulty wire service report, an inept reporter, an unreliable source. But aside from the fact that such a task would be almost impossible, it would miss a central point—that the system of reporting ensures that errors of fact and interpretation may be repeated, compounded, and reformulated as myths. In recent years the various components of the media have become extremely intertwined and dependent upon one another. The wire services, the nationally known newspapers, and the newsmagazines feed one another news and information. While the system undoubtedly speeds the flow of news to the public, it has encouraged a parrot-like character in which the various media segments tend to reproduce rather than examine one another's views.

In this respect the New York *Times'* caption proclaiming a NEW PATTERN assumes greater significance. Prior to its appearance in the *Times,* I talked with Jack Rosenthal, who had been working on a story on the relatively cool summer. When the subject of a new "shift" in violence came up I indicated that such allegations were false and misleading. Rosenthal wrote a thoughtful story, dwelling on police-community relations, civic programs, and the new community spirit among blacks. His story made no mention of a "new riot pattern." Apparently the caption writer had paid more attention to what *Newsweek* and the *Wall Street Journal* were saying than to his colleague at the *Times.*

The failure of the media to tell the complete story in the case of Cornell or the right story in the case of Cleveland goes beyond a lack of initiative or an inclination to sensationalize. It also indicates a bias—one which, notwithstanding Vice President Agnew's declarations, cuts *across* political and geographical lines. The media are no more aware of this bias than is the general public aware of its own. In part, we could call it a class bias in that those who comprise media staffs—reporters, editors, headline writers, etc.—are part of the vast American middle class and, as such, express its views, values, and standards.

Both the general public and the media share the same dislike of protestors; both are unable to understand violence as an expression of protest against oppressive conditions; both prefer the myth of orderly, peaceful change, extolling the virtues of private property and public decorum. People are expected to behave in a certain way; they just don't go around yelling and cursing or throwing rocks. Both will grant that it took a revolution to secure our independence and a civil war to end slavery (at least officially), but that was all long ago and somehow different. The bias also has elements of racism in that color is never far from the surface. It is difficult to say where the class bias begins and racist bias ends. These elements are inseparable and reenforce each other, and both manifest themselves in the thinking of the public and media alike.

A growing body of research shows that racial disorders are a part of the social process. The process includes an accumulation of grievances, a series of tension-heightening incidents such as police harassment, and a precipitating event such as an arrest which crystallizes the tensions and grievances that have mounted—the "last straw" that triggers the violence. The "typical rioter" is young, better educated than the average inner-city black, and more dissatisfied. He wants a better job but feels that prospective employers will discriminate against him. He is likely to be a long-term resident of the city. (In a survey in Detroit, 90 per cent of those arrested were from Detroit, 78 percent lived in the state, and only 1 per cent lived outside the state.) He is extremely proud of his race and is politically conscious. He is more interested in and informed about politics than blacks who are not involved in a disorder. He is also more inclined toward political activism. (In one survey, nearly 40 per cent of the participants in the disorder—as compared to only about 25 per cent of the nonparticipants—reported having been involved in civil rights activity.) Finally, he receives substantial support from the rest of his community, which does not participate but regards the violence as necessary and beneficial.

As important as the findings in these studies are, they have made virtually no impact on the vast majority of the public. Most Americans continue to believe that violence is caused by a tiny and insignificant minority, that "outside agitators" and "criminal elements" are mainly responsible for isolated outbursts that have little or no social significance. Intellectuals must share a portion of the blame for this situation. Having completed their studies, they have been notoriously reluctant to roll up their academic shirtsleeves and assume leadership in presenting their ideas to the public. There is a trace of condescension in their assumption that good ideas from above will somehow trickle down to the "masses of asses," as one academic I know calls them.

Greater responsibility for the failure to confront the public's resistance rests with the news media. They have failed to commit their power and prestige on behalf of such studies. They have failed to place the ideas before the public and push for reform in an aggressive, effective manner—settling for a splash of headlines and stories initially, and little followup. Instead the media have opted for the status quo, reflecting, sustaining, and perpetuating outworn beliefs of their predominantly white audience.

Historically the notion of plots and conspiracies has always had great currency in this country—and in other countries, too. Prior to the Civil War, Southerners frequently viewed abolitionists as "outside agitators" trying to stir up the happy slaves. Violent interracial clashes during World War I were said to have been instigated by the Bolsheviks, and the outbreak in Detroit in 1913 was attributed to an "Axis plot." The current wave of disorders has been blamed on individuals such as Stokely Carmichael and H. Rap Brown or, for those who like a more international flavor, "Communist infiltrators." In a survey of six Northern cities by the Lemberg Center, 77 per cent of all whites interviewed believed that "outside agitators" were a major contributing cause of disorders. When Los Angeles Mayor Sam Yorty recently blamed a rash of school disorders on a conspiracy of the Black Student Union, the Students for a Democratic Society, Communist sympathizers, and the National Council of Churches, he was following a long—though not very honorable—tradition.

Such allegations are usually made without a shred of evidence, except for an occasional "someone told me so." Nevertheless the media have frequently taken their cues from the public in formulating and circulating such reports. Misinterpretations of the events in Cleveland, along with assertions of a "new pattern" of premeditated violence, are blatant examples of this form of bias. But more often the bias is expressed in more subtle ways. For example, when rumors circulated that "outside agitators" were involved in a disturbance in Omaha, Neb., a news story appearing in the Arkansas *Gazette* last June 27 made reference to the rumors but also mentioned that the mayor had no evidence to support such reports. Yet, the headline above the story read: 'OUTSIDERS' LINKED TO OMAHA RIOTING.

A look at the way in which the disorders are written up reveals, tragically, that the majority of the media and the public share essentially the same view of the violence—as meaningless, purposeless, senseless, irrational. Media treatment of the disorders following the assassination of Rev. Martin Luther King, Jr., illustrates the point. The sense of loss and injury among blacks at the time of the assassination was extremely great—far greater than among whites. The unprecedented wave of disorders—approximately 200—was expressive of the anger, bitterness, resentment, frustration that black people everywhere felt.

How did the media handle the disorders? Stories in just two newspapers analyzed—the Buffalo *News* of April 9, 1968 (the day of Dr. King's funeral), and the Trenton *Times-Advertiser* one day later—are fairly typical. No attempt is made to place the violence in a social context. The reference to the assassination of Dr. King is perfunctory, with only a passing mention of his funeral and a few shouts about his death. Value-laden words receive unusual emphasis. The participants are "marauders," not men; they "rove" instead of run; they move in "gangs," not groups; they engage in "vandalism," not simply violence.

We have all grown so used to viewing blacks as stereotyped criminals that it is difficult to picture them in any other role; hence such frequent press concoctions as "roving gangs," "roving vandals," "roving gangs of rampaging teenagers," or, for variety, "a window-smashing rampage of roving gangs of Negro youths." The New York *Times* assertion last July 1 that "roving bands of ruffians" were involved in a disturbance in Middletown, Conn., seems somewhat feeble by comparison. The effect of such treatment by the media is to pander to the public's prejudice, reenforcing stereotypes, myths, and other outmoded beliefs. The media not only frighten the public but confuse it as well.

And let us not forget the effects on the news media. The proliferation of underground newspapers, radical publications, black journals, as well as underground radio stations on FM bands held by churches and universitites, indicates that the media are failing to reach certain groups, and that they still lack sensitivity, sophistication, and skepticism commensurate with their important and strategic position.

CRITICS AND CRITICISM

Spiro Agnew
SPEECH
NOVEMBER 20, 1969

Elected Vice President of the United States in 1968, Spiro Agnew has gained nationwide attention with his attacks on the mass media. The following speech was delivered by Vice President Agnew to the Montgomery, Alabama, Chamber of Commerce on November 20, 1969.

ONE week ago tonight I flew out to Des Moines, Iowa, and exercised my right to dissent.

There has been some criticism of what I had to say out there.

Let me give you a sampling.

One Congressman charged me with, and I quote, "A creeping socialistic scheme against the free enterprise broadcast industry." That is the first time in my memory anybody ever accused Ted Agnew of entertaining socialist ideas.

On Monday, largely because of this address, Mr. Humphrey charged the Nixon Administration with a "calculated attack" on the right of dissent and on the media today. Yet, it is widely known that Mr. Humphrey himself believes deeply that unfair coverage of the Democratic Convention in Chicago, by the same media, contributed to his defeat in November. Now, his wounds are apparently healed, and he casts his lot with those who were questioning his own political courage a year ago. But let us leave Mr. Humphrey to his own conscience. America already has too many politicians who would rather switch than fight.

Others charged that my purpose was to stifle dissent in this country. Nonsense. The expression of my views has produced enough rugged dissent in the last week to wear out a whole covey of commentators and columnists.

One critic charged that the speech was "disgraceful, ignorant and base," that it "leads us as a nation into an ugly era of the most fearsome suppression and intimidation." One national commentator, whose name is known to everyone in this room, said "I hesitate to get into the gutter with this guy." Another commentator charges that it was "one of the most sinister speeches I have ever heard made by a public official." The President of one network said it was an "unprecedented attempt to intimidate a news medium which depends for its existence upon government licenses." The President of another charged me with "an appeal to prejudice," and said it was evident that I would prefer the kind of television "that would be subservient to whatever political group happened to be in authority at the time."

And they say *I* have a thin skin.

Here are classic examples of overreaction. These attacks do not address themselves to the questions I have raised. In fairness, others —the majority of critics and commentators—did take up the main thrust of my address. And if the debate they have engaged in continues, our goal will surely be reached—a thorough self-examination by the networks of their own policies—and perhaps prejudices. That was my objective then; it is my objective now.

Now, let me repeat to you the thrust of my remarks the other night, and make some new points and raise some new issues.

I am opposed to censorship of television or the press in any form. I don't care whether censorship is imposed by government or whether it results from management in the choice and the presentation of the news by a little fraternity having similar social and political views. I am against censorship in all forms.

But a broader spectrum of national opinion *should* be represented among the commentators of the network news. Men who can articulate other points of view *should* be brought forward.

And a high wall of separation *should* be raised between what is news and what is commentary.

And the American people *should* be made aware of the trend toward the monopolization of the great public information vehicles and the concentration of more and more power over public opinion in fewer and fewer hands.

Should a conglomerate be formed that tied together a shoe company with a shirt company, some voice will rise up righteously to say that this is a great danger to the economy; and that the conglomerate ought to be broken up.

But a single company, in the nation's capital, holds control of the largest newspaper in Washington, D.C., *and* one of the four major television stations, *and* an all-news radio station, *and* one of the three major national news magazines—all grinding out the same editorial line—and this is not a subject you have seen debated on the editorial pages of the *Washington Post* or the *New York Times*.

For the purpose of clarity, before my thoughts are obliterated in the smoking typewriters of my friends in Washington and New York, let me emphasize I am not recommending the dismemberment of the Washington Post Company. I am merely pointing out that the public should be aware that these four powerful voices hearken to the same master.

I am merely raising these questions so that the American people will become aware of—and think of the implications of—the growing monopolization of the voices of public opinion on which we all depend —for our knowledge and for the basis of our views.

When the *Washington Times-Herald* died in the nation's capital, that was a political tragedy; and when the *New York Journal-American,* the *New York World-Telegram and Sun,* and *New York Mirror* and the *New York Herald-Tribune* all collapsed within this decade, that was a great, great political tragedy for the people of New York. The *New York Times* was a better newspaper when they were alive than it is now that they are gone.

What has happened in the city of New York has happened in other great cities in America.

Many, many strong independent voices have been stilled in this country in recent years. Lacking the vigor of competition, some of those that have survived have, let us face it, grown fat and irresponsible.

I offer an example. When 300 Congressmen and 59 Senators signed a letter endorsing the President's policy in Vietnam it was news— big news. Even the *Washington Post* and the *Baltimore Sun*—scarcely house organs of the Nixon Administration—placed it prominently on the front page.

Yet the next morning the *New York Times,* which considers itself America's paper of record, did not carry a word. Why?

If a theology student in Iowa should get up at a PTA luncheon in Sioux City and attack the President's Vietnam policy, my guess is that you would probably find it reported somewhere the next morning in the *New York Times.* But when 300 Congressmen endorse the President's Vietnam policy, the next morning it is apparently not considered news fit to print.

Just this Tuesday, when the Pope, the Spiritual Leader of half a billion Roman Catholics applauded the President's efforts to end the war in Vietnam, and endorsed the way he was proceeding—that news was on Page 11 of the *New York Times.* But the same day, a report about some burglars who broke into a souvenir shop at St. Peters and stole $9,000 worth of stamps and currency—that story made Page 3. How's that for news judgment?

A few weeks ago here in the South, I expressed my views about street and campus demonstrations. Here is how the *New York Times* responded:

"He," (that's me) "lambasted the nation's youth in sweeping and ignorant generalizations, when it is clear to all perceptive observers that American youth today is far more imbued with idealism, a sense of service and a deep humanitarianism than any generation in recent history, including particularly Mr. Agnew's (generation)."

That seems a peculiar slur on a generation that brought America out of the Great Depression without resorting to the extremes of either fascism or Communism. That seems a strange thing to say about an entire generation that helped to provide greater material blessings and personal freedom—out of that Depression—for more people than any other nation in history. We have not finished the task by any means—but we are still on the job.

Just as millions of young Americans in this generation have shown valor and courage and heroism in fighting the longest and least popular war in our history—so it was the young men of my generation who went ashore at Normandy under Eisenhower and with McArthur into the Phillipines.

Yes, my generation, like the current generation, made its own share of great mistakes and blunders. Among other things, we put too much confidence in Stalin and not enough in Winston Churchill.

But whatever freedom exists today in Western Europe and Japan exists because hundreds of thousands of young men in my generation are lying in graves in North Africa and France and Korea and a score of islands in the Western Pacific.

This might not be considered enough of a "sense of service" or a "deep humanitarianism" for the "*perceptive critics*" who write editorials for the *New York Times,* but it's good enough for me; and I am content to let history be the judge.

Now, let me talk briefly about this younger generation.

I have not and do not condemn this generation of young Americans. Like Edmund Burke, I would not know how to "draw up an indictment against a whole people." They are our sons and daughters. They contain in their numbers many gifted, idealistic and courageous young men and women.

But they also list in their numbers an arrogrant few who march under the flags and portraits of dictators, who intimidate and harass university professors, who use gutter obscenities to shout down speakers with whom they disagree, who openly profess their belief in the efficacy of violence in a democratic society.

The preceding generation had its own breed of losers—and our generation dealt with them through our courts, our laws and our system. The challenge now is for the new generation to put their own house in order.

Today, Dr. Syndey Hook writes of "storm troopers" on the campus; that "fanaticism seems to be in the saddle." Arnold Beichman writes of "young Jacobins" in our schools who "have cut down university administrators, forced curriculum changes, halted classes, closed campuses and set a nation-wide chill of fear through the university establishment." Walter Laqueur writes in *Commentary* that "the cultural and political idiocies perpetrated with impunity in this permissive age have gone clearly beyond the borders of what is acceptable for any society, however liberally it may be constructed."

George Kennan has devoted a brief, cogent and alarming book to the inherent dangers of what is taking place in our society and in our universities. Irving Kristol writes that our "radical students . . . find it possible to be genuinely heartsick at the injustice and brutalities of American society, while blandly approving of injustice and brutality committed in the name of 'the revolution'."

These are not names drawn at random from the letterhead of an Agnew-for-Vice-President Committee.

These are men more eloquent and erudite than I. They raise questions that I have tried to raise.

For among this generation of Americans there are hundreds who have burned their draft cards and scores who have deserted to Canada and Sweden to sit out the war. To some Americans, a small minority, these are the true young men of conscience in the coming generation. Voices are and will be raised in the Congress and beyond asking that amnesty should be provided for "these young and misguided American boys." And they will be coming home one day from Sweden and Canada, and from a small minority they will get a heroes' welcome.

They are not our heroes. Many of our heroes will not be coming home; some are coming back in hospital ships, without limbs or eyes, with scars they shall carry the rest of their lives.

Having witnessed firsthand the quiet courage of wives and parents receiving posthumously for their heroes Congressional Medals of Honor, how am I to react when people say, "Stop speaking out, Mr. Agnew, stop raising your voice."

Should I remain silent while what these heroes have done is vilified by some as "a dirty and immoral war" and criticized by others as no more than a war brought on by the chauvinistic, anti-communism of Presidents Kennedy, Johnson and Nixon?

These young men made heavy sacrifices so that a developing people on the rim of Asia might have a chance for freedom that they will not have if the ruthless men who rule in Hanoi should ever rule over Saigon. What is dirty or immoral about that?

One magazine this week said that I will go down as the "great polarizer" in American politics. Yet, when that large group of young Americans marched up Pennsylvania and Constitution Avenues last week—they sought to polarize the American people against the President's policy in Vietnam. And that was their right.

And so it is my right, and my duty, to stand up and speak out for the values in which I believe. How can you ask the man in the street in this country to stand up for what he believes if his own elected leaders weasel and cringe.

It is not an easy thing to wake up each morning to learn that some prominent man or institution has implied that you are a bigot, a racist or a fool.

I am not asking any immunity from criticism. That is the lot of the man in politics; we would have it no other way in this Democratic Society.

But my political and journalistic adversaries sometimes seem to be asking something more—that I circumscribe my rhetorical freedom, while they place no restrictions on theirs.

As President Kennedy once observed in a far more serious matter, that is like offering an apple for an orchard.

We do not accept those terms for continuing the national dialogue. The day when the network commentators and even gentlemen of the *New York Times* enjoyed a form of diplomatic immunity from comment and criticism of what they said—that day is over.

Just as a politician's words—wise and foolish—are dutifully recorded by the press and television to be thrown up to him at the appropriate time, so their words should likewise be recorded and likewise recalled.

When they go beyond fair comment and criticism they will be called upon to defend their statements and their positions just as we must defend ours. And when their criticism becomes excessive or unjust, we shall invite them down from their ivory towers to enjoy the rough and tumble of the public debate.

I do not seek to intimidate the press, the networks or anyone else from speaking out. But the time for blind acceptance of their opinions is past. And the time for naive belief in their neutrality is gone.

But, as to the future, all of us could do worse than take as our own the motto of William Lloyd Garrison who said: "I am in earnest. I will not equivocate. I will not excuse. I will not retreat a single inch. And I will be heard."

RESPONSES TO VICE PRESIDENT'S ATTACKS

The following remarks in reply to Vice President Agnew's speech of November 20, 1969, were printed in the New York Times *of November 21, 1969. Arthur Ochs Sulzberger is President and Publisher of the* New York Times; *Mrs. Katharane Graham is President of the* Washington Post *Company; Leonard H. Goldenson is President of A.B.C.; Reuven Frank is President of NBC News; and Dr. Frank Stanton is President of C.B.S.*

MR. SULZBERGER'S REPLY

Vice President Agnew is entitled to express his point of view, but he is in error when he implies that *The New York Times* ever sought or enjoyed immunity from comment and criticism. Indeed, all American institutions from the press to the Presidency should be the subjects of free and open debate.

It would be wise, however, for those involving themselves in such a discussion to be certain of their facts. Some of Mr. Agnew's statements are inaccurate.

The Vice President has accused us of avoiding the issue of monopoly journalism. Quite the opposite. In fact in an editorial on March 13, 1969, headed "Competition Not Monopoly," *The Times* stated: "The constitutional guarantee of freedom of the press provides the press with no warrant for seeking exemption from the laws prohibiting monopoly. If anything, the sanctity attached to press freedom by the First Amendment makes it the special obligation of the press to fight for the broadest extension of that freedom."

This is a sentiment that *The New York Times* has expressed repeatedly and still holds.

Report Is Printed

Mr. Agnew is again mistaken when he says that *The Times* did not "carry a word" on the story about the Congressmen and Senators signing a letter endorsing the President's policy in Vietnam. *The New*

York Times printed the story. Unfortunately, it failed to make the edition that reached Washington but was carried in a later edition of *The Times.* Moreover, *The Times* has given considerable attention to that story as it developed. In the paper of Nov. 6, there was a story on Page 11. In the paper of Nov. 7, there was a front page story that the House Foreign Affairs Committee had approved a resolution endorsing President Nixon's "efforts to negotiate a just peace in Vietnam." In the paper of Nov. 13, there was the story to which the Vice President referred. In the paper of Nov. 14, President Nixon's visit to the House and the Senate to convey his appreciation to those who supported his Vietnam policy was the lead story. That story again reported the fact that more than 300 Congressmen and 59 Senators had signed the resolution.

As to the assertion that the story about the Pope appeared on Page 11 while a less important story was printed on Page 3, the Vice President unfortunately does not understand some of the complicated problems of making up a newspaper. Many important stories have to appear on pages other than Page 1 and a story that appears on Page 3 or Page 6 is not necessarily considered more important than a story that appears on Page 11 or 13.

It is the basic credo of *The Times* that news and editorial opinion are kept separate and that opinion should appear only on the editorial page. We shall continue to follow that credo.

MRS. GRAHAM'S REPLY

Vice President Agnew's remarks about the Washington Post Company are not supported by the facts.

The *Washington Post, Newsweek,* WTOP-TV, and WTOP Radio decidedly do not "grind out the same editorial line."

It is long-standing policy of the Post Company to enlist in each of its enterprises the best professional journalists we can find and give them a maximum of freedom in which to work. Each branch is operated autonomously. They compete vigorously with one another. They disagree on many issues. We think that the result is journalism of a high caliber that is notable for a diversity of voices on a wide range of public issues.

As to the voices of public opinion in the Washington area, they are plentiful and diverse. Washington is one of the most competitive communications cities in America by any objective standards. It is one of only three cities left with three major newspapers under separate ownership, all of them first rate.

In addition to the four major television stations, there are three ultra-high frequency stations. Radio is even more competitive in the area with some 35 outlets.

MR. GOLDENSON'S STATEMENT

As I said last week, after the Vice President's first speech, I firmly believe that in our free society the ultimate judges of the reliability of our news presentation will be the viewing public.

Again I leave it to the public to determine whether the Vice President's renewed attack today is an attempt to intimidate and discredit not only television news reporting but other major news media. Personally, I believe it is.

I hope we are not facing a period in the history of our nation when high Government officials try to act both as judge and jury on the issue of a free press.

MR. FRANK'S STATEMENT

In Vice President Agnew's second speech on the press, he seems to have lowered his voice, but is seeking new targets.

His first speech concentrated on the news operations of the television networks. He said that because they reached many more people than *The New York Times,* they were not entitled to the protection of press freedom.

His current attack is aimed primarily at *The Washington Post* and *The New York Times* and particularly at the "news judgment" of *The Times.* We do not welcome this sort of Government intervention directed against newspapers any more than we relish it when it strikes at broadcast news.

DR. STANTON'S STATEMENT

Apparently the Vice President is embarked upon a campaign, despite his rhetoric to the contrary, to intimidate the news media into reporting only what he wants to hear. We repeat what we said in reference to his attack last week: Whatever the deficiencies of a free press, they are minor compared to those of a press which would be subservient to the executive power of Government.

James Reston
THE LAGGARD PRESS

"Change is the biggest story in the world today," states James Reston of the New York Times. It is also, paradoxically, the one story not covered sufficiently by the press. Not only must the newspaper do "all it can to make people aware of change," contends Mr. Reston, it must become a force in preparing people for change as well.

SOMETHING seems to be wrong with the newspaper press. Everybody is either criticizing us, or what is worse, ignoring us. Arthur Schlesinger, Jr., told the American Historical Association in Chicago the other day that after working in the White House, he was convinced that newspapers were an unreliable guide for the historian. In Britain the courts have been tossing reporters in jail for refusing to tell where they got their news. In Washington Pierre Salinger is accusing us of managing the news and vice versa. In Cleveland and New York we have had a newspaper strike and lockout for over three months. And when you suggest that the duty to print newspapers in a democracy is more important than the right to strike or lockout, even newspaper folk look at you as if you were out of date and maybe out of your mind. . . .

I think we are in trouble because we have not kept up with the needs of the age. Change is the biggest story in the world today, and we are not covering it adequately; change in the size and movement of our people; change in the nature, location, and availability of jobs; violent change in the cities and on the land; change in the relations between village and town, town and city, city and state, state and nation; and, of course, change in the relations between the empires that are falling and empires that are rising, the old states that are going down and the new ones that are coming up. The population of the country was 97 million in 1913; it is over 187 million now. The labor force of the country has more than doubled—from 30 million to over 71 million—and the farm workers have dropped from 13.5 million in 1913 to 4.5 million now. We have gone in this time from a predominantly rural to a primarily urban society, from an isolated country with a defense budget in 1913 of $250 million to the most internationalist and involved nation in all history, with a defense budget of $56.7 billion. There were no radio or television stations in 1913, but 2,500 daily newspapers. This total has declined since then to 1,850. . . .

We are very good at reporting change when it is violent. When the bulldozers start to change property values at home or the guns produce change in Cuba or Vietnam, we are there. But we were not very good about reporting the economic and social conditions in Cuba that produced Castro, and we're remarkably indifferent to the unemployed in Pittsburgh and the social and economic conditions in Harlan County, Kentucky, and the Appalachian South.

What we have done in these last fifty years, I think, is to transfer the reporting habits of the police court and the county court house to the great capitals of the world. This was necessary. In fact, I wish we had retained a little more of the muck-raking zeal of those days. But essentially we are—with, of course, notable exceptions—concentrating on the violence of the world as we concentrated on the violence of the police station, and this leaves a vast uncovered area of change.

It is not necessarily violent change that is going to transform the world. In fact, by concentrating on the violent troubles in Berlin, Vietnam, the Congo, Cuba, and elsewhere, we have created the impression that our overseas troubles are endless and maybe even insoluble, whereas the truth is that the United States has handled the violent changes of the past generation fairly well. It is not the earthquakes but the tides of history that are bothering us. It is the slow, quieter changes of the family, the scientific laboratory, and the electronic computer that are changing the fabric of the world, and it is the reporting of these changes that leaves so much to be desired.

The question here is merely one of degree. I am not suggesting that we leave spot news to the radio and television. I am merely saying that we should give as much space to this deeper strata of news as we do, say, to women's fashions. We do not make fashion news compete for space with Washington spot news. We say that we are going to allocate a few columns to fashions "for another reason." I think we should do at least as much for reports of these quiet revolutions in our cities, laboratories, factories, and farms. And the "other reason" here is fairly plain: for unless we report these changes, our people will not adapt to them, and every civilization must either adapt or perish.

When Woodrow Wilson called the reporters to his office for the first time in 1913, he said to them: "The news is the atmosphere of public affairs. Unless you get the right setting to affairs—disperse the right impression—things go wrong. . . . " The atmosphere of change was in the air in 1913 when Wilson made that remark, but we failed to make our people conscious of it, and a world war broke out the following year. We have been in four wars in these fifty years, and unless we adjust to change, we shall probably have some more.

Is the American newspaper doing all it can to make people aware of change? The answers, of course, vary a great deal, but in my view too many newspapers are not only underplaying change on their news pages, but are deploring change, inciting opposition to change, and perpetuating rather than destroying popular illusion on their editorial pages.

Part of the trouble, I believe, is that we have not really thought through a modern definition of news. Nobody questions that a splashy revolution in Guatemala is news, but file 1,000 words on the social and political conditions there that will probably cause a revolution next year, and see what happens on the desk of most American papers. Maybe you'll get it in if it's a dull day, and maybe you won't. Sometimes I think we'll do anything for Latin America except read about it. Things don't have to "happen" to be news. They can just be going on quietly, like the unemployment in Pittsburgh or the boom in Houston, or the allocation of most of our scientists to the Pentagon, the Space Agency, and the Atomic Energy Commission. Ideas are news, but they don't always get into the paper. Let Chairman Miller of the Republican National Committee say for the fiftieth time that we should blockade Cuba and tear down the wall in Berlin, and he will be sure to get in the press, but let some thoughtful but unknown professor suggest that we should have a peace plan for Cuba in case one day Castro collapses—which is not a bad idea—and he'll be lucky to get a brief notice outside his home town.

I think we have to rethink not only our definition of news but the allocation of our reporters. We are not covering our own country as well as we should—maybe not even as well as we cover some other countries. Like officials in Washington, we suffer from Afghanistanism: if it's far away, it's news, but if it's close at home, it's sociology. You can get the cream of the graduation class at Columbia to go to Ethiopia for the Peace Corps or *The New York Times,* but try to get them to find out what's going on in the south side of Chicago!

This would change, I'm sure, if we gave men time to do a serious job of reporting on the south side of Chicago and let them move on from there to probe into other areas of poverty and unrest. Also, as this kind of material increased in our newspapers the attitude of the public toward newspapers would change for the better, and the quality of the men attracted to our profession would improve. For unless I'm wildly mistaken, the people of this country would welcome thoughtful reporting of important changes in our society, and might increase their support and respect for the American newspaper as a result. . . .

Marya Mannes
WHAT'S WRONG WITH OUR PRESS

Marya Mannes, one of America's most outspoken social critics, examines our press and condemns its resistance to change. Her observations sound a warning to the nation's press, a warning that they ignore at their own peril.

NOTE: *In 1960, the Women's National Press Club invited two speakers to address the Association of Newspaper Editors. One was Mrs. Clare Boothe Luce, the other Mrs. Eleanor Roosevelt, and each was to speak for twenty minutes on the subject "What's Wrong with Our Press?" Shortly before the event, Mrs. Roosevelt suffered a minor accident, and I was asked to substitute for her.*

It is, I think, pertinent to remark here that although this speech had wide repercussions in Washington and across the country, only the Woman's Page of The Washington Post *featured it prominently and no single newspaper printed it in full or in substantial part. Time, understandably, omitted it entirely, and of the news magazines only* The Reporter, *to which I was attached, published a slightly condensed text.*

NEWSPAPERS have two great advantages over television. They can be used by men as barriers against their wives. It is still the only effective screen against the morning features of the loved one, and, as such, performs a unique human service. The second advantage is that you can't line a garbage pail with a television set—it's usually the other way around.

But here are some interesting statistics from a little, and little known, survey by Mr. Roper called "The Public's Reaction to Television Following the Quiz Investigations." In it he asks everybody but me this question: Suppose you could continue to have only one of the follow-ing—radio, television, newspapers, or magazines—which would you prefer? Newspapers came in second: Forty-two per cent said if they could only have one, they would keep television. Thirty-two per cent said if they could only have one, they would keep newspapers.

Even so, newspaper people should be much happier than the magazine people, because only four per cent said they needed magazines, as against nineteen per cent for radio.

But listen to this. Mr. Roper asked these same harried people: "If you get conflicting or different reports of the same news story from radio, television, the magazines, and the newspapers, which of the four ver-sions would you be most inclined to believe?" Thirty-two per cent believe newspapers as against thirty per cent who believe television. But then something really strange happens. When Mr. Roper asked his guinea pigs *which* of these media they would be *least* inclined to believe, the newspapers topped the list. In a big way, too. Twenty-four per cent don't believe newspapers as against nine per cent who don't believe television. And though I'm as leery of certain polls as anyone, this margin of credulity is too wide to be discounted.

The fact is that although network television still allots too little time to the vital service of informing the public, it does a better job in that little time than the nation's press as a whole. And when I speak of the nation's press as a whole, I am *not* speaking of the five or six splendid newspapers—and the one great newspaper—which serve the world as models of responsible public information. I am speaking of the local press which in hundreds of American communities is the *only* news available, aside from those recitals of ticker tape that pass for radio news, and which defaults on its obligations to the public.

Why do I think network TV does a better job of informing than these papers? Well, let's get the partisan bit over with. Television lives on advertising to an even greater extent than newspapers, and since advertising is big business, advertising is by nature Republican. Yet nowhere in network newscasts or network commentaries on current events have I encountered the intense partisanship, the often rabid bias that colors the editorial pages of the majority of newspapers in this country. Douglass Cater, in his book *The Fourth Branch of Gov-ernment,* confines himself to only one pungent footnote on this sub-ject. "I have deliberately avoided," he writes, "getting into the pre-dominantly one-party nature of newspaper ownership. It is a fact of life." This particular fact of life is a shameful one: that newspapers whose duty it is to inform the American public give them only one side of the issues that affect them profoundly—the Republican side. This is shameful not only for Democrats—they have survived it before and will survive it again—but for the maturity of our people. Some of the same papers which loudly extol the virtues of free enterprise and a free press are consistently failing to print the facts on which a people can form a balanced and independent opinion. That balanced and independent opinion is our only real security as a nation.

Now, very often, television coverage of news is superficial and inadequate. Very often the picture takes precedence over the point. But by and large the news reports and commentaries on CBS and NBC and ABC make every effort to present viewers with more than one aspect of an issue, either by letting opposing spokesmen have their say, or by outlining the positions held by both major parties on the subject involved.

Television also provides a wide range of opinion by setting up four or five experts and letting them knock each other down. What has the local press of this nature? Is it discharging its duty to diversity by printing snippets of opinion from unqualified readers? Is this exploring an issue?

Television may not have a Lippmann or a Reston, but then, what papers in America can claim an Eric Sevareid, a Walter Cronkite, a Huntley or a Brinkley, or—although he is invisible—an Edward Morgan?

Another thing. Among the leading commentators on television, you find no Pegler, no Winchell, no Fulton Lewis Jr. Fortunately for the American public, television does not tolerate the kind of distortion of fact, the kind of partisan virulence and personal peeve, that many newspapers not only welcome but encourage. In its entertainment, television caters far too much to the lowest instincts of man, particularly the lust for violence and—at the opposite end of the spectrum— the urge to escape from reality into sedation. But there is one appetite it does not feed and which the partisan newspapers of the nation do: the appetite for hate—hate of whatever is different. I do not find on television the kind of editorials chronic in the New York tabloids as well as in many local papers across the country where the techniques of demagoguery prevail: Rouse the Rabble by Routing Reason.

A newspaper has the right—the duty even—to assume an attitude, to take a position. But it has an equally sacred right to explain that position in the light of the opposing one, to document that position, and to bolster it, not with emotion but with fact.

Here, of course, is where background information helps the public to draw its conclusions. TV does a great deal of this in the form of documentaries, and you can of course say that they have the time and the money to do this and you haven't. Yet across this wide country, and with the exception of a handful of syndicated columns, I fail to find in any local paper any attempt, however minimal, to strengthen this muscle of digestion, without which news can neither nourish nor inform. It can only stuff. Between the opinions of the editor and the bare statements of the wire services there is nothing, nothing, that is, except a collection of snippets used as fillers between the ads and picked at random.

One of the greatest and most justified criticisms of television has been that in appealing to the largest audience possible, it neglects minority audiences and minority tastes. This is still largely true. But there is, perhaps, one program a day and many, of course, on Sunday which an intelligent man or woman can enjoy and derive interest from. In my trips east or west or north or south, I pick up the local paper to find this enjoyment or interest—in vain. Now, surely there's something wrong here. Many of these places I've visited—and I'm sure this is true of the whole country—have college communities where highly intelligent and talented people live, whether they are teachers or doctors or lawyers or musicians or scientists. What is there for them in the paper, usually the only paper, of their town? What features are provided for these people? What stimulation? How many times have I heard them say: "If you want to see what a really bad paper is like, read our sheet." When a local paper has a monopoly in a region, as most of them do, why is it necessary to aim at the lowest common denominator?

I believe that over a period of decades newspapers have become a habit rather than a function. They have held their franchise so long that change has become inadmissible. I do not know, in fact, of any medium that has changed as little in the last twenty years as the daily press. And this resistance to change is the end of growth—which, in turn, marks the end of usefulness.

Change means trouble, change means work, change means cost. It is easier to print wire services dispatches than have a reporter on the beat. It is easier to buy syndicated columns than find—and train—local talent. It is easier to let the ads dictate the format than develop a format that elevates news above dogfood. It is easier to write editorial copy that appeals to emotion rather than reason. And in handling straight news, it is easier to assume the pious mantle of objectivity than to edit. To quote Eric Sevareid: "Our rigid formulae of so-called objectivity, beginning with the wire agency bulletins and reports—the warp and woof of what the papers print . . . our flat, one-dimensional handling of news, have given the lie the same prominence and impact that truth is given. They have elevated the influence of fools to that of wise men; the ignorant to the level of the learned; the evil to the level of the good." This featureless objectivity is nothing less than the editor's abdication of responsibility and is just as dangerous as the long and subtle processing of fact to fit a policy that characterizes certain weekly magazines. The one is dereliction; the other is deception. And both may provide a reason for the decline of public confidence in their press.

This is, to me, a tragedy. I am a printed-word woman myself, and I still think the word was not only in the beginning but will be in the end. No picture can ever be an adequate substitute. The word will prevail; that is, if you, who are its guardians, treat it with the respect it deserves. For if you degrade and cheapen the word too long, the people will turn to the picture. They are beginning to turn to the picture now. Not in New York, maybe, not in Washington, D.C., or St. Louis, or two or three other cities, but in hundreds of towns across the country. Oh, they will buy your papers—to hold up at breakfast or to line the trash can or to light a fire. But not to learn. And you may wake up one day to find you have lost the greatest power entrusted to men: to inform a free people.

NEWS AND THE WHOLE TRUTH

Complaining that "too much of our news is one-dimensional," Elmer Davis, long one of America's most respected and recognized radio news voices finds that our journalism is "not yet good enough." The following selection appeared in his influential book, But We Were Born Free.

EACH spring the members of the American Newspaper Publishers Association assemble in convention and spend a good deal of their time eulogizing themselves. Conventions of editors and reporters, whether for newspapers or radio news, are more practical and less complacent. The American news business, press and radio, certainly deserves some eulogies; it is the most copious in the world, and I think its average quality is at least as good as any other's. But it is not yet good enough. Too often we tell the customers not what is really going on, but what seems to be going on. And I am not referring to the small minority of newspapers, and the smaller minority of newspapermen, who don't want to tell the truth, but to the great majority who do want to tell the truth but often fall short.

Too much of our news is one-dimensional, when truth has three dimensions (or maybe more); we still have inadequate defenses against men who try to load the news with propaganda; and in some fields the vast and increasing complexity of the news makes it continually more difficult—especially for us Washington reporters—to tell the public what really happened. Some of these failings are due to encrusted habits of the news business, which can be changed only slowly, but which many men are now trying to change; some of them will be harder to cure because they are only the reverse side of some of our greatest merits, and it is difficult to see how to get rid of them without endangering the merits too.

The merits which entail the worst drawbacks are competition and the striving for objectivity, and we should be much worse off without either. But objectivity often leans over backward so far that it makes the news business merely a transmission belt for pretentious phonies. As for competition, there is no doubt that the nation is much better served by three wire services—the Associated Press, the United Press and the International News Service, sometimes supplemented by the English Reuters—and by several radio networks than it would be by monopoly in either field. But competition means an overemphasis on speed, as has been noted by the Associated Press Managing Editors (not the editors of the AP but the men who use its service); and sometimes it leads to an exaggerated build-up.

Like most radio newsmen, I am heavily dependent on the wire services. I am supposed to be aware of all the world's news and to report what seems to me most important or that to which I can add something in the way of interpretation. But I can't cover it all myself—not even all that happens in Washington; usually I cover about one story a day on foot, get angles or elucidations on half a dozen others by telephone, and must depend on the wire services for the rest. Experience has taught me, when the versions of the same story given by two wire services differ materially, to prefer the less exciting; the other might have been souped up to beat the competition.

President Truman announced his decision not to run again at the end of his speech at the Jefferson-Jackson Day dinner on March 29, 1952 —an extemporaneous addition to a script distributed several hours in advance. All the wire services sent out the text, of course; early editions of the Sunday papers were going to press and had to have it at the earliest moment. The UP and INS merely sent out the text; the AP, desirous of making everything clear (and maybe of getting the jump on the competition), prefaced it with a lead saying that the President made no disclosure of his intentions. Papers carrying that lead were on the street as he was disclosing his intentions. At least one radio station—a good one, too—writing its eleven-o'clock news out of the AP, went on the air and said that he had made no disclosure of his intentions; whereas many of the listeners a few minutes earlier had heard the President say he wouldn't run.

I do not suppose that any of the wire services ever consciously sacrifices accuracy to speed; but speed is what counts most, because what every wire service wants is to get newspapers to use its story rather than its competitors' stories. I have seen many service messages on press-association wires boasting about how many minutes, or even how many seconds, they were ahead of the competition, how their story got the play. I have seldom if ever seen a message saying, "While our story was unfortunately a few minutes behind time, it had more truth in it." Yet these outfits live, and must live, by competition; and we are better off with that competition, whatever its shortcomings, than we should be without it. One of the wire services has a motto, "Get it there first—but first get it right." I am sure they all try to do that; I am not sure that a wire service which actually succeeded in doing it would last long against the competition.

Nine days before the Germans surrendered in 1945 there was a great, though brief, flurry over an AP report from San Francisco—where the constituent assembly of the United Nations was then meeting—that they had surrendered and an announcement could be expected at any moment. The story was sent by one of the ablest reporters in the country; he got it from a person described as a high American official, who wouldn't let his name be used—something that happens every day; and it may have been mass self-delusion that persuaded many people that the high official was the Secretary of State, who would have known. Actually it was Senator Connally; but he might have known too; and if the reporter had stopped to check up with the Secretary of State or anybody else, the competition might have got the story out ahead of him. So it was left to the President of the United States to do the checking up and find out that the story was false.

That time, the AP got a beat on a surrender that didn't happen; nine days later it got a beat on the one that did happen—because one of its correspondents broke a release date that fifteen other correspondents observed. Now some of those hold-for-release regulations of the SHAEF public-relations officers—imposed in an endeavor to get simultaneous release in all Allied capitals—may have seemed ridiculous; the German radio was already announcing the surrender. Nevertheless the sixteen correspondents who had covered the actual ceremony had all promised to hold the story till a certain hour. Fifteen of them did; one of them did not. If that incident had been repeated once or twice it would have made it extremely difficult for any correspondent to get any news.

Here the fault clearly lay with the pressure of competition. I am told, by a man who should know, that the three principal AP correspondents on the Western front had identical instructions; besides competing with everybody else they were competing with one another, presumably on the theory that that would keep them on their toes. It is not surprising that one of them got so far up on his toes that he fell over on his face.

It was the United Press that ended the old war four days early in 1918 —an incident now remembered chiefly because Roy Howard, who was responsible for what was then the greatest boner in American news history, was able enough to live it down. He happened to be in a position to see, quite legitimately, what appeared to be an official dispatch;

and he flashed it without checking up on it. It was in contradiction to the known intention of ending the war four days later; but I do not suppose there was or is a reporter for any wire service, American or foreign, who would not have done what Roy Howard did. It is hard to say how much actual harm was done, aside from taking the edge off the celebration of the real armistice; but there is some reason to believe that the message that fooled Howard was planted by a German agent in Paris, who presumably hoped that it would do harm.

Now these were not bad reporters; they were all good reporters, among the best; but they were all in too big a hurry, for fear somebody else would beat them to it. We have seen many forecasts of what will happen in the next war, if we have one. I do not know what the course of operations will be; the one thing I feel safe in predicting is that some American reporter will end it a few days before it actually ends, and the families of men who were killed after he said it was over will, for the rest of their lives, be convinced that you can't believe what you see in the papers.

William J. Lederer
WHAT THE PRESS CAN DO

Concerned with the shortcomings of the American press, William J. Lederer, in this selection from his book A Nation of Sheep, *makes some specific recommendations on what the press can do to "improve its product."*

A PAPER cannot be well-edited for foreign news if the staff is ill-informed on world events. I suggest that papers subscribe to the American Universities Field Staff Reports. In my opinion, they represent the most distinguished reporting-in-depth there is on world affairs. Also, I recommend subscribing to the airmail editions of *The Economist, The New York Times,* and *The Asahi Evening News.*

Beyond that, we need newspapers managed by people who realize the importance of what they are doing. We need foreign correspondents who have special qualifications for the areas they are to report, who have studied these areas and are competent in the language of the people whose activity they are to report. Theodore White, one of our distinguished correspondents, says "A fast pencil and a good pair of legs aren't enough for a foreign correspondent." Some editors need to learn that. On the strategic news desks that handle the cabled dispatches to prepare them for the newspaper we need educated men who understand the information they are handling. They need time to consider it, to look up references in the well-stocked library that every newspaper should have and few do have, to write in background if it is needed. They need authority to hold back a report if it looks doubtful, confused or inadequate, until they can get a story that makes sense to them and informs the reader. They need to be free of the insensate time pressure to rush into type the latest bulletin even if it adds nothing but confusion to what they had earlier. *The Christian Science Monitor* will wait a day if necessary to make sure that its story means something. Or they will come in several days later with full background treatment, when most papers have forgotten the subject in the rush to the latest sensation. Continuity is one of the greatest needs of the reader on important issues, and especially if they are remote and unfamiliar to him. Continuity on anything is one of the most serious lacks in most newspapers. You'd think they were in business only today, or anticipated a wholly new set of readers each day to whom they owe no responsibility for what they got them excited about yesterday. Readers need to know how the story came out; what happened after yesterday's banner headline. If the newspaper is the poor man's university, as it claims to be, it needs to take a leaf from the universities, to staff with trained people and give them time to read and study and authority to exercise trained judgment in the interest of an informed report for the reader. We are a long way short of that kind of service of information, and the crises of our times increasingly demand it.

It costs nothing (except perhaps a bit of sensationalism) to make the headlines agree with the text of the story—especially not make headlines state an event as fact, but in the body of the piece hint that it is rumor.

Foreign news often is not read because: (a) it is not well written; (b) the strange names and what has gone on before are unknown to the reader. The papers should provide a box giving a synopsis of pertinent information.

An effort should be made to reduce the practice of ascribing stories to unknown people such as "Diplomatic sources say," and "According to high Washington officials," to a minimum. Protecting an important news source is understandable. But this dodge is being used as a cover for half the unconfirmed rumors floating around bars and restaurants. The reader deserves better treatment than this.

Last, reporters should be paid more than the mechanics in the back room. The editorial part of a paper (or TV station or radio station) is what makes it good or bad. Today reporters frequently not only are paid less than linotype operators, but they have more pressure on them. They must have an incentive, and time to read and think.

If a correspondent goes on a free junket (when commercial airlines or steamers are available) provided by the U.S. Government, a foreign government, or a private commercial organization, we, the readers, deserve to know that someone with publicity in mind is paying for the trip. There should be a boxed notice such as: "Japan Air Lines paid our reporter's expenses for a thirty-day tour to Japan. Equivalent value of tickets, housing, and meals is $3600." If the writer has his expenses paid by a foreign government, the reporter is acting as a foreign agent—even if his article is entirely factual. I suggest that editors study the Department of Justice's ruling for this. (Incidentally, there was one journalist who wrote several flattering books on President Rhee. Readers had no way of knowing that the author was being paid by Rhee.)

Suggesting steps to improve the press coverage of foreign affairs is an almost impossible assignment because publishing a good newspaper in this hectic age is a most difficult job. There is little doubt that the average reporter is a dedicated man who will risk his life to get a story. But where international news is concerned, the story must travel a long and tenuous path between point of origin and publication at home. First, the reporter must find the news and then dig out the facts from an alien environment. Next, the story must be cabled to America, sometimes from a place where there are few communications facilities and where it is subject to local censorship.

Upon arriving in the United States the story is analyzed by the editors for value and perspective. An immediate decision must be made as to which geographic areas in America might have an interest in it (I am speaking of the wire services which supply eighty per cent of our foreign news). The story is then retransmitted to area headquarters, which reanalyzes the story before putting it on the wires to individual papers. When it arrives at the local paper a third evaluation process takes place. Should it go on page one or be buried on page twelve? When this has been decided then a headline—limited to a specified number of letters—must be supplied in a matter of minutes. Everything is done in a mad rush because late news is considered no news.

Even though the editor and reporters may wish to fill the paper with important national and international news, there usually are two inhibiting presences hovering over them: the publisher and the business manager. The paper must make money or there will be no paper at all. In the opinion of most newspaper executives, the only way to avoid bankruptcy is to give the customers what they want.

The customers apparently don't want foreign news. They generally buy a paper to read of local scandals, comic strips, society news, advice to the lovelorn, horoscopes, sports, and other entertaining features.

The press is dependent on the two wire services for foreign news. These gauge their coverage to the average demands of their client papers. What is needed is a higher level of demand, more informed and more critical, to provide more adequate foreign reporting to match our global responsibilities.

With the exception of a small number of rich, well-established papers, magazines, and broadcasting systems, publishers cannot afford their own adequate foreign-news staffs.

There are a few suggestions above on how the press can improve its product, but part of the problem rests with the customers. If the average citizen is not interested in more than a mediocre press on international matters, then a mediocre press is what he will continue to get. If he clamors long and hard enough for a wider and more significant news coverage, then the chances are good he will get something better.

If your newspaper, television station, or magazine is inadequate (and the chances are that it is), then you share a large percentage of the guilt. Only if you express a demand for a more informed and informing American journalism will those who own the presses be seriously moved to provide it.

Thomas Schroth
THE ROLE OF THE PRESS
IN A DEMOCRATIC GOVERNMENT

Once described as "the fourth branch of government," the press does indeed contribute greatly to the functioning of the American system. Stories are written or featured at the discretion of the newspaperman. Personalities and ideas can be sold to the public. Thomas Schroth, Executive Editor of Con-gressional Quarterly, examines the importance of the role of the press in a democratic government and notes what he considers to be "a very unhealthy situation."

IT WAS probably an Englishman, Macaulay, in 1828, who first re-ferred to the press as the fourth estate. "The gallery in which the reporters sit," he said, "has become a fourth estate of the realm."

Thomas Jefferson indicated with remarkable accuracy the current and enduring attitude of the press and the people toward the press when he wrote, "Were it left to me to decide whether we should have a government without newspapers or newspapers without government I should not hesitate for a moment to prefer the latter."

Thomas Jefferson at the beginning of this country also emphasized the necessity of the press to be free—a theme that runs deep in Ameri-can life today. "No government," Jefferson said, "ought to be without censors; and where the press is free, none ever will." Jefferson not only stressed freedom of the press but the obligation of the press to criticize and oversee the conduct of government.

Jefferson also said, "When the press is free and every man able to read, all is safe." Here he referred to the role of the press as the com-municator to the people on what government is doing.

Thus the free press watches and criticizes the government and informs the people.

Democracy in the United States could not operate without this role of communicator played by the press. And government would be far less perfect without the constant role of critic played by a responsible press.

The press has not always pleased men in public life, despite their recognition of its vital role. Indeed, it was Jefferson, angry with the treatment he was getting from the press, who said, "The man who never looks into a newspaper is better informed than he who reads them, inasmuch as he who knows nothing is nearer the truth than he whose mind is filled with falsehoods and errors."

It is doubtful whether there was a President since Jefferson who did not feel similar complaints about the press. Most of them have not hesitated to utter them. But angry and dissatisfied as they may get with the press, few men in high public office in America have underrated the importance of the press in making government work. For the press is a participant in the American governmental process. It is a "fourth branch of government," a term Douglass Cater used for the title of his book on this subject. The "other" three branches would be quite different in their operation and probably not as effective if it were not for the press.

The federal government of the United States is divided into a multitude of power centers. Principally, there are three: the executive branch, the legislative branch, and the judiciary. But these are all fragmented.

The judiciary branch has many district courts and circuit courts and the Supreme Court.

The legislative branch is divided into two main sections; each section, House and Senate, is further greatly broken up by the committee system. Each committee is a small legislature in itself. In 1885, Woodrow Wilson said in *Congressional Government:* "The leaders of the House are the chairmen of the standing committees. Indeed, to be entirely accurate the House has as many leaders as there are leading classes of legislation. Each committee goes its own way at its own pace." By the 1960's, the situation had not changed greatly.

The executive department has a multitude of power centers—the White House, the State Department, the Commerce Department, the Defense Department, the Army, Navy and Air Force within the Defense Department, among others. Each has its ax to grind and each has a particular goal or message or purpose which it wishes to pursue.

It is fair to say that the press tends to place some order upon these power relationships. In many cases it is the reporter who decides, in his judgment of news values, whether the President should be heard first, whether the chairman of a congressional committee should be heard first, whether the Secretary of Defense should receive greater attention on a particular day than the Secretary of State.

243
Thomas Schroth
THE ROLE OF THE
PRESS IN A
DEMOCRATIC
GOVERNMENT

The experienced politician, of course, can draw attention to his particular activities. For example, President Lyndon B. Johnson seized the center stage with his intense activity in the first few weeks of his administration—putting in the shadows somewhat the actions of the Congress and other parts of the government. In the early 1950's, Senator Joseph R. McCarthy showed great talent in keeping the spotlight of the press on his person and on his various activities.

But what the people know, what they read, what they listen to, is in large part and in the final act of decision determined by the press— by the editors and reporters who, exercising their news judgment, choose what they are going to write and what they are going to print in their newspapers and put on their television networks and radio stations. As Cater said, the reporter "is the indispensable broker and middle man among the sub-governments of Washington. He can choose from among the myriad events that seethe beneath the surface of government, which to describe, which to ignore."

As the American democracy simply would not work if the American people were not informed about what government is doing, one can see the great importance of the role played by the American press.

Take President Johnson's "war on poverty": if this "war" were going to be successful, if Congress were going to be persuaded to pass the necessary legislation, if the people were going to provide the essential support that a broad governmental attack on a social phenomenon such as poverty needed, the support of the American people had to be generated by explanation and broad exposition to the various poverty programs. Thus the President had to speak of it frequently. The press and broadcasters recorded what he had to say, and the readers and the listeners of America gradually became involved with this national purpose.

Another example: the civil rights debate in the Senate of the United States. One of the explanations for the prolonged debate in 1963–64 was that the public needed to be informed of the arguments for and against civil rights. The southerners felt that they would have an opportunity to draw attention to what they considered bad points in the bill, and the civil rights leaders felt that there was an opportunity for them to draw attention to the need for legislation in this field and to the humanitarian aspects of the bill.

The privileges granted to the press in the nation's capital are remarkable when compared with other countries. For example, a Washington reporter has ready access to the President himself at formal press conferences and on many informal occasions. The reporter can ask the President questions that congressmen and lobbyists and other members of the executive branch rarely have the opportunity to ask. Washington reporters have ready access to the highest offices in the administration and are often given more informative interviews by Cabinet members than are given to members of Congress or congressional committees.

Reporters are constantly in attendance during congressional hearings when they are open—about two-thirds of them are. And reporters have immediate access to most members of Congress.

Thus, Washington reporters can go from one news source to another, comparing, getting responses, and building a news story into what amounts to the formation of government policy. Very little governmental policy is made without some reference to its news value. It is well known that there are some programs in the federal government, foreign and domestic, which are more popular than other programs. For example, the Peace Corps was popular. It had news value. It was easy to sell to the American people, as opposed to, say, economic aid to foreign nations. Economic aid had always been much more difficult to sell than military aid. Thus, in the last decade administrations have tended to stress military aid to other nations rather than economic aid and to tie the two together into one legislative package. All this emphasis was greatly influenced by the news value of the programs involved.

There is a basic conflict of interest between the public official and the reporter. The public official wants to make policy with as few distractions as possible. He fears premature publicity. It is not too much of a generalization to say that the typical public official would prefer to develop a policy, resolve the conflicts within government, and then announce the policy and say, "This is our policy." On the other hand, the reporter is constantly seeking to be first in getting the news, to winnow out any new developments in policy. He automatically rejects the idea that policy should not be discussed until it is finalized. A conscientious Washington reporter is against such secrecy. That's part of his creed. The reporter feels policy is going to be best if it is publicized while it is being made and before it becomes set. Indeed, he feels that the molding of policy is the people's work and that the people must be in on the process of development of policy. Thus, the maximum publicity during the early stages is just as important as the final announcement of policy as far as the reporter is concerned.

There is another potential conflict between the press and government, which is found in the concept that the reporter is an ally of government, is one who should share the responsibility of announcing—or even making—policy, in effect, of governing the nation in the tense situation that surrounds the cold war era in which we live. This is directly opposed by the concept of the press as a critic, as a censor of government, whereby the people can examine government actions and then exert their influence on government actions (for the press also reports the public's reactions to the government).

245
Thomas Schroth
THE ROLE OF THE
PRESS IN A
DEMOCRATIC
GOVERNMENT

If the press moves too far in the direction of being a participant, it seems to me it would lose its essential role; that is, the role of the critic. It may be that a really warm friendship between a high official and a member of the press corps is basically impossible, for the press must always look with a certain amount of suspicion on the actions of public officials and the press must always be ready to criticize, regardless of how close personally the reporter is to the public official. Criticism and constant surveillance of government by an alert and intelligent press is essential to the successful working of a democracy.

In this connection, comment is suggested on remarks by several government officials who decried the unlimited freedom of the press to pry into and print government secrets. They question whether the people have a right to know in all cases. Too much publicity in the press, they say, could greatly assist our adversaries. Shrewd government reporting which ferrets out, prematurely, disarmament proposals, for example, are damaging to the country, they say. They even question whether the American reader really feels a need to be informed on such details as the U.S. disarmament negotiation position.

All this, it seems to me, comes close to saying that our government should be run by an elite and that this elite should decide what the U.S. disarmament negotiation should be; that this elite decides what is good and what is bad for the U.S. in its relations with other countries. Of course, important military and even diplomatic secrets should be guarded by the U.S. officials at the proper times, but are "proper times" as many and as complete as felt by many of our government officials?

The United States Government that runs with the maximum knowledge—in advance—of the people of the country is going to be the best government. I believe that the American people are vitally interested in, for example, the United States disarmament negotiations position and in all other foreign, military, and domestic positions taken by the United States Government in their name. Every effort should be made to inform the people—in advance—of what those positions are going to be and to develop through the press a consensus which indicates the feeling of this country and of its people—who are ultimately sovereign in our country. Even difficult-to-understand policies of this country in such technical fields as nuclear energy and disarmament are the business of the people, and it is the job of the reporter to get that information to the people, with or without the co-operation of the bureaucracy.

As it is now, our secrecy in certain matters in the nuclear field, the military field, and the disarmament field is so ridiculous that the Soviet Union undoubtedly knows more about some military programs and disarmament plans of this country than members of Congress or the press or the people of this country. That is a very unhealthy situation.

S. L. A. Marshall
PRESS FAILURE IN VIETNAM

S. L. A. Marshall was the official army historian of European Theater Operations during World War II and is a Brigadier General (USA, Retired). For many years he served the Detroit News as its military analyst. In the following article, Brigadier General Marshall criticizes the United States press corps in Vietnam for not presenting a balanced reporting of the war.

TWO months ago, following my return to the United States from Vietnam, Major General John Norton and the main body of his First Cavalry Division Air Mobile fought an important battle in the extreme west of the Central Highlands of South Vietnam. The battle was remarkable for many reasons, including the fact that it did not make one lead headline in this country.

The Division had been campaigning for months on ground much closer to its large fortified perimeter next to An Khe, inland from the east coast about 30 miles. On the Bon Song plain next to the sea, in the hills inland from the port of Tuy Hoa and among the high mountains directly northeast of its own base, its brigades had taken on major enemy forces, exterminated most of them and driven the others from the field.

Then as August opened, the great body of the First Cavalry was lifted and committed more than 60 miles westward, beyond Plei Me near the Cambodian border, in a countryside dominated by rugged peaks, covered with dense jungle and rain forest, and permeated by numerous streams. The radical switch of scene and action took less than 12 hours. For speed and distance, there is no mass movement of troops to compare with it in military history.

Thus began Operation Paul Revere II, the euphemism chosen by the political authorities to cloak this main trial-at-arms in Vietnam. It ended on August 25, and by that time Norton had committed 14 Battalions, six of them his own, to the battle line. The statistics of this battle are eye-opening; it was the real whopper of the summer. The actual body count of enemy dead was 861, which under the conditions of jungle warfare, with the enemy risking fanatically to extract his slain, indicates destruction of twice that number. Two hundred-and-two prisoners were captured, along with more than 300 weapons, many of them crew-served. Confirmed as engaging on the other side were nine specific North Vietnamese Battalions.

So here in aggregate was a battle of forces far larger than those at San Juan Hill and El Caney combined, bigger and more impressive than Pork Chop Hill by any measure, bloodier than Cantigny, and lasting as long as Belleau Wood. But no understanding of its proportions—indeed, scarcely any awareness of its existence, though it involved many of their sons—was conveyed to the people of the United States. Those who noted the press reports at all were entitled to the impression that the cavalrymen were off on another wild goose chase which might incidentally result in some slight drawing of blood.

Why is this so? The Army procedure of playing down the sanguinary character of operations in the Central Highlands by labeling each engagement with some prominent but long-dead American's name is not to be blamed (though this gentility seems naive and definitely confuses history). It is not the duty of the Army to function as war reporter to the nation, conducting interviews and writing feature stories; and in any event official communiqués seem to have passed out of style.

The deployed Army is there, ready and anxious to serve representatives of all information media. Its people are eager to talk. They feel strongly that public recognition of the fighting performance of the troops is good for morale. Nor does the Army hesitate to talk of the grimmer aspects of the ordeal—losses, privation, shortages, and heartbreaking incidents—because officers know these are part of the story.

Individual battles, ever the mainstream of the fighting story in Vietnam as in any other war, continue to be ignored solely because the majority of U.S. correspondents in Saigon don't give a damn about them. Perhaps the reporters are ignorant of war and do not wish to expose their innocence, or so fearful of the front that they cannot endure the thought of staying with it. Or perhaps they stay chained to their desks in the wretched and rapidly-deteriorating city because of managing editors who deem any other kinds of "war" stories more sensational, more worth having, than what happens to troops.

In any case, the overwhelming majority of correspondents do not get to the front; and in that regard at least, the American press con-

tinues to be derelict in its main responsibility. The story of the war
is not being told in its daily columns; there we find only the tangents
and sidebars.

To put it another way, there is a cynical faddishness to war reporting
out of Vietnam that contrasts diametrically with every prior performance, including Korea and Lebanon. Today's average correspondent prefers a piece that will make people on the home front squirm
and agonize. Never before, in any war, has there been so much concentration on the off-beat yarn to the exclusion of a balanced accounting of how operations are being conducted.

Even the television crews are guilty of this attitude, though as a group,
they are quite ready to cope with battle risks off and on, and go forward more than others. Their trouble is they want blood on the moon
every night. It has to be a picture of a stricken field or of some poor
wounded man mumbling unintelligibly as he is littered to the waiting
chopper.

The off-beat yarns fall into several familiar patterns, none of which
promises a beat any longer, though collectively they are beaten to
death. Any demonstration or riot, and especially a Buddhist demonstration-riot, is sure-fire copy. So is the terrorist incident within the
city, even though it merely scuttles a worn-out barge and may have
been an act of private vengeance.

Then there is the thing-that-went-wrong story. Hapless civilians have
been killed in every war fought by the United States, but only in Vietnam, where they are far less common than in France during the invasion or in Korea, do they command first-page treatment every time.

The same goes for the story about soldiers dying from their own air
bombs, mortar fire or artillery shells. Though it was never the case in
previous wars when such incidents were more frequent and with less
reason, this, too, is now a dependable bell-ringer. If one correspondent could compile a large enough file of writings about these accidents, he might cop the Pulitzer prize for war reporting.

The war is being covered primarily for all bleeding hearts and for
Senator Fulbright, who casts about for a way to stop it by frightening
and shocking the citizenry. It is not being reported for simple souls
who would like to know how it is being fought and how good are the
chances that the South Vietnamese and American forces and their
allies can bring off a military victory.

Jack Norton's good battle of August in and around the la Drang valley
was not exceptional in being overlooked. The same has to be said of
Operations Austin II, Crazy Horse, Hawthorne II, and Nathan Hale,
fought while I was forward with troops in the weeks of May, June and

early July. Each of these was a major battle in terms of the numbers of troops engaged and blows dealt the enemy (Paul Revere I was minor). None was fully reported to the American people.

There was one flash of press interest during Hawthorne II (the Battle of Toumorong) when Captain Carpenter called down napalm on his own company. Flocks of correspondents winged north from Saigon after the President mentioned the incident and stayed forward almost one day to interview Carpenter on his life and loves—to the complete disgust of West Point's one-time Lonesome End. The episode stays dear in my memory because among the visitors was a 30-year-old "war reporter" for a national news weekly who, on hearing from Colonel Ted Mataxis that I was doing a book on the battles during the southwest monsoon, said to me: "General, if you want to know how the fighting here is working out, you must go to Hong Kong and talk to my bureau chief; he's the only man who understands that side of the war." I needed a double take to be sure that he wasn't pulling my leg.

There are a few who stay with it, who recognize that the name of the game is Being With Troops, and requires sharing their risks part of the time. The story of Sam Castan of *Look* magazine needs no one to point up its moral. He accepted the risks in Operation Crazy Horse and because his luck ran out, paid the supreme sacrifice, though I am sure he would not have had it any other way. Possibly some feeling for what is right and what is not is necessary.

I would also mention Charley Black of Columbus, Georgia, Bob Boos of the Associated Press and good old Jim Lucas of Scripps Howard. Jim has a new book of war stories out on Vietnam; time will put him in the company of Ernie Pyle and R. H. D. There are other stickers with the Marines and in III Corps zone; I apologize to them that I do not list their names. In eight weeks in the field I saw but three newsmen. My time was spent in II Corps zone, since it is self-defeating to attempt covering too much.

But I would still risk one generalization: The only ones who are willing to stay with it, and who believe that the man-against-man play on the fire line is the thing, are correspondents like Black, Boos and Lucas who served the United States under fire in earlier wars. Past service has made them incapable of trying for the name without having the game.

There are said to be 350 "war correspondents" in Saigon. That is more than were in Korea and as many as we had in European Theater in World War II. They are legion, compared to what the national press sent forth to cover the deployments on the American Expeditionary Force under General Pershing in 1917. Any scolding of them would be invidious, since I have no awareness of their personal problems —how their wives feel about danger and urge them to play it safe, what orders and rockets shower on them from the boss's desk, or how their uninformed imaginations exaggerate one man's dangers in war.

It is enough to say to them that they may be defaulting on their one great opportunity to achieve a journalistic success that will make life more pleasant for them and their families in the future. The war in Vietnam is the most fascinating, protean and story-filled conflict in which the U.S. forces have ever engaged. Its action is kaleidoscopic, its small-picture dramas and human interest angles are infinite in number, and its surprises are unending. Hundreds of outstanding stories are missed. The writer who cannot get a book and a larger reputation out of Vietnam within a brief span should quit the business.

Any reporter can make a clean break from the sit-in posture simply by insisting that his post is forward and his professional integrity is at stake. American dailies do not readily throw away the initial $3,500 investment required to set up a correspondent in Vietnam. In any case, the man has a choice to make, for his main chance to mature as a writer is certainly not in the noxious atmosphere of Saigon. It is not that the official briefings are bad; on the contrary, they have a high level of competence. The deplorable thing is that young writers too lazy to gather the facts themselves sit around and sneer at all that is said. With the conference reeking of pseudo sophistication and half-baked cynicism, perspective inevitably becomes blurred. The result is an accenting of the negative and trivial story that obscures the truly important.

For some part of the failure of the press corps in Vietnam in earlier years, the Government bureaucracy, including the military, was indeed responsible. But that is an old story and is no longer true. Today American correspondents are given freer access to battle fronts and bases, with readier and more agreeable facilities for moving about than they were ever accorded in any war. The commanders give them a warmer welcome and take them into confidence more fully than in times past. When they travel, they are freeloaders and some of them, even on short hauls for brief stays, have the nerve to take a trunk along. Still, the field Public Information Officers often have to journey to Saigon and convince the reporters that something very special is brewing before they will get off their duffs for a few days.

I have refrained from saying anything about how this failure of the press contributes to the blighting and confusing of American public opinion regarding the war and the national prospects in it. Indeed, the topic is best dropped; there is no way to prove that the press failure is more baneful than the deliberate effort of a few statesmen in Washington—and of some speakers before the UN General Assembly—to mislead public opinion by newly raising false issues and aggravating old fears. Our time is the heyday of the fogmakers, and there seems to be no choice but to suffer them.

Far removed from all of this wavering and doubt, our Army in Vietnam hews to the line. Troops understand their mission, know what they are doing, and do it splendidly. Men like General Norton and his soldiers are above feeling hurt that their deeds go unsung and will be little noted in the future. The pity is that a national will might polarize around this solid, shining and reassuring performance, if we were but permitted to view it.

REPORTING VIETNAM:
TWO REPLIES

Responding to the preceding article by S. L. A. Marshall attacking Vietnam war coverage are two reporters who were there. The first selection is by Malcolm W. Browne, a 1964 Pulitzer Prize winner who has spent over five years reporting from Vietnam. The second is by Dale Minor who spent time on special assignment in Vietnam and is the author of The Information War.

Malcolm W. Browne

GENERAL S. L. A. Marshall's disgusting polemic, "Press Failure in Vietnam," is an insult to the memory of Bernie Kolenberg, Jerry Rose, Dickie Chapelle and Sam Castan—American reporters who died covering the Vietnam war. It is an offense against the other 87 reporters wounded there, some of them maimed, and a dishonorable slur on those doomed to become casualties in the years ahead. There have been eyes blown out, hands permanently crippled (and for a cameraman, this is the end of a career), feet lamed by spike traps, ligaments and tendons wrecked by grenade and shell fragments, and countless bullet wounds.

It is one more gratuitous attack on the Vietnam press corps, of a type that has come all too frequently in the past four years from Marshall, the editors of *Time* magazine, Joe Alsop, Keyes Beech of the Chicago *Daily News,* the late Marguerite Higgins and Jim Lucas. All well over 40 years old, they have delighted in deprecating their younger colleagues, often in a distinctly "sour grapes" tone. This is particularly true when they find themselves outpaced day after day, not only in the running war reportage (definitely a young man's game) but in the

253

writing of sober political background stories—at which the older men, theoretically, benefit from long experience.

Marshall, in effect, declares that American newsmen (except for some of those from his own generation) are mostly chicken. Not only are they too frightened to cover the war in the field, he says, but they cynically "sit around and sneer." The General also infers cowardice in reporters who abruptly leave the "front," as he calls it, to cover political disturbances in Saigon.

Let us touch first on this matter of cowardice (and let the reader remember that many of us have had to fight for our lives to get out of Vietnam ambushes, and we have often had to act more like soldiers than newsmen). The General evidently has never had his lungs seared by tear gas in a Saigon riot; never been chased through a score of blocks by mobs of homicidal teenagers and agitators armed with torches, bricks, machetes and iron pipes; never been beaten into unconsciousness by rioters or police; never had his wife threatened by political gangs (many of us have our wives with us); never been arrested for having legitimately covered the news.

Marshall imagines that this is merely another miniature World War II or Korea, and all we need are reporters with guts, like those who landed in the first waves at Anzio or Omaha Beach. (Incidentally, one of the reporters who did land at Anzio and a lot of other murderous beaches, Homer Bigart of the New York *Times,* has somewhat different views from Marshall. Bigart's brilliant work in Vietnam in 1962 involved a great deal of dangerous war coverage, but he was also one of the first to discover that Vietnam was not just another World War II or Korea. And he was 57 at the time.)

It is well to look at perspectives. Marshall spent about three months in Vietnam this past summer. I recall that he was out for a week or so in 1962 with former CIA Chief Allen Dulles to investigate GI morale. So let us say he has spent around four months in Vietnam in recent years.

But Vietnam is no quickie war like World War II or Korea. For the U.S., World War II lasted three years and eight months; Korea lasted three years and one month. In terms of substantial American involvement, the Vietnam war has been going on for five years already, and no end is in sight.

Granted, Vietnam has been a slow-burning war compared with earlier ones. But this has not made it any safer or easier for war correspondents. And some of us have been covering the Vietnam war almost from the beginning. People like Mert Perry and Francois Sully (*Newsweek*), Peter Arnett and Horst Faas (*Associated Press*), Beverly Deepe (*freelance*), Michel Renard (*freelance*), Neil Sheehan (New York *Times*) and many others have laid their lives on the line—not ten, but hundreds of times in the past five years.

The difference between the reporter who has been in Vietnam five years and the one who has been there only about four months is essentially one of maturity and perspective. To be sure, the engagement at Ia Drang was important, but perhaps somewhat less so for a reporter who has campaigned many times before in the Ia Drang valley than for a relatively green observer like General Marshall.

The August Ia Drang fight was the latest in a continuing series. American newsmen were with General Khanh's forces there in early 1964, and during the bloody battle of February this year, when casualties on both sides were far higher than in the August fight. Arnett, Faas, Al Chang, Jim Pickerell, Dirck Halstead and many others have narrowly cheated death many a time at Ia Drang as well as elsewhere in the bleak border zone.

And we will all carry brutal memories for the rest of our days from datelines like Song Be, Binh Gia, Ap Bac, Ba Gia, Plei Me, Dong Xoai, Cai Lai, Bong Son (which Marshall incorrectly spells) and hundreds of others. At the time, they all seemed pretty big and important to us, and they did to our editors, too. Now, with the war still rolling on like the Mekong River, one begins to wonder. Did any of those battles secure any vital piece of real estate for one side or the other? Did any of them result in a breakthrough? Did any of them permanently eliminate a major belligerent unit?

The answers, of course, are No. This is not a war for real estate like World War II and Korea, and there is no front. There are hundreds of highly mobile hostile and friendly units engaged in endless maneuvers, always seeking an advantage in one way or another. When a hill, ridgeline or hamlet becomes an objective for one side or the other, it is important for a few hours or days. When the fight is over, the winner frequently abandons the objective. And despite the fine success of the First Cavalry (Air Mobile) up in the Ia Drang area last August, I would be delighted to buy both a drink and 10 gallons of gasoline for General Marshall if he would be willing to drive a jeep up that valley today without benefit of an escort of at least a regiment of troops.

When a place like Ia Drang gets battled over a number of times (there will be many more fights there, I'm sure) it ceases to be front-page news. It is a fact that 52,000 Americans are killed each year in auto accidents, yet auto accidents generally are not front-page news because they are too common to be news. I am not arguing whether this is right or wrong, but it is a fact.

Given this situation, the intelligent reporter will pace himself. The veterans spend more time in the field than anyone else, but they pick their operations carefully. They know that the average big search-and-clear or hunter-killer operation is unlikely to be interesting. These operations are planned in advance, and are so massive and cumbersome that the Vietcong generally has plenty of time to move his important forces out of the way.

This does not make for easy operations, either for the troops or the correspondents, since they still must face exhausting jungle marches, heat prostration, red ants, various jungle sicknesses, and most of all, enemy harassment in the form of sniping, mines and booby traps. For the troops, there are few tangible results beyond the rice caches burned and the handful of suspects piled up. For the correspondents there is little "hard" copy; reporters must rely heavily on the sidelights Marshall deprecates to get any copy at all.

On the other hand, there are countless operations that do draw a great deal of blood, and are interesting, if hair-raising, to both troops and correspondents. Most often they are small company- or battalion-sized operations that go without fanfare or elaborate preparation. These are the operations that stand a good chance of coming to grips with the Vietcong.

But the correspondent who depends on an invitation from some well-meaning public information officer will all too often wait in vain for a tip on an interesting engagement. The veterans have long ago learned to take official invitations with a grain of salt and follow their instinct as to where the action will be. Often on hunches, correspondents have ignored the official invitations of big, planned operations, say by the First Cavalry Division out of An Khe, and instead have driven their own cars to some town in the Mekong River delta or up to Hau Nghia Province to get in on a smaller operation. Working on basically the principle of independent initiative, the AP Saigon bureau won three Pulitzer Prizes in three successive years. Those prizes did not result from the "cynical sit-in" approach Marshall charges, but from hard soldiering and good sense. Most of all they came from a sense for news, and being in the right place at the right time.

Marshall declares that correspondents freeload on the U.S. Armed Forces in Vietnam. For a visiting fireman like Marshall, I imagine this was true. For most of us, a bunk costs a dollar a night, meals cost about a buck a piece, cases of C Rations are available at $12 each, fatigues, helmets and jungle gear must be purchased on the Saigon black market, and when we get shot, it costs us $70 a day to get patched up at the Navy Hospital in Saigon. (Jim Pickerell was in that hospital for two weeks after getting a bullet through his leg, and it runs into money for a free-lance). When we get killed, the Armed Forces charge us about $140 (plus other expenses) to get the loan of an aluminum casket and a MATS flight to Travis Air Force Base.

Sadly, there is a kernel of truth in Marshall's charges. The newsmen in Vietnam are not all hard-driving men and women. Washington has traditionally been a haven for a certain number of performing seals who have written their dispatches and analyses from the hand-outs, briefings, leaks and other standard sources that involve a minimum of labor and initiative. Inevitably, Saigon has become infested with some of these people, and they are no different in Saigon from what they are in Washington. There are also "draftees" in the news corps, some of whom are merely anxious to finish their tours as "volunteers" and return to domestic news assignments. Their primary motivation is survival.

Finally, there are those who treat every war in modern times as a kind of sporting event, writing each dispatch as a hard-hitting cheer for the home team. These men are important for military morale. Probably the finest of this type in American journalistic history was Ernie Pyle. But in my opinion, they tell us almost nothing about how a war is going, even though they tell us in meaning detail what our GIs are doing and suffering. I submit that in a war like Vietnam it is good to know how our GIs are getting along, but it is vastly more important to know what the war is all about, where it seems to be going and what the Vietnamese are doing and thinking. That is the job the young correspondents Marshall so despises have done supremely well— better, indeed than the American government at any time during the conflict.

The Vietnamese enemy obviously has something on the ball that earlier enemies of the United States have lacked. Korea, for instance, is a nation with a population roughtly comparable in size to that of North and South Vietnam. The North Korean Army was fairly well equipped and trained when it attacked the South in 1950, and it gained ground fast. Even so, a million-man North Chinese expeditionary force had to come in to pull the fat out of the fire for the Korean Communists. But despite this, the combined enemy forces never swept the United Nations into the sea.

In Vietnam, however, no evidence has been produced to show that any more Vietnamese are fighting in the enemy infantry ranks (although Russian missile advisors and Chinese experts are helping out in the North). But the combined Vietcong and North Vietnamese forces manage to keep going, holding their base areas fairly secure, making up their battle losses and continuing to inflict bloody attrition on their Saigon and American enemies. This has been accomplished despite 345,000 American servicemen in Vietnam, and support of groups in Thailand, the Seventh Fleet, the Air Force and South Vietnam's own government forces totalling well over half a million men.

It is not within the scope of this article to discuss the reasons for Vietcong tenacity. But they are a primary concern for most of the veteran correspondents in Vietnam. While it is fine to entertain the American public with breezy gung-ho stories about the Vietnam war, it is selling America short to say only this.

If the young correspondents covering Vietnam are more cynical than those covering earlier wars, they are also smarter and generally far better informed. As a group, they drink less and work harder. (I trust that General Marshall has not forgotten the atmosphere at the press billets in Seoul during the latter part of the Korean War.) In some ways, they are perhaps more cautious. As then, they lack the luxury of gigantic stories like Normandy, where a newsman stood a great chance of being killed, but also had a monumental story to compensate for the risk.

In Vietnam, there are little Normandies every day, and they kill soldiers and newsmen just as dead as the big one in 1944. The only difference is that now most of them are worth only a few paragraphs on page 37. If you're going to die covering a war, it's a lot better to do it covering something important (not necessarily big) than spilling out your guts over a random enemy mine you stepped on while covering a massive operation resulting in "no significant enemy contact."

The hard core of newsmen in Vietnam grow weary of the endless ranting from their detractors. From the Pentagon or White House it is predictable. From journalistic colleagues it is professional back stabbing—as contemptible in a newsman as it is in any other professional.

It would be good to see a truce where each writer on Vietnam began tending his own garden and sticking to the business at hand—covering Vietnam. Despite Marshall, Alsop, Beech, Assistant Secretary of Defense Arthur Sylvester, *Time* magazine and some others, that is what the hard core of the Vietnam press corps has been doing all along. Fortunately for America, this hard core is the leader in coverage. Let the others keep pace if they can.

Dale Minor

IT MAY not be the duty of the Army, as S. L. A. Marshall says, "to function as war reporter to the nation . . ." (though the number of men it employs in that capacity might mislead people). But it is also not the duty of the correspondent to look after the morale of the troops, or to provide images for the polarization of a national will, as Marshall suggests it should. What the General has written is yet another catalogue of all the hackneyed charges made by detractors of the American press in Vietnam since Diem, and to a similar purpose.

While the allegation that "the overwhelming majority of correspondents do not get to the front" (a dependable old bell-ringer if ever there was one) serves as Marshall's launching pad, a re-definition of the reporter's function and an attempt to confine "the game" to areas in which the military mind is at ease, seem to be his destination. Several years ago, another American general expressed a similar attitude toward the press when he snapped at the New York *Times'* Homer Bigart, "Why the hell don't you get on the team?"

If one wants to play the statistical game, one might suggest the General do a little more research. He might compare the casualty figures among correspondents in Vietnam since the American build-up with figures for a comparable period during the Korean War. He might also take a closer look at the figure of 350 he gives for the number of working correspondents in Vietnam today.

If Marshall's interest is *reporters* working for American news outlets, he will find, I believe, less than 100 working in the country at any given moment—at times considerably less—after subtracting from the list photographers, technical members of TV crews, newsmen and crews accredited to non-American news organizations, wives accredited but working only in Saigon, newsmen on rotation in Hong Kong or elsewhere, and last, but far from least, the steady stream of journalistic visitors who are registered on arrival and therefore get their names on the next monthly list, only to be gone by the time the list is published. This last category, reporters and columnists whose tour is a one or two week affair spent flitting about the country from one briefing to another (and in whose copy and columns are often planted officialdom's complaint about the regular press), is responsible for the huge turnover in the Saigon press corps: More than 1,100 accredited between January 1 and the end of June, while the total monthly number remained near the 350 mark.

Were the General able to spend some time with the regular members of the American press in Vietnam, he might not only learn something of their personal and professional problems, about which he professes his ignorance but also of Vietnam's problems, about which he does not profess his ignorance though he profusely indicates it. He might also, being an honest man, have to admit to making a specious, if all too common, identification: the least cowardly with the sneering-cynical. My own observation of many Saigon briefings has been that the troublemakers are generally those who do gain the facts themselves and who do get about the country, while the "sit-in" more often writes his file straight from the handout and usually can be depended upon to echo the party line.

But while I find most of Marshall's charges inaccurate, exaggerated or even ill-conceived, what really disturbs me is the conclusion they all point to, his definition of the proper role of the reporter—"the name of the game." "The name of the game is Being With Troops." Cosy figure. The name of *whose* game? The game of the correspondent assigned to Vietnam is properly named Vietnam; and Being With Troops, while an important part of the "game" at this juncture, nonetheless remains only a part.

There is an understandable tendency among military men in Vietnam to *wish* that military activity were the only important element in the Vietnam story. But it becomes less understandable, and even dangerous, when they wish it so strongly that they convince themselves (and others), in the face of all contrary evidence, by denying the relevance or importance of anything not within their professional scope and control. This phenomenon has produced a constant source of friction between the military and civilian sides of the U.S. Mission.

The General does not mention the internal crisis that shook South Vietnam during a good portion of his stay in the spring and summer of this year except obliquely, in a discussion of what he calls "off-beat yarns." Among these he includes "any demonstration or riot and especially a Buddhist demonstration-riot." Are we to assume, then, that in the General's view, search and destroy operation number one-hundred-and-so-and-so is an urgently important story, while an attempt (nearly successful) to topple the Ky government and possibly the entire U.S. effort with it, is nothing more than an off-beat yarn played up out of press perversity?

It seems that what the General demands is a "war correspondent" out of the crusade of the '40's—that romantic figure who acted more as the civilian adjunct of the Public Information Office, more a propagandist for home-fried morale—epitomized by the saintly Ernie Pyle—than a critical observer of the scene. Surely, that was a time when those with Marshall's turn of mind were happier, when almost all problems were military and had military solutions, when everyone was, indeed, "on the team" and in agreement about "the name of the game."

I've never been quite sure just what a "bleeding-heart" is supposed to be. Something vile, I know. S. L. A. Marshall says that's who the war is being covered for, and from his complaints I deduce them to be wishy-washy types who are squeamish about general slaughter, bombed villages, defoliated crops and a civilian-military casualty ratio of 10-1, and/or people who have questions about the moral and political validity of current American policy there.

What the General apparently desires is reporting of the war for those who simply want to know "how it is being fought" and how good the chances are of victory. Being With Troops is all and only, says Marshall, and don't confuse public opinion regarding the war with negative side-bars and offbeat tangents about what the Vietnamese feel and do, and what is happening to them.

Man, talk about cynical faddishness!

John Tebbel
GLOBAL FREEDOM OF THE PRESS:
A SLOW STRANGULATION

Contending that "the struggle for press freedom never ends," John Tebbel, Professor of Journalism at New York University and frequent contributor to Saturday Review, *examines the world's press and its various degrees of freedom.*

BY ANY measurement, freedom of the press in the world is suffering from slow strangulation. With colonels and generals, past and present, in control of so many governments, and more subtle curbs operative in nearly all the others, few nations can claim a free press today, and their number continues to diminish.

The concept of "freedom" itself becomes a matter of semantics. One new African country proudly asserts that its Constitution absolutely guarantees freedom of the press because anyone may own or start a newspaper, and there is no pre-publication censorship. The same Constitution, however, provides that anyone who wishes to operate a paper must be licensed by the government, which appears to see no inconsistency in these provisions.

Newspapers in every country have two common problems: their relationship with government and the economic struggle to survive. In either case, the outlook is not encouraging. The dominant aspect of late twentieth-century international politics has been the decline of popular democratic government. As James Reston has pointed out, the kind of government to which the United States, the United Kingdom, and most of the Western European countries subscribe has not only made little progress but could hardly be described as even popular in other areas of the world. Freedom of the press cannot be expected to prosper in such a global environment.

A key element in the struggle between the Soviet Union and the Government of Czechoslovakia was freedom of the press, a Western concept so alien to orthodox Communist ideology that the Russians experience honest difficulty in understanding it. To them, it is a simple matter. The press exists to serve the people, who are the government. If the press criticizes the government, it is criticizing the people and therefore is committing a treasonous act.

Because the conflict between concepts is so dramatic in Eastern Europe, it is easy to overlook the fact that authoritarian control of the press is the rule in large parts of the world. A military junta commands Greece, and military men control Yugoslavia, Spain, Argentina, Brazil, Bolivia, Nicaragua, Paraguay, El Salvador, and Cuba. In Africa, they dominate Algeria, Nigeria, Ghana, the Congo, Upper Volta, Dahomey, the Central African Republic, Sierra Leone, Togo, Biafra, and Burundi. Dictatorial civilian regimes rule in South Africa, Rhodesia, and Angola, and of course in the Soviet Union and Eastern Europe. Generals and colonels are in control from the United Arab Republic to Pakistan, Thailand, Iraq, Burma, Indonesia, North and South Korea, Taiwan, South and North Vietnam, and China.

In all of these countries, the press is controlled by government in greater or less degree, from rigid censorship and complete direction of what is printed to various methods of intimidation, overt or subtle. The semantics of ideology sometimes present the control as the will of the people, and therefore "democratic," but by the standards of the Western democracies there is no free press. Even where newspapers and magazines have some degree of freedom, radio and television are state controlled.

Nor are the Western democracies themselves immune. The struggle for press freedom never ends. In the United Kingdom, the newspapers must contend with severely restrictive libel and contempt of court laws (and recently, as in the case of the *London Observer,* with contempt of Parliament as well). The British trust that their government will never severely abuse the absolute control it possesses over radio and television. In America, the battle is against government at every level from the White House down to the county courthouse, in the fight to get into print what politicians want to conceal, for whatever reason.

The First Amendment guarantees that the American press will win some of these skirmishes, at least; but meanwhile, especially on the national level, it is losing the largest contest, involving the use of public relations techniques to control and manage the news.

In brief, the outlook for freedom of the press in the world is a dark one. Two years ago, an attempt was made to measure world press freedom statistically. The Freedom of Information Center at the School of Journalism, University of Missouri, compiled its information from a survey questionnaire circulated to various sets of judges, including scholars, foreign correspondents, and other journalists, who were asked to rate given countries according to a list of criteria devised by the Center. In this survey, the press was termed free in fifty-five countries, controlled in twenty-nine, and in a transitional state in ten others. Twenty-one countries were unranked.

265
John Tebbel
GLOBAL FREEDOM
OF THE PRESS:
A SLOW
STRANGULATION

A year later, according to the results of a second survey released last spring, the score showed forty-seven free, twenty-six controlled, eleven transitional, and thirty-one unranked. Translated to population terms, these figures mean that presently 43.3 per cent of the world's peoples enjoy a free press, 41.1 per cent read a controlled press, 9 per cent are in a transitional stage, and 6.6 per cent are unranked. While the Center warned of some technical difficulties in making comparisons, it concluded that "the picture of world press freedom emerging for 1967 was one of more losses than gains." The survey affirms that no region of the world has gained in press freedom between the two attempts at measurement.

It may be impossible to measure press freedom statistically with any degree of accuracy, because so many variables are involved and so many differences of opinion exist about virtually every aspect of it, but there is abundant evidence to support the conviction that the media are slowly losing the battle. In the coming era of world satellite communications, governments may eventually dictate what is transmitted, by virtue of international agreements. Today, in much of the world, freedom of the press is not even a dream in the hearts of the people. In the Western democracies where it still exists, those who enjoy its benefits constantly jeopardize it by their apathy.

There is a fundamental difference in attitude between most of the developing countries and the older nations. In the culture of the latter, such basic concepts as individual freedom, freedom of expression, and the rights of man are, if not taken for granted, at least regarded as essential to the functioning of representative government. But to most people in the developing countries, these are new ideas which excite them and embarrass their political leaders. The authority of these leaders rests on custom and tradition. Freedom of the press can only be a threat to that authority, and so they are against it more often than not. Thus, the idea of a free press functioning as a mainspring in a democratic society is opposed to authoritarian censorship in many of these countries, and conflict is the result.

Authoritarianism, however, is only the most obvious means of curtailing or stifling press freedom. In America, for example, no one but the extremists of Left and Right would argue seriously that the press is controlled, in the usual sense of the word. Yet it is not easy to cite ourselves as completely and gloriously free when it is possible for unions to hold a life-or-death power over individual papers, or when access to public records and proceedings can be and is denied to the press by every unit of government from the federal to the county courthouse—not to mention the further controls which bar and bench are presently trying to impose.

Control can be achieved by more subtle means than the presence of a government which, either by law or without it, regulates the conduct of the press directly. The harsh libel restrictions in British law, and the rigid controls exerted by the bench over the coverage of legal proceedings, constitute effective control of the press in the U. K.

There is also the control exerted by near monopoly, as in the case of West Germany, where the central issue in the press freedom controversy concerns the extraordinary degree to which the Axel Springer newspaper-book-magazine empire monopolizes the nation's output of printed material. Dealing with this kind of control is not an easy matter in a country such as Germany, where the relatively simple question of monopoly is so deeply complicated by political considerations.

Still another kind of control which makes press freedom so hard to realize is the matter of newspaper ownership by unions or by religious bodies, as is so often the case in Europe. How independent can a newspaper be under such ownership? In some instances, there is as much freedom as there would be if the control were in the hands of a private entrepreneur, but in others the news columns, as well as the editorials, are heavily weighted by whatever political viewpoint the union or religion is promoting.

For that matter, private ownership can produce as complete control of the press as authoritarian government. The difference is between one and several points of view. But if the private owners are at the same time heavily involved in political or trade union activity, or are closely allied to a regime by financial or other ties, the differing viewpoints will not represent variations of opinion, but only sources of propaganda. This is true, in varying degree, in many European countries. There are several nations in the world where newspaper editors and publishers are also professional politicians, sitting in legislative bodies or otherwise occupying public positions.

With press freedom either under attack or already extinguished in so much of the world, it might be supposed that there would be unanimity of viewpoint among those still able to discuss the question. Yet delegates to the 1967 Commonwealth Press Union conference in London found themselves deeply divided about press freedom and how it should be defined. The Union's press freedom committee had produced a document on the subject which embodied and expanded the terms of a resolution passed at the 1965 conference, but this proved to be unacceptable to most of the delegates.

267
John Tebbel
**GLOBAL FREEDOM
OF THE PRESS:
A SLOW
STRANGULATION**

Representatives of Canada, New Zealand, and the West Indies were disturbed by a comment attached to the report which suggested that the Canadian and New Zealand press was not truly free because the countries discriminated against foreign publishers. (Canada withholds a tax concession from those publishers. New Zealand forbids foreigners to hold more than a quarter of the shares in any publishing company.) The Canadians and New Zealanders contended that this was a matter of press ownership, not press freedom. Their law, the Canadians argued further, prevented United States companies from annexing Canadian firms, and in any case, community interests would be better served by local papers, locally owned.

Lord Thomson of Fleet, answering these views, condemned them as "narrow nationalism" and "selfish interests." The Canadian-born international press magnate asserted that any obstruction of the press by government constituted an infringement of press freedom. Nevertheless, the conference upheld the 1965 resolution but eliminated all references to other countries, and to discrimination.

While the professionals quibble over semantics, there is steadily growing censorship and manipulation of the press everywhere. Sometimes it takes the form of force. More often, it is indirect, as in controlling the supply of newsprint, withdrawing government-controlled advertising, denying access to the government for news, or helping papers loyal to the government.

We are, in short, slowly losing a freedom on which open societies must ultimately depend. Dictators of every stripe, and authoritarian governments of all kinds, are natural enemies of press freedom. Apathy and indifference among people who possess that freedom can be equally fatal.

Rick Friedman
A NEGRO LEADER LOOKS AT THE PRESS

In the following article Rick Friedman, feature writer for Editor and Publisher, *discusses with Whitney Young, Jr., Executive Director of the National Urban League, the special problems and responsibilities journalism faces reporting the current racial situation in America. The article originally appeared in* Editor and Publisher *in the July 18, 1964, issue.*

SITTING in his mid-Manhattan National Urban League office, Whitney M. Young, Jr., appearing relaxed, smoking a cigarette and taking advantage of a short break in a tight schedule, summed up civil rights news reporting this way:

"Newspapers, despite superb spot coverage, have been guilty of emphasizing the conflicts between the whites and Negroes and minimizing, if not completely ignoring, areas of cooperation between the two groups. The in-depth series too often is the exception to this rule. We need more of them."

GETTING ALONG

Leaning forward to crush out the cigarette, he elaborated. "Floyd Patterson moves out of Scarsdale because of racial problems and this makes news. But for 12 to 15 years, there have been situations in the suburbs where Negro kids are the most popular ones in the neighborhood.

"Yet, to the general public, conflict is the norm. Negroes and whites getting along in the same neighborhood are considered oddballs. The public thinks that any white person who cooperates is offbeat.

269

"Big Business in this country, the principals of major corporations, the top people in government—it's easier for us to enter into discussion with them today than it was in the past. Before, they watched civil rights like it was a spectator sport.

"Now, they realize that business is being hurt, that it doesn't do them any good to have the Klan represent America overseas, to have free enterprise shown as not working for the American non-white. These people realize now that the real test of free enterprise is when it helps those who may be different.

"Now, we walk into the offices of presidents of the largest corporations at THEIR request. They want to know what they can do. Now, we speak before groups of city managers, mayors, industrial boards, builders, real estate federations who never had a Negro on their programs before.

"But these positive, new positions taken by American industry are not always played up in our press. Newspapers are not informing readers of what the role-models of the country are doing to advance civil rights."

But aren't many of these corporations that invite you to private breakfasts and luncheons, reluctant to let the press know about them?

"Sure," Mr. Young admitted. "But the press has to convince these men it's to their own interest for such stories about them to be publicized; that if the public thinks these corporations aren't discriminating, such stories could improve their images. The Urban League has been glad to cooperate with the press in breaking down resistance to getting the real stories from corporations doing their part in advancing civil rights."

VIOLENCE IN HARLEM

Mr. Young moved to what he considered a second error in civil rights coverage. "Too many newspapers give the impression that violence, vandalism, crime, murder are new things in Harlem—and give them a racial overtone. The truth is that violence has been a way of life in Harlem for years, just as it has been in white, poverty-struck communities.

"The big difference today is that, in addition to Negroes getting killed, some white persons are also getting killed. Now, the white community finally cares. Now, many newspapers are trying to identify a problem that was always there before white people were getting killed."

He paused to light another cigarette. "My own wife isn't safe in Harlem. The single fact of color is no guarantee of her safety. I don't want Harlem safe just for white people. I want Harlem safe for ALL human beings.

"Contrast this poor coverage with the superb stories the press has done on the war on poverty—almost totally free of racial overtones. The *New York Times* and the *Washington Post* are two examples."

IRRESPONSIBLE LEADERS

The third area of bad reporting, according to Mr. Young, was when some newspapers promote and project irresponsible Negro civil rights leaders. Often it is the press itself that makes these men leaders, Mr. Young contended.

"Somebody gets up and says he's going to start an all-Negro political party and the next day there are headlines, front page stories, editorials. But does any one pick up the phone to find out that this man has no backing, no members, no money and no power?

"The World's Fair stall-ins were the same type of bad reporting. Responsible leaders in Philadelphia, Cincinnati or Boston could have told any reporter who asked that they were not going to send in cars to have them impounded on the Long Island Expressway. Anyone who checked could have found out that the stall-in people had poor organization, no money. All the national Negro organizations were opposed to it.

"Something happens in civil rights and the newspapers call up outstanding personalities like James Baldwin or Louis Lomax or Willie Mays and ask what they think. Baldwin and Lomax are excellent writers but they are responsible to nobody but themselves. They are responsible to no organization so they can make statements that get front page space.

"I don't question the integrity of their statements. But do newspapers call Frank Sinatra to comment on foreign policy? Or John O'Hara to comment on wheat to Russia? The racial situation is complex and it takes organization, know-how to comment on it. Lomax can say what he wants. I have to speak for the Urban League, its thousands of members and its 56-year-tradition.

"The press gives somebody such as Malcolm X a chance to air his views. Then when he does, they rush in panicky and report them."

Are you suggesting that the press ignore someone such as Malcolm X?

"No. But I expect the press to report him objectively. When Malcolm X draws a crowd in Harlem, not 10 in 1,000 would follow him to a separate state or to Africa. Let the press find out who in the crowd would follow him. Let the press report Malcolm X in a more subjective way instead of just saying he's out to start rifle clubs. Let the press find out how many would follow him, where he gets his money, whether he's a con man or not, who is behind him.

"Let the press put him in proper context and cover him just as they do James Hoffa."

Mr. Young named the United Council on Civil Rights as an example of responsible Negro leadership. It is made up of heads of seven leading Negro civil rights organizations—Wilkins (NAACP), King (SCLC), Foreman (SNCC), Farmer (CORE), Mr. Young, Mrs. Dorothy Height, National Council on Negro Women, and Jack Greenberg, head of the NAACP Legal Defense Fund. These leaders meet regularly to decide what collective action they will take on civil rights.

But hasn't the press covered these meetings?

"They know about the meetings and when we hold them. We've been written up. But they don't seek us out when something like the Christmas boycott idea pops up. Baldwin, Lomax, Rep. Adam Clayton Powell pushed it. Our United Council rejected it because a boycott would hurt a lot of small retailers who employ Negroes. As with the stall-ins, we felt the Christmas boycott would be almost useless—any demonstration is useless when it's not focused, not specific.

"This was another failure on the part of the press to project responsible Negro leadership, the kind of leadership which produced the March on Washington last year. After that march, we suggested that Negroes keep marching to libraries, adult education centers, retraining centers, PTA meetings, if they wanted to put meaning into the March on Washington. It was almost a year before a wire service picked up this plea."

But adult education, job retraining, they don't present as dramatic a story to reporters as Malcolm X or the stall-in, do they?

"To a good reporter, job retraining is dramatic. Otherwise, he's lazy, has no creativity, no imagination," Mr. Young countered.

"When the Urban League takes 40 girls about to become domestic workers and retrains them so that 30 of the 40 are now working with major corporations, that's *dramatic,* isn't it? The *New York Herald-Tribune* showed how a beautiful piece could be done on this subject.

"The press should be informing the public of this positive aspect of civil rights."

AMERICAN TRADITION

Mr. Young lit another cigarette. "The press has failed to tell its readers that what the Negro is doing is nothing more than what Americans have been doing since Susan B. Anthony and the Woman Suffragists right up through the labor movement.

"But let a Jesse Gray show up overnight and create a rent strike and it gets top play."

Doesn't it deserve top press play?

"All I'm asking is for a little more balance in newspapers. For somebody to pick up a phone and talk to more responsible sources. In these critical times, the press cannot afford to give incorrect information. Reporters have to look beneath the headlines, to the person who can deliver the correct story."

What about the positive side of civil rights press coverage? Do you think there is one?

"Sure," Mr. Young said. "Many newspapers have helped gain public acceptance on civil rights laws in not only school desegregation but in other areas such as fair housing and employment. Depth reporting in this area has been outstanding.

"These laws got good local support from newspapers. Newspapers made segregation something undesirable. In many areas, it became unfashionable to discriminate openly. Last Summer, the *Chicago Daily News* did a series on civil rights that ran an entire month. It was a top job.

"Because of newspapers, many people no longer feel free to articulate primitive prejudices. So some of these same people form a new rationale, a more polite one and the word 'nigger' no longer is the thing to say unless these same people get delayed on the Triborough Bridge by a civil rights demonstration.

"I think the challenge to newspapers now is to make sure people don't accomplish their old segregationist objectives with new, more subtle schemes, ones that involve property, standards of education, a new vocabulary such as *neighborhood school concept.*

"This is the real challenge to newspapers, to all media—make it as much a status symbol to have diversity as it once was to have sameness. Make the norm inclusiveness instead of exclusiveness. Make people see that their own self-interests will be served by integration. Assure the insecure, frightened, unsophisticated who surround themselves with sameness that diversity won't put them in danger.

"The real challenge to the press is to create the kind of climate where people will have to apologize for anything that is all-white, except their own families, as a sign of insecurity."

Gerald Grant
THE "NEW JOURNALISM" WE NEED

"We don't need a whole new breed of novelists in action; we need more cogent journalism that tells us about problems rather than sketching conflict," contends Gerald Grant, former reporter for the Washington Post *and currently a Teaching Fellow at Harvard.*

SEVERAL months after Benjamin Bradlee left *Newsweek* to become managing editor of the Washington *Post,* a series of staff shakeups began. After the first wave one of the editors invited a dozen young city staff reporters to lunch. As he sipped his Dubonnet on the rocks we nervously wondered about our fate. Most of what he said now escapes me. But I have a vivid recollection of his curiosity about the social circles we traveled in. Whom did we see? What parties did we go to? Whom did we know? His point was that a good deal of what went on in Washington could be learned at dinner parties—or at least that those who were able to establish a social relationship with sources after working hours were most likely to be privileged to the inside story on the job. Some of the best journalists in Washington had grown in reputation as their sources had grown in responsibility; in some cases they had been lucky enough to be classmates.

At the time his message struck me as mildly offensive. Not that it was pointless; his own prominent social connections had not hurt his career. As I look back, however, his inquiry no longer strikes me as saying so much about upward mobility of journalists as about patterns of thought in journalism. His comments underscored the idea that talent in journalism is often a skill for finding out what somebody *else* thinks or knows about something. It may be an oversimplification, yet it is true that lively concern for whom a journalist knows reflects weak appreciation for how he thinks.

What separates most journalists from the few great ones is that the latter are not content with knowing what their sources think. They exhibit an independent intelligence that seeks to wrest meaning from the torrent of events rather than acting as mere transmission belts. They ask better questions because they have a better concept of what the "story" is.

There are some journalists who think, as Richard Hofstadter has said, in terms of configuration and style, thus delineating patterns as well as describing events. One recalls the work of Philip Meyer of the Knight Newspapers, who has effectively used social science skills to analyze current issues; of the perceptive reporting of Joseph Lelyveld and Anthony Lukas of the New York *Times;* of the probing exemplified by the work of Laurence Stern's and Richard Harwood's Insight Teams on the Washington *Post.* There has been a gratifying tendency on a number of papers such as *Newsday* and the Los Angeles *Times* to give reporters the time and freedom to do serious, thoughtful journalism. But as Daniel P. Moynihan said in his brilliant eulogy for Paul Niven, "[Journalism is] that most underdeveloped, least realized of professions. Not a profession at all, really. Rather a craft seeking to become such out of the need to impose form on an activity so vastly expanded in volume and significance as desperately to need the stabilizing influence of procedure and precedent and regularity."

Max Ways, in a *Fortune* article last October entitled "What's Wrong with News: It Isn't New Enough," attributes journalism's shortcomings to its failure to adopt new forms and new definitions of "the story." As a result of applying old yardsticks to events, he says, journalism continues to focus on what can be easily measured and told, to the neglect of more complex and important events unfolding in the society. But were the yardsticks ever any good? My guess is that journalism in 1870 failed in much the same ways it does today. The underlying explanation, then as now, is the kind of mental habits and attitudes most journalists bring to bear on events.

Journalists work by a code that makes many of them moral eunuchs. The professional, in print at least, generally pretends to be without opinions or convictions. His objectivity differs from that of the scientist who demands freedom to develop a fresh hypothesis but then remains objective in the sense that he will look in an unprejudiced way at the results of his experimentation.

Reportorial objectivity has been under vigorous attack by the "New Journalists." Citing Norman Mailer and others, they rightly sense that newsroom objectivity may result in untruth. It masks feelings and stifles imagination. More importantly, it can produce a trained incapacity for thought in the young journalist. Unconsciously he comes to believe that what he thinks doesn't matter. He regards himself as a conduit. The reporter calls an expert for a quote as an unfortunate shortcut to thinking the problem through himself. He asks not what do I think, but what do they think? That can be a habit difficult to break. He seldom has a sense of personal responsibility for what he writes.

Gerald Grant
THE "NEW JOURNALISM" WE NEED

This is why Michael Arlen, writing in *Living Room War,* is right when he characterizes much current journalism as propaganda. Not that experts shouldn't be interviewed, or that reporters must be philosopher-kings; but they should be something more than tape recorders. Most journalists are caught in a nether world. They are neither men of action, forced to confront a problem by struggling with it in an operational sense, nor men of true imagination or contemplation.

Yet uncritical enthusiasm for the New Journalism of passion and advocacy may cost more in the loss of the valuable skepticism of the traditional newspaperman than can be gained through the new involvement. The trouble with advocacy may be that it leads writers who haven't thought or felt much to portray cardboard emotions. Most readers would rather hear the experts. The challenge is to make sense out of the experts and of events. We don't need a whole new breed of novelists in action; we need more cogent journalism that tells us about problems rather than sketching conflict, that gives us the arguments rather than two sets of opposing conclusions. We do not need more passion but more intellect, more understanding.

While there are heartening signs of change, it remains depressingly true that the rewards in journalism tend not to go to the writer who painstakingly thinks a problem through and expresses the subtleties, but to the author of jazzy personality-pieces, scoops, and exposés. Exposés are nominated for prizes (often rightly so, of course) while a complicated piece of analysis wins the epithet "thumbsucker." These attitudes are related to the city-room environment where keen—often counter-productive—competition encourages reporters to jealously guard their scoops and current projects even from their co-workers. There is no incentive for the kind of intellectual sharing and discussion of first drafts that is common in an academic community or in any profession where the contributions and criticisms of one's colleagues are considered essential.

Work tends to be defined as scurrying about and asking questions. It is the rare reporter who has the fortitude to sit at his desk and read a book on a subject he intends to write about. Not infrequently one reads a long newspaper series—in which hundreds of man hours of reporting and travel time have been invested—and it is glaringly obvious that some of the most basic books written in that field have not been glanced at by the writers. I once asked Nicholas von Hoffman of the Washington *Post* how he avoided the usual pitfalls of newspaper writing. His exaggerated reply: "I never read newspapers."

Interestingly, von Hoffman was in his thirties when he turned to journalism, having been a community-action organizer with Saul Alinsky. Perhaps that thought-provoking apprenticeship also protected him from learning the bad intellectual habits that are bred into many young reporters. There may be something of a pattern in his experience, although it could just as well be explained by genetic endowment. The careers of a number of exceptional journalists reveal some catalytic intellectual experience outside the newsroom: Walter Lippmann's association with Santayana and his diplomatic experience; David Broder's opportunity to break out of the usual journalistic formulas on the *Congressional Quarterly;* Nick Kotz's background of Phi Beta Kappa and study at the London School of Economics before his present assignment with the Des Moines *Register* and *Tribune;* Willie Morris' residence at Oxford before tackling the *Texas Observer,* and now the editorship of *Harper's;* Anthony Lewis' immersing himself in the Harvard Law School as a Nieman Fellow before doing his exceptional reporting on the U.S. Surpreme Court; Alan Barth's sojourn with the Schlesingers while he was a Nieman; Joseph Lelyveld's Fulbright year in Southeast Asia before joining the *Times.*

Journalists pride themselves on being generalist-specialists. Ridicule of academic specialities ranks high as newsroom sport. Yet the methods by which journalists are trained tend to be extremely narrow, even though most are probably college graduates. On most large papers today reporters specialize early in fields in which few have any general background: transportation, politics, education, or perhaps even elementary education. But the academic, whose specialty or current research may be narrowly focused, usually has had a broad intellectual base that emphasizes the interrelationships of knowledge and common methods of inquiry. The journalist learns his lore on the job. He is steeped in the concrete and specific phenomena pertaining to his beat, learning in the syncretic, associative way. Thus, he often lacks a broad conceptual framework of his subject, or a method of analysis. Hence he is usually very good in predicting what will happen tomorrow, but seldom about the shape of things five years from now. Similarly, he often remains unaware of historical parallels of current events, or of cross-cultural comparisons.

The aims of journalism differ crucially from those of scholarship. The academic investigating police behavior, for instance, wants to tell it all once, thoroughly, exhaustively. His intellectual aim is to formulate a theory or model that will explain the seemingly variable surface events, and perhaps predict the shape of things to come. The newspaper has a vested interest in the concrete and specific, in telling the same story again and again in a way that makes it sound new and different. Thirteen petty robberies must be written in a way to make them sound as different and interesting as possible.

Both approaches have their strength, however. If the journalist often obscures the general truth in mountains of fact, the scholar frequently remains blinded to the specific truth of a particular situation because of his faith in his abstractions, and occasionally, his ideology. Noam Chomsky has shown in *American Power and the New Mandarins* how frequently the latter is true. He convincingly pairs Neil Sheehan's description in the New York *Times* of fetid slums in Saigon with some scholarly accounts of the supposed benefits of American-sponsored "Urbanization" in Vietnam. He writes:

Many have remarked on the striking difference between the way the press and the visiting scholar describe what they see in Vietnam. It should occasion no surprise. Each is pursuing his own craft. The reporter's job is to describe what he sees before his eyes; many have done so with courage and even brilliance. The scholarly adviser and colonial administrator, on the other hand, is concerned to justify what he has done and what he hopes to do, and—if an expert as well—to construct an appropriate ideological cover, to show that we are just and righteous in what we do, and to put nagging doubts to rest.

Paradoxically, the limited generalization characteristic of most journalism is often a great strength. It doesn't care what the general theory is, but what is true in this particular instance. Ignorance of what is supposed to be true may have the productive result of puncturing myth or forcing scholars to re-evaluate old evidence.

Much more could be said of the sins of academe—of its petty jealousies, blindnesses, and irrelevancies. My aim, however, has been to probe the roots of what Norman Isaacs of the Louisville *Courier-Journal* once called the "mental prearrangement" that passes for thought among many journalists. More weight could be given to exceptions to some of the norms cited. But the point is precisely that there are such norms, though they are increasingly being violated.

The more general question that obtrudes is how can the norms be changed? To begin with, journalism schools could profitably follow the developments of law, education, and business schools whose faculties are no longer top-heavy with former practitioners, although they have an important place. Faculty are needed from the academic disciplines who are interested in applying their knowledge to the problems of mass media and who will teach students more thoughtful modes of analysis in a realistic setting. Such new faculty could also play a vital role in strengthening journalism schools' much-neglected role of critically assessing the performance of the press.

Newspapers should also recruit from law schools and graduate schools of sociology and political science. A great many more skilled young academics in the social sciences could be attracted to new careers in the mass media if given responsibility to tackle significant issues.

Newspapers need not become miniature graduate schools, but neither should they produce the kind of shabby analysis that they do of city budgets and school reading scores. Personnel practices must change. Salaries must rise. Sabbaticals should become standard. Research assistants will be needed. Change might be so drastic as to free the average reporter from drudgery and scut work in the way that the average elementary school teacher has been liberated in New York City. The costs of carrying out these suggestions might prove a considerable financial drain on many smaller papers—at least until their benefits could be established. For that reason, such programs ought to be worthy of foundation support.

But these are long-term changes. What about now? Newspapers have only begun to take advantage of outside expertise. Academic skepticism of "newspaper writing" can be overcome with the right kind of assurances from sensitive editors that copy will be responsibly handled (not to mention massage of professorial egos with promises of the right kind of display). This puts a premium on editors who are aware of the outside expert's area of competence and interest and who can frame issues in an intellectually stimulating way. Outsiders should also be involved in seminar-like lunches, planning sessions and critiques of coverage. This use of experts as "consultants" has become fairly common among magazines but is employed less frequently by newspapers.

A bolder necessary step is to go beyond hiring the free-lance talents of academics to hiring the academics themselves. But the twist here is to employ them for their skill as teachers, as catalysts who would develop new concepts and methods of reporting. Distinguished teachers and thinkers could be brought to newspapers for short periods to head special projects and reporting teams. Some might come on sabbatical; others for only a semester or a few months or weeks. They might come from think tanks, foundations, publishing houses, and universities as well as from the ranks of freelances and other diverse social critics. Why not ask Ralph Nader, Saul Alinsky, or James Baldwin as well as sociologist Nathan Glazer, psychologist Robert Coles, economist Robert Lekachman? There are scores of candidates, though perhaps not all as well known, in every large city.

Under such a system, a small team of reporters might be assigned to work for a month preparing a series on the police, or an assessment of educational programs in the slums, or a survey of changing racial attitudes. They might work with a political scientist, a sociologist, a social psychologist. They would read and jointly discuss several books and perhaps a half-dozen relevant articles, attempting to define issues, identify historical trends, decide where reportorial energies should be directed.

Instead of rushing out to interview sources, reporters might spend time digging into census documents, examining attitudinal research, and drawing some conclusions of their own. There would be some debate about what the story is—with one result that the series would not be, like so many others, merely an elaboration of the obvious. Interviews would not be sought until there was some evaluation of what had been written, what the questions were, and the kinds of sources that could best answer them. In the case of the racial attitude series, reporters would have a chance to learn about constructing a survey, how data is fed into a computer, and some elementary notions about principles of statistical inference.

David Riesman, commenting on a draft of this article, noted that more reflective social scientists are under attack today by some of their radical activist colleagues. Although generally enthusiastic about the suggestions here, he added, "I could imagine the ironies of academicians in the newsroom being more journalistic than the journalists."

One should not overlook the benefits that would accrue to academics as a result of immersion in the newsroom. They would come away with a more realistic sense of the possible, of how complicated things really are in the concrete. It might broaden the outlook of many scholars about what their fields of inquiry ought to include. It could prove an interesting testing ground for many kinds of hypotheses and have benefits in research terms, including research about the mass media. New and better academic publications might be another by-product. The hostility of many journalists toward academics—perhaps a result of their unconscious resentment at their dependence on the experts— might be reduced. There might be a similar gain in understanding on the part of the academics, who are frequently jealous of the journalists' power (and angry at what they regard as its misuse), and who sometimes resent journalists who "cream off" the fruits of their research.

The whole notion of a newspaper as an educational institution— internally as well as externally—is central to this concept. The possibilities of encouraging greater cross-fertilization within the newsroom are limitless. Outsiders would be astonished at how little information or expertise is exchanged or developed among newspaper staffs, which have an exceptional range of talent and great opportunities for such development. A consulting firm like Arthur D. Little would close tomorrow if internal staff growth processes were as moribund as those on even our largest newspapers. Newspapermen, though they would vigorously deny it, jealously guard their imagined status and small prerogatives within the newsroom, and nothing in the way the place operates is likely to encourage them to do otherwise. One way is to bring in a catalyst from whom all learn as they teach each other. The multiplier effects of such a process could be surprising. Journalism could expand your mind.

APPENDIX:
HISTORICAL READINGS

To understand more fully many of the issues raised in Journalism: Readings in the Mass Media, *a look backward may be helpful. The concept of freedom of the press has a long history. The debate over the role and responsibility of the journalist did not begin yesterday. Much of what we take for granted today once had to be fought for and defined. The following six statements represent significant expressions of the human spirit in its attempt to gain the freedom to print the news and the truth. They should provide a historical framework within which to understand and assess the contemporary newspaper and its critics.*

APPENDIX
PSYCHIATRIC TRAINING

John Milton
AREOPAGITICA

John Milton (1608-1674) in addition to being one of the great poets of the English language, was a staunch advocate for freedom of speech and freedom of the press.

I DENY not, but that it is of greatest concernment in the Church and Commonwealth, to have vigilant eye how books demean themselves as well as men; and thereafter to confine, imprison, and do sharpest justice on them as malefactors. For books are not absolutely dead things, but do contain a potency of life in them to be as active as that soul was whose progeny they are; nay, they do preserve as in a vial the purest efficacy and extraction of that living intellect that bred them. I know they are as lively, and as vigorously productive, as those fabulous dragon's teeth, and being sown up and down, may chance to spring up armed men. And yet, on the other hand, unless wariness be used, as good almost kill a man as kill a good book: who kills a man kills a reasonable creature, God's image; but he who destroys a good book, kills reason itself, kills the image of God, as it were in the eye. Many a man lives a burden to the earth; but a good book is the precious life-blood of a master spirit, embalmed and treasured up on purpose to a life beyond life. 'Tis true, no age can restore a life, whereof perhaps there is no great loss; and revolutions of ages do not oft recover the loss of a rejected truth, for the want of which whole nations fare the worse.

We should be wary therefore what persecution we raise against the living labors of public men, how we spill that seasoned life of man, preserved and stored up in books; since we see a kind of homicide may be thus committed, sometimes a martyrdom, and if it extend to the whole impression, a kind of massacre, whereof the execution ends not in the slaying of an elemental life, but strikes at that ethereal and fifth essence, the breath of reason itself, slays an immortality rather than a life. But lest I should be condemned of introducing license, while I oppose licensing, I refuse not the pains to be so much historical as will serve to show what hath been done by ancient and famous commonwealths against this disorder, till the very time that this project of licensing crept out of the Inquisition, was catched up by our prelates, and hath caught some of our presbyters.

■ ■ ■

But some will say, What though the inventors were bad, the thing for all that may be good? It may be so; yet if that thing be no such deep invention, but obvious, and easy for any man to light on, and yet best and wisest commonwealths through all ages and occasions have forborne to use it, and falsest seducers and oppressors of men were the first who took it up, and to no other purpose but to obstruct and hinder the first approach of Reformation, I am of those who believe it will be a harder alchemy than Lullius ever knew to sublimate any good use out of such an invention. Yet this only is what I request to gain from this reason, that it may be held a dangerous and suspicious fruit, as certainly it deserves, for the tree that bore it, until I can dissect one by one the properties it has.

■ ■ ■

I cannot praise a fugitive and cloistered virtue, unexercised and unbreathed, that never sallies out and sees her adversary, but slinks out of the race, where that immortal garland is to be run for, not without dust and heat. Assuredly we bring not innocence into the world, we bring impurity much rather; that which purifies us is trial, and trial is by what is contrary. That virtue therefore which is but a youngling in the contemplation of evil, and knows not the utmost that vice promises to her followers, and rejects it, is but a blank virtue, not a pure; her whiteness is but an excremental whiteness; which was the reason why our sage and serious poet Spenser, whom I dare be known to think a better teacher than Scotus or Aquinas, describing true temperance under the person of Guion, brings him in with his palmer through the cave of Mammon, and the bower of earthly bliss, that he might see and know, and yet abstain. Since therefore the knowledge and survey of vice is in this world so necessary to the constituting of human virtue, and the scanning of error to the confirmation of truth, how can we more safely and with less danger scout into the regions of sin and falsity than by reading all manner of tractates and hearing all manner of reason? And this is the benefit which may be had of books promiscuously read.

But of the harm that may result hence three kinds are usually reckoned. First, is feared the infection that may spread; but then all human learning and controversy in religious points must remove out of the world, yea, the Bible itself; for that ofttimes relates blasphemy not nicely, it describes the carnal sense of wicked men not unelegantly, it brings in holiest men passionately murmuring against Providence through all the argument of Epicurus: in other great disputes it answers dubiously and darkly to the common reader: and ask a Talmudist what ails the modesty of his marginal Keri, that Moses and all the prophets cannot persuade him to pronounce the textual Chetiv. For these causes we all know the Bible itself put by the Papist into the first rank of prohibited books. The ancientest fathers must be next removed, as Clement of Alexandria, and the Eusebian book of evangelic preparation, transmitting our ears through a hoard of heathenish obscenities to receive the Gospel. Who finds not that Irenaeus, Epiphanius, Jerome, and others discover more heresies than they well confute, and that oft for heresy which is the truer opinion? Nor boots it to say for these, and all the heathen writers of greatest infection, if it must be thought so, with whom is bound up the life of human learning, that they writ in an unknown tongue, so long as we are sure those languages are known as well to the worst of men, who are both most able, and most diligent to instil the poison they suck, first into the courts of princes, acquainting them with the choicest delights, and criticisms of sin. As perhaps did that Petronius whom Nero called his Arbiter, the master of his revels; and the notorious ribald of Arezzo, dreaded and yet dear to the Italian courtiers. I name not him for posterity's sake, whom Harry the Eighth named in merriment his Vicar of Hell. By which compendious way all the contagion that foreign books can infuse will find a passage to the people far easier and shorter than an Indian voyage, though it could be sailed either by the north of Cataio eastward, or of Canada westward, while our Spanish licensing gags the English press never so severely. But on the other side that infection which is from books of controversy in religion is more doubtful and dangerous to the learned than to the ignorant; and yet those books must be permitted untouched by the licenser. It will be hard to instance where any ignorant man hath been ever seduced by any papistical book in English, unless it were commended and expounded to him by some of that clergy: and indeed all such tractates, whether false or true, are as the prophecy of Isaiah was to the eunuch, not to be understood without a guide. But of our priests and doctors how many have been corrupted by studying the comments of Jesuits and Sorbonists, and how fast they could transfuse that corruption into the people, our experience is both late and sad. It is not forgot since the acute and distinct Arminius was perverted merely by the perusing of a nameless discourse written at Delft, which at first he took in hand to confute.

Seeing, therefore, that those books, and those in great abundance which are likeliest to taint both life and doctrine, cannot be suppressed without the fall of learning, and of all ability in disputation, and that these books of either sort are most and soonest catching to the learned (from whom to the common people whatever is heretical or dissolute may quickly be conveyed), and that evil manners are as perfectly learnt without books a thousand other ways which cannot be stopped, and evil doctrine not with books can propagate, except a teacher guide, which he might also do without writing, and so beyond prohibiting, I am not able to unfold how this cautelous enterprise of licensing can be exempted from the number of vain and impossible attempts. And he who were pleasantly disposed could not well avoid to liken it to the exploit of that gallant man who thought to pound up the crows by shutting his park gate. Besides another inconvenience, if learned men be the first receivers out of books and dispreaders both of vice and error, how shall the licensers themselves be confided in, unless we can confer upon them, or they assume to themselves above all others in the land, the grace of infallibility and uncorruptedness? And again if it be true, that a wise man, like a good refiner, can gather gold out of the drossiest volume, and that a fool will be a fool with the best book, yea, or without book; there is no reason that we should deprive a wise man of an advantage to his wisdom, while we seek to restrain from a fool that which being restrained will be no hindrance to his folly. For if there should be so much exactness always used to keep that from him which is unfit for his reading, we should in the judgment of Aristotle not only, but of Solomon and of our Savior, not vouchsafe him good precepts and by consequence not willingly admit him to good books; as being certain that a wise man will make better use of an idle pamphlet than a fool will do of sacred Scripture.

'Tis next alleged we must not expose ourselves to temptations without necessity, and next to that, not employ our time in vain things. To both these objections one answer will serve, out of the grounds already laid, that to all men such books are not temptations, nor vanities, but useful drugs and materials wherewith to temper and compose effective and strong medicines, which man's life cannot want. The rest, as children and childish men, who have not the art to qualify and prepare these working minerals, well may be exhorted to forbear, but hindered forcibly they cannot be by all the licensing that Sainted Inquisition could ever yet contrive: which is what I promised to deliver next, That this order of licensing conduces nothing to the end for which it was framed and hath almost prevented me by being clear already while thus much hath been explaining. See the ingenuity of Truth, who, when she gets a free and willing hand, opens herself faster than the pace of method and discourse can overtake her. It was the task which I began with, to show that no nation, or well instituted state, if they valued books at all, did ever use this way of licensing; and it might be answered, that this is a piece of prudence lately discovered. To which I return, that as it was a thing slight and obvious to think on, for if it had been difficult to find out, there wanted not among them long since, who suggested such a course; which they not following, leave us a pattern of their judgment that it was not the not knowing, but the not approving, which was the cause of their not using it. . . . If we think to regulate printing, thereby to rectify manners, we must regulate all recreations and pastimes, all that is delightful to man. No music must be heard, no song be set or sung, but what is grave and Doric. There must be licensing dancers, that no gesture, motion, or deportment be taught our youth but what by their allowance shall be thought honest; for such Plato was provided of; it will ask more than the work of twenty licensers to examine all the lutes, violins, and the guitars in every house; they must not be suffered to prattle as they do, but must be licensed what they may say. And who shall silence all the airs and madrigals that whisper softness in chambers? The windows also, and the balconies must be thought on; there are shrewd books with dangerous frontispieces set to sale; who shall prohibit them, shall twenty licensers? The villages also must have their visitors to inquire what lectures the bagpipe and the rebeck reads even to the ballatry, and the gamut of every municipal fiddler, for these are the countryman's Arcadias, and his Monte Mayors. Next, what more national corruption, for which England hears ill abroad, than household gluttony: who shall be the rectors of our daily rioting? And what shall be done to inhibit the multitudes that frequent those houses where drunkenness is sold and harbored? Our garments also should be referred to the licensing of some more sober workmasters to see them cut into a less wanton garb. Who shall regulate all the mixed conversation of our youth, male and female together, as is the fashion of this country; who shall still appoint what shall be discoursed, what presumed, and no further? Lastly, who shall forbid and separate all idle resort, all evil company? These things will be, and must be; but how they shall be least hurtful, how least enticing, herein consists the grave and governing wisdom of a state. To sequester out of the world into Atlantic and Utopian polities, which never can be drawn into use, will not mend our condition; but to ordain wisely as in this world of evil, in the midst whereof God hath placed us unavoidably. Nor is it Plato's licensing of books will do this, which necessarily pulls along with it so many other kinds of licensing, as will make us all both ridiculous and weary, and yet frustrate; but those unwritten, or at least unconstraining laws of virtuous education, religious and civil nurture, which Plato there mentions as the bonds and ligaments of the commonwealth, the pillars and the sustainers of every written statute; these they be which will bear chief sway in such matters as these, when all licensing will be easily eluded. Impunity and remissness, for certain, are the bane of a commonwealth, but here the great art lies, to discern in what the law is to bid restraint and punishment, and in what things persuasion only is to work. If every action which is good or evil in man at ripe years were to be under pittance, and prescription, and compulsion, what were virtue but a name, what praise could be then due to well-doing, what gramercy to be sober, just, or continent? Many there be that complain of divine providence for suffering Adam to transgress; foolish tongues! when God gave him reason, he gave him freedom to choose, for reason is but choosing; he had been else a mere artificial Adam, such an Adam as he is in the motions. We ourselves esteem not of that obedience, or love, or gift, which is of force. God therefore left him free, set before him a provoking object, ever almost in his eyes; herein consisted his merit, herein the right of his reward, the praise of his abstinence. Wherefore did he create passions within us, pleasures round about us, but that these rightly tempered are the very ingredients of virtue? They are not skilful considerers of human things who imagine to remove sin by removing the matter of sin; for, besides that it is a huge heap increasing under the very act of diminishing, though some part of it may for a time be withdrawn from some persons, it cannot from all, in such a universal thing as books are; and when this is done, yet the sin remains entire. Though ye take from a covetous man all his treasure, he has yet one jewel left, ye cannot bereave him of his covetousness. Banish all objects of lust, shut up all youth into the severest discipline that can be exercised in any hermitage, ye cannot make them chaste that came not thither so: such great care and wisdom is required to the right managing of this point. Suppose we could expel sin by this means; look how much we thus expel of sin, so much we expel of virtue: for the matter of them both is the same; remove that, and ye remove them both alike. This justifies the high providence of God, who, though he commands us temperance, justice, continence, yet pours out before us, even to a profuseness, all desirable things, and gives us minds that can wander beyond all limit and satiety. Why should we then affect a rigor contrary to the manner of God and of nature, by abridging or scanting those means, which books freely permitted are, both to the trial of virtue, and to the exercise of truth? It would be better done, to learn that the law must needs be frivolous, which goes to restrain things, uncertainly and yet equally working to good, and to evil. And were I the chooser, a dram of well doing should be preferred before many times as much the forcible hindrance of evil doing. For God sure esteems the growth and completing of one virtuous person, more than the restraint of ten vicious. And albeit whatever thing we hear or see, sitting, walking, travelling, or conversing, may be fitly called our book, and is of the same effect that writings are, yet grant the thing to be prohibited were only books, it appears that this Order hitherto is far insufficient to the end which it intends. Do we not see, not once or oftener, but weekly that continued courtlibel against the Parliament and City, printed, as the wet sheets can witness, and dispersed among us, for all that licensing can do? Yet this is the prime service a man would think, wherein this Order should give proof of itself. If it were executed, you'll say. But certain, if execution be remiss or blindfold now, and in this particular, what will it be hereafter and in other books? If then the Order shall not be in vain and frustrate, behold a new labor, Lords and Commons, ye must repeal and proscribe all scandalous and unlicensed books already printed and divulged; after ye have drawn them up into a list, that all may know which are condemned, and which not; and ordain that no foreign books be delivered out of custody, till they have been read over. This office will require the whole time of not a few overseers, and those no vulgar men. There be also books which are partly useful and excellent, partly culpable and pernicious; this work will ask as many more officials, to make expurgations, and expunctions, that the Commonwealth of Learning be not damnified. In fine, when the multitude of books increase upon their hands, ye must be fain to catalogue all those printers who are found frequently offending, and forbid the importation of their whole suspected typography. In a word, that this Order may be exact, and not deficient, ye must reform it perfectly according to the model of Trent and Seville, which I know ye abhor to do. Yet though ye should condescend to this, which God forbid, the Order still would be but fruitless and defective to that end whereto ye meant it. If to prevent sects and schisms, who is so unread and so uncatechized in story, that hath not heard of many sects refusing books as a hindrance, and preserving their doctrine unmixed for many ages, only by unwritten traditions? The Christian faith, for that was once a schism, is not unknown to have spread all over Asia, ere any Gospel or Epistle was seen in writing. If the amendment of manners be aimed at, look into Italy and Spain, whether those places be one scruple the better, the honester, the wiser, the chaster, since all the inquisitional rigor that hath been executed upon books.

Another reason, whereby to make it plain that this Order will miss the end it seeks, consider by the quality which ought to be in every licenser. It cannot be denied but that he who is made judge to sit upon the birth or death of books whether they may be wafted into this world or not had need to be a man above the common measure, both studious, learned, and judicious; there may be else no mean mistakes in the censure of what is passable or not; which is also no mean injury. If he be of such worth as behooves him, there cannot be a more tedious and unpleasing journeywork, a greater loss of time levied upon his head, than to be made the perpetual reader of unchosen books and pamphlets, oft times huge volumes. There is no book that is acceptable unless at certain seasons; but to be enjoined the reading of that at all times, and in a hand scarcely legible, whereof three pages would not down at any time in the fairest print, is an imposition which I cannot believe how he that values time, and his own studies, or is but of a sensible nostril, should be able to endure. In this one thing I crave leave of the present licensers to be pardoned for so thinking, who doubtless took this office up, looking on it through their obedience to the Parliament, whose command perhaps made all things seem easy and unlaborious to them; but that this short trial hath wearied them out already, their own expressions and excuses to them who make so many journeys to solicit their license, are testimony enough. Seeing therefore those who now possess the employment, by all evident signs wish themselves well rid of it, and that no man of worth, none that is not a plain unthrift of his own hours is ever likely to succeed them, except he mean to put himself to the salary of a press corrector, we may easily foresee what kind of licensers we are to expect hereafter, either ignorant, imperious, and remiss, or basely pecuniary. This is what I had to show, wherein this Order cannot conduce to that end, whereof it bears the intention.

I lastly proceed from the no good it can do to the manifest hurt it causes, in being first the greatest discouragement and affront that can be offered to learning, and to learned men.

■   ■   ■

He who is not trusted with his own actions, his drift not being known to be evil, and standing to the hazard of law and penalty, has no great argument to think himself reputed in the Commonwealth wherein he was born, for other than a fool or a foreigner. When a man writes to the world, he summons up all his reason and deliberation to assist him; he searches, meditates, is industrious, and likely consults and confers with his judicious friends; after all which done he takes himself to be informed in what he writes, as well as any that writ before him; if in this the most consummate act of his fidelity and ripeness, no years, no industry, no former proof of his abilities can bring him to that state of maturity, as not to be still mistrusted and suspected, unless he carry all his considerate diligence, all his midnight watchings, and expense of Palladian oil, to the hasty view of an unleisured licenser, perhaps much his younger, perhaps far his inferior in judgment, perhaps one who never knew the labor of book-writing, and if he be not repulsed, or slighted, must appear in print like a puny with his guardian, and his censor's hand on the back of his title to be his bail and surety, that he is no idiot, or seducer, it cannot be but a dishonor and derogation to the author, to the book, to the privilege and dignity of learning. And what if the author shall be one so copious of fancy as to have many things well worth the adding come into his mind after licensing, while the book is yet under the press, which not seldom happens to the best and diligentest writers; and that perhaps a dozen times in one book? The printer dares not go beyond his licensed copy; so often then must the author trudge to his leavegiver, that those his news insertions may be viewed; and many a jaunt will be made, ere that licenser, for it must be the same man, can either be found, or found at leisure; meanwhile either the press must stand still, which is no small damage, or the author lose his accuratest thoughts, and send the book forth worse than he had made it, which to a diligent writer is the greatest melancholy and vexation that can befall. And how can a man teach with authority, which is the life of teaching, how can he be a doctor in his book as he ought to be, or else he had better be silent, whenas all he teaches, all he delivers, is but under the tuition, under the correction of his patriarchal licenser to blot or alter what precisely accords not with the hide-bound humor which he calls his judgment? When every acute reader upon the first sight of a pedantic license will be ready with these like words to ding the book a quoit's distance from him, "I hate a pupil teacher, I endure not an instructor that comes to me under the wardship of an overseeing fist. I know nothing of the licenser, but that I have his own hand here for his arrogance; who shall warrant me his judgment?" "The State, sir," replies the stationer; but has a quick return, "The State shall be my governors, but not my critics; they may be mistaken in the choice of a licenser, as easily as this licenser may be mistaken in an author; this is some common stuff"; and he might add from Sir Francis Bacon, that "such authorized books are but the language of the times." For though a licenser should happen to be judicious more than ordinary, which will be a great jeopardy of the next succession, yet his very office, and his commission, enjoins him to let pass nothing but what is vulgarly received already. Nay, which is more lamentable, if the work of any deceased author, though never so famous in his lifetime, and even to this day, come to their hands for license to be printed, or reprinted, if there be found in his book one sentence of a venturous edge, uttered in the height of zeal, and who knows whether it might not be the dictate of a divine spirit, yet not suiting with every low decrepit humor of their own, though it were Knox himself, the Reformer of a Kingdom, that spake it, they will not pardon him their dash: the sense of that great man shall to all posterity be lost for the fearfulness, or the presumptuous rashness, of a perfunctory licenser. And to what an author this violence hath been lately done, and in what book of greatest consequence to be faithfully published, I could now instance, but shall forbear till a more convenient season. Yet if these things be not resented seriously and timely by them who have the remedy in their power, but that such iron molds as these shall have authority to gnaw out the choicest periods of exquisitest books, and to commit such a treacherous fraud against the orphan remainders of worthiest men after death, the more sorrow will belong to that hapless race of men, whose misfortune it is to have understanding. Henceforth let no man care to learn, or care to be more than worldly wise, for certainly in higher matters to be ignorant and slothful, to be a common steadfast dunce will be the only pleasant life, and only in request.

And as it is a particular disesteem of every knowing person alive, and most injurious to the written labors and monuments of the dead, so to me it seems an undervaluing and vilifying of the whole nation. I cannot set so light by all the invention, the art, the wit, the grave and solid judgment which is in England, as that it can be comprehended in any twenty capacities how good soever, much less that it should not pass except their superintendence be over it, except it be sifted and strained with their strainers, that it should be uncurrent without their manual stamp. Truth and understanding are not such wares as to be monopolized and traded in by tickets and statutes and standards. We must not think to make a staple commodity of all the knowledge in the land, to mark and license it like our broadcloth, and our woolpacks. What is it but a servitude like that imposed by the Philistines, not to be allowed the sharpening of our own axes and coulters, but we must repair from all quarters to twenty licensing forges. Had any one written and divulged erroneous things and scandalous to honest life, misusing and forfeiting the esteem had of his reason among men, if after conviction this only censure were adjudged him, that he never henceforth write but what were first examined by an appointed officer, whose hand should be annexed to pass his credit for him, that now he might be safely read, it could not be apprehended less than a disgraceful punishment. Whence to include the whole nation, and those that never yet thus offended, under such a diffident and suspectful prohibition, may plainly be understood what a disparagement it is. So much the more, whenas debtors and delinquents may walk abroad without a keeper, but unoffensive books must not stir forth without a visible jailer in their title. Nor is it to the common people less than a reproach; for if we be so jealous over them, as that we dare not trust them with an English pamphlet, what do we but censure them for a giddy, vicious, and ungrounded people; in such a sick and weak state of faith and discretion as to be able to take nothing down but through the pipe of a licenser. That this is care or love of them we cannot pretend, whenas in those popish places where the laity are most hated and despised the same strictness is used over them. Wisdom we cannot call it, because it stops but one breach of license, nor that neither: whenas those corruptions which it seeks to prevent break in faster at other doors which cannot be shut.

And in conclusion it reflects to the disrepute of our ministers also, of whose labors we should hope better, and of the proficiency which their flock reaps by them, than that after all this light of the Gospel which is, and is to be, and all this continual preaching, they should still be frequented with such an unprincipled, unedified, and laic rabble as that the whiff of every new pamphlet should stagger them out of their catechism and Christian walking. This may have much reason to discourage the ministers when such a low conceit is had of all their exhortations, and the benefiting of their hearers, as that they are not thought fit to be turned loose to three sheets of paper without a licenser; that all the sermons, all the lectures preached, printed, vented in such numbers, and such volumes, as have now well-nigh made all other books unsalable, should not be armor enough against one single Enchiridion, without the castle of St. Angelo of an Imprimatur.

And lest some should persuade ye, Lords and Commons, that these arguments of learned men's discouragement at this your Order are mere flourishes, and not real, I could recount what I have seen and heard in other countries, where this kind of inquisition tyrannizes; when I have sat among their learned men, for that honor I had, and been counted happy to be born in such a place of philosophic freedom as they supposed England was, while themselves did nothing but bemoan the servile condition into which learning amongst them was brought; that this was it which had damped the glory of Italian wits; that nothing had been there written now these many years but flattery and fustian. There it was that I found and visited the famous Galileo, grown old, a prisoner to the Inquisition, for thinking in astronomy otherwise than the Franciscan and Dominican licensers thought.

Andrew Hamilton
DEFENSE OF
JOHN PETER ZENGER

Andrew Hamilton (c. 1676–1741) was a lawyer who won recognition for his stirring defense of John Peter Zenger, the printer who dared to write anti-government comments.

I BEG leave to insist that the right of complaining or remonstrating is natural; and the restraint upon this natural right is the law only, and that those restraints can only extend to what is false; for as it is truth alone which can excuse or justify any man for complaining of a bad administration, I as frankly agree that nothing ought to excuse a man who raises a false charge or accusation, even against a private person, and that no manner of allowance ought to be made to him who does so against a public magistrate.

Truth ought to govern the whole affair of libels, and yet the party accused runs risk enough even then; for if he fails of proving every tittle of what he has wrote, and to the satisfaction of the court and jury too, he may find to his cost that when the prosecution is set on foot by men in power, it seldom wants friends to favor it. And from thence (it is said) has arisen the great diversity of opinions among judges about what words were or were not scandalous or libelous. I believe it will be granted that there is not greater uncertainty in any part of the law than about words of scandal; it would be misspending of the court's time to mention the cases, they may be said to be numberless; and therefore the uttermost care ought to be taken in following precedents. . . .

If . . . . there is so great an uncertainty among judges (learned and great men) in matters of this kind; if power has had so great an influence on judges, how cautious ought we to be in determining by their judgments, especially in the plantations, and in the case of libels? There is heresy in law, as well as in religion, and both have changed very much; and we well know that it is not two centuries ago that a man would have been burnt as an heretic for owning such opinions in matters of religion as are publicly wrote and printed at this day. They were fallible men, it seems, and we take the liberty not only to differ from them in religious opinion, but to condemn them and their opinions too; and I must presume that, in taking these freedoms in thinking and speaking about matters of faith and religion, we are in the right: for, though it is said there are very great liberties of this kind taken in New York, yet I have heard of no information preferred by Mr. Attorney for any offenses of this sort. From which I think it is pretty clear, that in New York a man may make very free with his God, but he must take special care what he says of his Governor.

It is agreed upon by all men that this is a reign of liberty, and while men keep within the bounds of truth, I hope they may with safety both speak and write their sentiments of the conduct of men in power—I mean of that part of their conduct only which affects the liberty or property of the people under their administration; were this to be denied, then the next step may make them slaves. For what notions can be entertained of slavery beyond that of suffering the greatest injuries and oppressions without the liberty of complaining; or if they do, to be destroyed, body and estate, for so doing?

It is said and insisted upon by Mr. Attorney that government is a sacred thing; that it is to be supported and reverenced; it is government that protects our persons and estates; that prevents treasons, murders, robberies, riots, and all the train of evils that overturns kingdoms and states and ruins particular persons; and if those in the administration, especially the supreme magistrate, must have all their conduct censured by private men, government cannot subsist. This is called a licentiousness not to be tolerated. It is said that it brings the rulers of the people into contempt, and their authority not to be regarded, and so in the end the laws cannot be put in execution. These I say, and such as these, are the general topics insisted upon by men in power, and their advocates.

But I wish it might be considered at the same time how often it has happened that the abuse of power has been the primary cause of these evils, and that it was the injustice and oppression of these great men, which has commonly brought them into contempt with the people. The craft and art of such men is great, and who, that is the least acquainted with history or law, can be ignorant of the specious pretenses which have often been made use of by men in power to introduce arbitrary rule and destroy the liberties of a free people. . . .

The danger is great, in proportion to the mischief that may happen through our too great credulity. A proper confidence in a court is commendable; but as the verdict (whatever it is) will be yours, you ought to refer no part of your duty to the discretion of other persons. If you should be of opinion that there is no falsehood in Mr. Zenger's papers, you will, nay (pardon me for the expression) you ought to say so; because you don't know whether others (I mean the court) may be of that opinion. It is your right to do so, and there is much depending upon your resolution, as well as upon your integrity.

The loss of liberty to a generous mind is worse than death; and yet we know there have been those in all ages, who for the sake of preferment, or some imaginary honor, have freely lent a helping hand to oppress, nay to destory, their country.

This brings to my mind that saying of the immortal Brutus, when he looked upon the creatures of Caesar, who were very great men, but by no means good men. "You Romans," said Brutus, "if yet I may call you so, consider what you are doing; remember that you are assisting Caesar to forge those very chains which one day he will make yourselves wear." This is what every man (that values freedom) ought to consider: he should act by judgment and not by affection or self-interest; for, where those prevail, no ties of either country or kindred are regarded, as upon the other hand, the man who loves his country prefers its liberty to all other considerations, well knowing that without liberty, life is a misery. . . .

Power may justly be compared to a great river: while kept within its due bounds, [it] is both beautiful and useful; but when it overflows its banks, it is then too impetuous to be stemmed—it bears down all before it and brings destruction and desolation wherever it comes. If then this is the nature of power, let us at least do our duty, and like wise men (who value freedom) use our utmost care to support liberty, the only bulwark against lawless power, which in all ages has sacrificed to its wild lust and boundless ambition the blood of the best men that ever lived.

I hope to be pardoned, Sir, for my zeal upon this occasion; it is an old and wise caution that when our neighbor's house is on fire, we ought to take care of our own. For though, blessed be God, I live in a government where liberty is well understood and freely enjoyed, yet experience has shown us all (I'm sure it has to me) that a bad precedent in one government is soon set up for an authority in another; and therefore I cannot but think it mine, and every honest man's duty, that (while we pay all due obedience to men in authority) we ought at the same time to be upon our guard against power wherever we apprehend that it may affect ourselves or our fellow-subjects.

I am truly very unequal to such an undertaking on many accounts. And you see I labor under the weight of many years, and am borne down with great infirmities of body; yet old and weak as I am, I should think it my duty, if required, to go to the utmost part of the land where my service could be of any use in assisting to quench the flame of prosecutions upon informations, set on foot by the government, to deprive a people of the right of remonstrating (and complaining too) of the arbitrary attempts of men in power. Men who injure and oppress the people under their administration provoke them to cry out and complain; and then make that very complaint the foundation for new oppressions and prosecutions. I wish I could say there were no instances of this kind.

But to conclude: The question before the court and you, gentlemen of the jury, is not of small nor private concern, it is not the cause of a poor printer, nor of New York alone, which you are now trying. No! It may in its consequence affect every freeman that lives under a British government on the main of America. It is the best cause. It is the cause of liberty; and I make no doubt but your upright conduct, this day, will not only entitle you to the love and esteem of your fellow-citizens, but every man who prefers freedom to a life of slavery will bless and honor you as men who have baffled the attempt of tyranny; and by an impartial and uncorrupt verdict, have laid a noble foundation for securing to ourselves, our posterity, and our neighbors, that to which nature and the laws of our country have given us a right—the liberty, both of exposing and opposing arbitrary power (in these parts of the world, at least), by speaking and writing truth.

Benjamin Franklin
APOLOGY FOR PRINTERS

Benjamin Franklin (1706–1790), inventor, diplomat, philosopher, and states-man, was also a noted printer and fighter for freedom of the press.

BEING frequently censur'd and condemn'd by different Persons for printing Things which they say ought not to be printed, I have some-times thought it might be necessary to make a standing Apology for my self, and publish it once a Year, to be read upon all Occasions of that Nature. Much Business has hitherto hindered the execution of this Design; but having very lately given extraordinary Offence by printing an Advertisement with a certain N.B. at the End of it, I find an Apology more particularly requisite at this Juncture, tho' it happens when I have not yet Leisure to write such a thing in the proper Form, and only in a loose manner throw those Considerations together which should have been the Substance of it.

I request all who are angry with me on the Account of printing things they don't like, calmly to consider these following Particulars

1. That the Opinions of Men are almost as various as their Faces; an Observation general enough to become a common Proverb, *So many Men so many Minds.*

2. That the Business of Printing has chiefly to do with Men's Opinions; most things that are printed tending to promote some, or oppose others.

3. That hence arises the peculiar Unhappiness of that Business, which other Callings are no way liable to; they who follow Printing being scarce able to do any thing in their way of getting a Living, which shall

not probably give Offence to some, and perhaps to many; whereas the Smith, the Shoemaker, the Carpenter, or the Man of any other Trade, may work indifferently for People of all Persuasions, without offending any of them: and the Merchant may buy and sell with Jews, Turks, Hereticks, and Infidels of all sorts, and get Money by every one of them, without giving Offence to the most orthodox, of any sort; or suffering the least Censure or Ill-will on the Account from any Man whatever.

4. That it is as unreasonable in any one Man or Set of Men to expect to be pleas'd with every thing that is printed, as to think that nobody ought to be pleas'd but themselves.

5. Printers are educated in the Belief, that when Men differ in Opinion, both Sides ought equally to have the Advantage of being heard by the Publick; and that when Truth and Error have fair Play, the former is always an overmatch for the latter: Hence they chearfully serve all contending Writers that pay them well, without regarding on which side they are of the Question in Dispute.

6. Being thus continually employ'd in serving all Parties, Printers naturally acquire a vast Unconcernedness as to the right or wrong Opinions contain'd in what they print; regarding it only as the Matter of their daily labour: They print things full of Spleen and Animosity, with the utmost Calmness and Indifference, and without the least Ill-will to the Persons reflected on; who nevertheless unjustly think the Printer as much their Enemy as the Author, and join both together in their Resentment.

7. That it is unreasonable to imagine Printers approve of every thing they print, and to censure them on any particular thing accordingly; since in the way of their Business they print such great variety of things opposite and contradictory. It is likewise as unreasonable what some assert, *That Printers ought not to print any Thing but what they approve;* since if all of the Business should make such a Resolution, and abide by it, an End would thereby be put to Free Writing, and the World would afterwards have nothing to read but what happen'd to be the Opinions of Printers.

8. That if all Printers were determin'd not to print any thing till they were sure it would offend no body, there would be very little printed.

9. That if they sometimes print vicious or silly things not worth reading, it may not be because they approve such things themselves, but because the People are so viciously and corruptly educated that good things are not encouraged. I have known a very numerous Impression of *Robin Hood's Songs'* go off in this Province at 2/per Book, in less than a Twelvemonth; when a small Quantity of *David's Psalms* (an excellent version) have lain upon my Hands above twice the Time.

10. That notwithstanding what might be urg'd in behalf of a Man's being allow'd to do in the Way of his Business whatever he is paid for, yet Printers do continually discourage the Printing of great Numbers of bad things, and stifle them in the Birth. I my self have constantly refused to print any thing that might countenance Vice, or promote Immorality; tho' by complying in such Cases with the corrupt Taste of the Majority, I might have got much Money. I have also always refus'd to print such things as might do real Injury to any Person, how much soever I have been solicited, and tempted with Offers of great Pay; and how much soever I have by refusing got the Ill-will of those who would have employ'd me. I have heretofore fallen under the Resentment of large Bodies of Men, for refusing absolutely to print any of their Party or Personal Reflections. In this Manner I have made my self many Enemies, and the constant Fatigue of denying is almost insupportable. But the Publick being unacquainted with all this, whenever the poor Printer happens either through Ignorance or much Persuasion, to do any thing that is generally thought worthy of Blame, he meets with no more Friendship of Favour on the above Account, than if there were no Merit in't at all. Thus, as Waller says,

> *Poets lose half the Praise they would have got*
> *Were it but known what they discreetly blot;*

yet are censur'd for every bad Line found in their Works with the utmost Severity.

I come now to the particular Case of the N.B. above-mention'd, about which there has been more Clamour against me, than ever before on any other Account. In the Hurry of other Business an Advertisement was brought to me to be printed; it signified that such a Ship lying at such a Wharff, would sail for Barbadoes in such a Time, and that Freighters and Passengers might agree with the Captain at such a Place; so far is what's common; But at the Bottom this odd Thing was added, N.B. *No Sea Hens nor Black Gowns will be admitted on any Terms.* I printed it, and receiv'd my Money; and the Advertisement was stuck up around the Town as usual. I had not so much Curiosity at that time as to enquire the Meaning of it, nor did I in the least imagine it would give so much Offence. Several good Men are very angry with me on this Occasion; they are pleas'd to say I have too much Sense to do such things ignorantly; that if they were Printers they would not have done such a thing on any consideration; that it could proceed from nothing but my abundant Malice against Religion and the Clergy: They therefore declare they will not take any more of my Papers, nor have any farther Dealings with me; but will hinder me of all the Custom they can. All this is very hard!

I believe it had been better if I had refused to print the said Advertisement. However, 'tis done and cannot be revok'd. I have only the following few Particulars to offer, some of them in my behalf, by way of Mitigation, and some not much to the Purpose; but I desire none of them may be read when the Reader is not in a very good Humour.

1. That I really did it without the least Malice, and imagin'd the N.B. was plac'd there only to make the Advertisement star'd at, and more generally read.

2. That I never saw the Word *Sea-Hens* before in my Life; nor have I yet ask'd the meaning of it; and tho' I had certainly known that *Black Gowns* in that Place signified the Clergy of the Church of England, yet I have the confidence in the generous good Temper of such of them as I know, as to be well satisfied such a trifling mention of their Habit gives them no Disturbance.

3. That most of the Clergy in this and the neighbouring Provinces, are my Customers, and some of them my very good Friends; and I must be very malicious indeed, or very stupid, to print this thing for a small Profit, if I had thought it would have given them just Cause of Offence.

4. That if I have much Malice against the Clergy, and withal such Sense; 'tis strange I never write or talk against the Clergy my self. Some have observed that 'tis a fruitful Topic, and the easiest to be witty upon of all others. I can print any thing I write at less Charge than others' yet I appeal to the Publick that I am never guilty this way, and to all my Acquaintance as to my Conversation.

5. That if a Man of Sense had Malice enough to desire to injure the Clergy, this is the foolishest Thing he could possibly contrive for that Purpose.

6. That I got Five Shillings by it.

7. That none who are angry with me would have given me so much to let it alone.

8. That if all People of different Opinions in this Province would engage to give me as much for not printing things they don't like, as I can get by printing them, I should probably live a very easy Life; and if all Printers were every where so dealt by, there would be very little printed.

9. That I am oblig'd to all who take my Paper, and am willing to think they do it out of meer Friendship. I only desire they would think the same when I deal with them. I think those who leave off, that they have taken it so long. But I beg they would not endeavour to dissuade others, for that will look like Malice.

10. That 'tis impossible any Man should know what he would do if he was a Printer.

11. That notwithstanding the Rashness and inexperience of Youth, which is most likely to be prevail'd with to do things that ought not to be done; yet I have avoided printing such Things as usually give Offence either to Church or State, more than any Printer that has followed the Business in this Province before.

12. And lastly, That I have printed above a Thousand Advertisements which made not the least mention of *Sea-Hens* or *Black Gowns;* and this being the first Offence, I have the more Reason to expect Forgiveness.

I take leave to conclude with an old Fable, which some of my Readers have heard before, and some have not.

"A certain well-meaning Man and his Son, were travelling towards a Market Town, with an Ass which they had to sell. The Road was bad; and the old Man therefore rid, but the Son went a-foot. The first Passenger they met, asked the Father if he was not ashamed to ride by himself, and suffer the poor Lad to wade along thro' the Mire; this induced him to take up his Son behind him: He had not travelled far, when he met others, who said, they were two unmerciful Lubbers to get both on the Back of that poor Ass, in such a deep Road. Upon this the old Man gets off, and let his Son ride alone. The next they met called the Lad a graceless, rascally young Jackanapes, to ride in that Manner thro' the Dirt, while his aged Father trudged along on Foot; and they said the old Man was a Fool, for suffering it. He then bid his Son come down, and walk with him, and they travell'd on leading the Ass by the Halter; 'till they met another Company, who called them a Couple of sensless Blockheads, for going both on Foot in such a dirty Way, when they had an empty Ass with them, which they might ride upon. The old Man could bear no longer; My Son, said he, it grieves me much that we cannot please all these People: Let us throw the Ass over the next Bridge, and be no farther troubled with him."

Had the old Man been seen acting this last Resolution, he would probably have been call'd a Fool for troubling himself about the different Opinions of all that were pleas'd to find Fault with him: Therefore, tho' I have a Temper almost as complying as his, I intend not to imitate him in this last Particular. I consider the Variety of Humours among Men, and despair of pleasing every Body; yet I shall not therefore leave off Printing. I shall continue my Business. I shall not burn my Press and melt my Letters.

A FREE PRESS IN A DEMOCRACY

Thomas Jefferson (1743-1826), third President of the United States and author of the Declaration of Independence, often wrote about freedom of the press as demonstrated in the following passages written at various stages of his career.

NO GOVERNMENT ought to be without censors; and where the press is free, no one ever will. If virtuous, it need not fear the fair operation of attack and defense. Nature has given to man no other means of sifting out the truth, either in religion, law, or politics.

■　　■　　■

A coalition of sentiments is not for the interest of the printers. They, like the clergy, live by the zeal they can kindle, and the schisms they can create. It is contest of opinion in politics as well as religion which makes us take great interest in them, and bestow our money liberally on those who furnish aliment to our appetite. . . . So the printers can never leave us in a state of perfect rest and union of opinion. They would be no longer useful, and would have to go to the plough.

■　　■　　■

Indeed the abuses of the freedom of the press here have been carried to a length never before known or borne by any civilized nation. But it is so difficult to draw a clear line of separation between the abuse and the wholesome use of the press, that as yet we have found it better to trust the public judgment, rather than the magistrate, with the discrimination between truth and falsehood. And hitherto the public judgment has performed that office with wonderful correctness.

. . .

No experiment can be more interesting than that we are now trying, and which we trust will end in establishing the fact that man may be governed by reason and truth. Our first object should therefore be to leave open to him all the avenues to truth. The most effectual hitherto found is the freedom of the press. It is therefore the first shut up by those who fear the investigation of their actions. The firmness with which the people have withstood the late abuses of the press, the discernment they have manifested between truth and falsehood show that they may safely be trusted to hear everything true and false and to form a correct judgment between them. As little is it necessary to impose on their senses or dazzle their minds by pomp, splendor or forms. Instead of this artificial, how much surer is that real respect which results from the use of their reason and the habit of bringing every thing to the test of common sense.

. . .

I have lent myself willingly as the subject of a great experiment, which was to prove that an administration, conducting itself with integrity and common understanding, cannot be battered down, even by the falsehoods of a licentious press, and consequently still less by the press as restrained within the legal and wholesome limits of truth. This experiment was wanting for the world to demonstrate the falsehood of the pretext that freedom of the press is incompatible with orderly government. . . . [A true press] is a noble institution, equally the friend of science and of civil liberty.

. . .

The artillery of the press has been leveled against us, charged with whatsoever its licentiousness could devise or dare. These abuses of an institution so important to freedom and science, are deeply to be regretted, inasmuch as they tend to lessen its usefulness, and to sap its safety; they might, indeed, have been corrected by the wholesome punishments reserved and provided by the laws of the several States against falsehood and defamation; but public duties more urgent press on the time of public servants, and the offenders have therefore been left to find their punishment in the public indignation.

Nor was it uninteresting to the world, that an experiment should be fairly and fully made, whether freedom of discussion, unaided by power, is not sufficient for the propagation and protection of truth —whether a government, conducting itself in the true spirit of its constitution, with zeal and purity, and doing no act which it would be unwilling the whole world should witness, can be written down by falsehood and defamation. The experiment has been tried; you have witnessed the scene; our fellow citizens have looked on, cool and collected; they saw the latent source from which these outrages proceeded, they gathered around their public functionaries, and when the constitution called them to the decision by suffrage, they pronounced their verdict, honorable to those who had served them, and consolatory to the friend of man, who believes he may be intrusted with his own affairs.

No inference is here intended, that the laws, provided by the State against false and defamatory publications, should not be enforced; he who has time, renders a service to public morals and public tranquility, in reforming these abuses by the salutary coercions of the law; but the experiment is noted, to prove that, since truth and reason have maintained their ground against false opinions in league with false facts, the press, confined to truth, needs no other legal restraint; the public judgment will correct false reasonings and opinions, on a full hearing of all parties; and no other definite line can be drawn between the inestimable liberty of the press and its demoralizing licentiousness. If there be still improprieties which the rule would not restrain, its supplement must be sought in the censorship of public opinion.

■   ■   ■

It is a melancholy truth, that a suppression of the press could not more completely deprive the nation of its benefits, than is done by its abandoned prostitution to falsehood. Nothing can now be believed which is seen in a newspaper. Truth itself becomes suspicious by being put into that polluted vehicle. The real extent of this state of misinformation is known only to those who are in situations to confront facts within their knowledge with the lies of the day. I really look with commiseration over the great body of my fellow citizens, who, reading newspapers, live and die in the belief, that they have known something of what has been passing in the world in their time; whereas the accounts they have read in newspapers are just as true a history of any other period of the world as of the present, except that the real names of the day are affixed to their fables. General facts may indeed be collected from them, such as that Europe is now at war, that Bonaparte has been a successful warrior . . . , but no details can be relied on. I will add, that the man who never looks into a newspaper is better informed that he who reads them; inasmuch as he who knows nothing is nearer to truth than he whose mind is filled with falsehoods and errors. . . .

Perhaps an editor might begin a reformation in some way as this. Divide his paper into four chapters, heading the 1st, Truths. 2d, Probabilities. 3d, Possibilities. 4th, Lies. The first chapter would be very short.

■ ■ ■

I deplore . . . the putrid state into which our newspapers have passed, and the malignity, the vulgarity, and mendacious spirit of those who write them. . . . These ordures are rapidly depraving the public taste.

It is however an evil for which there is no remedy, our liberty depends on the freedom of the press, and that cannot be limited without being lost.

James Fenimore Cooper
ON THE PRESS

James Fenimore Cooper (1789-1851) gained fame with his Leatherstocking Tales, *adventurous stories of the American frontier. The following selections are from his political study* The American Democrat.

IT WOULD seem that providence, for some of its own great ends, has denied to man any particular blessing, which his own waywardness is not destined to lessen, if not entirely to neutralize. In nothing connected with human happiness, is this grave truth more apparent than in the history of the press.

In despotisms, where the weakness of the bodies of nations, is derived from an ignorance of their force, and from the want of means to act in concert, the press is the lever by which the thrones of tyrants and prejudices are the most easily overturned, and, under such circumstances, men often contend for privileges in its behalf, that become dangerous to the peace of society, when civil and political rights are obtained.

In a popular government, so far from according an entire immunity from penalities to the press, its abuses are those which society is required, by its very safety, to visit with its heaviest punishments. In a democracy, misleading the publick mind, as regards facts, characters, or principles, is corrupting all that is dear to society at its source, opinion being the fountain whence justice, honors, and the laws, equally flow.

It is a misfortune that necessity has induced men to accord greater license to this formidable engine, in order to obtain liberty, than can be borne with less important objects in view; for the press, like fire, is an excellent servant, but a terrible master.

It may be taken as a rule, that without the liberty of the press, there can be no popular liberty in a nation, and with its licentiousness, neither publick honesty, justice, nor a proper regard for character. Of the two, perhaps, that people is the happiest which is deprived altogether of a free press, since private honesty, and healthful tone of the publick mind are not incompatible with narrow institutions though neither can well exist under the constant corrupting action of a licentious press.

The governing principle connected with this interest, would seem to depend on a general law, which, under abuses, converts the most beneficial moral agents to be the greatest enemies of the race. The press is equally capable of being made the instrument of elevating man to the highest point of which his faculties admit, or of depressing him to the lowest.

In struggling for liberty and emancipation from errors and prejudices, men have not always paused to reflect on the influence of the agents they have employed, when those agents, from contending with a powerful enemy, shall have become conquerors, and have begun to look about them for the fruits of victory. The press, so efficient as the opponent of tyrants, may become despotic itself; it may substitute new errors for those it has eradicated, and, like an individual spoiled by success, may generally abuse its advantages.

Many false notions have been introduced into society, in the desire to vindicate the rights of so powerful an agent. Of these, one of the worst is the admission of a claim in the press to interfere, in any manner, with private character. The good of such an interference, is at the best but doubtful, and the oppression, in those cases in which injustice is done, is of the most intolerable and irreparable kind.

It would be a proper and a just, though an insufficient atonement, in cases of established libel, to vest a power in the courts to compel the libeller to publish, for a series of weeks, or months, or even years, his own condemnation in his own columns, that the antidote might accompany the poison; though it is to be feared, that the possession of popular rights is still too recent, to permit the majority of men to entertain correct notions concerning an instrument that, they rightly fancy, has been so serviceable in the conflict they have just escaped.

It ought never to be forgotten, that the press, contending for natural but forbidden rights, is no more like the press when these rights are obtained, than the man struggling with adversity, and chastened by misfortune, is like the man flushed with success and corrupted by prosperity.

The history of the press is every where the same. In its infancy it is timid, distrustful, and dependant on truth for success. As it acquires confidence with force, it propagates just opinions with energy; scattering errors and repelling falsehood, until it prevails; when abuses rush in, confounding principles, truths, and all else that is estimable, until it becomes a serious matter of doubt, whether a community derives most good or evil, from the institution.

ON THE LIBERTY OF THE PRESS

What is called the liberty of the press, is very generally misconceived. In despotic, or narrow governments, persons, styled censors, are appointed to examine the columns of journals, *before the latter are issued*, with power to suppress all offensive or injurious articles. This, of course, is putting the press under the control of government, and the press is not a free press, since it cannot publish what its editors please. By the liberty of the press, we are to understand, only, an exemption from this restraint, or a condition of things which enables the citizen to publish what he please, as he can utter what he may please with his tongue.

All men, in a civilized country, however, are responsible for what they say, or publish. If a man speak slander against another, he is liable to the individual injured, in damages. If a man publish a libel, he incurs the same liability. Some persons suppose that the press possesses privileges, in this respect, that are not accorded to individuals; but the reverse is the fact, as a man may utter with impunity, that which he cannot publish with impunity. The distinction arises from the greater circulation, and the greater power to injure, of a published libel, than of a spoken slander. The editor of a journal, therefore, does not possess the same immunities as an editor, that he possesses as a private citizen. Without such a distinction the community would possess a set of men in its bosom, who would enjoy a power to tyrannize over it, with impunity, through its means of publicity.

The liberty of the press, in principle, resembles the liberty to bear arms. In the one case, the constitution guaranties a right to publish; in the other, a right to keep a musket; but he who injures his neighbor with his publications may be punished, as he who injures his neighbor with his musket may be punished.

The constitution of the United States does not guaranty even the right to publish, except as against the laws of congress, as has been previously stated; the real liberty of the press depending altogether on the provisions of the several state governments, in common with most of the other liberties and rights of the citizen.

ON THE AMERICAN PRESS

The newspaper press of this country is distinquished from that of Europe in several essential particulars. While there are more prints, they are generally of a lower character. If follows that in all in which they are useful, their utility is more diffused through society, and in all in which they are hurtful, the injury they inflict is more wide-spread and corrupting.

The great number of newspapers in America, is a cause of there being so little capital, and consequently so little intelligence, employed in their management. It is also a reason of the inexactitude of much of the news they circulate. It requires a larger investment of capital than is usual in this country, to obtain correct information; while, on the other hand, the great competition renders editors reckless and impatient to fill their columns. To these circumstances may be added the greater influence of vague and unfounded rumours in a vast and thinly settled country, than on a compact population, covering a small surface.

Discreet and observing men have questioned, whether, after excluding the notices of deaths and marriages, one half of the circumstances that are related in the newspapers of America, as facts, are true in their essential features; and, in cases connected with party politics, it may be questioned if even so large a proportion can be set down as accurate.

This is a terrible picture to contemplate, for when the number of prints is remembered, and the avidity with which they are read is brought into the account, we are made to perceive that the entire nation, in a moral sense, breathes an atmosphere of falsehoods. There is little use, however, in concealing the truth; on the contrary, the dread in which publick men and writers commonly stand of the power of the press to injure them, has permitted the evil to extend so far, that it is scarcely exceeding the bounds of a just alarm, to say that the country cannot much longer exist in safety, under the malign influence that now overshadows it. Any one, who has lived long enough to note changes of the sort, must have perceived how fast men of probity and virtue are loosing their influence in the country, to be superseded by those who scarcely deem an affectation of the higher qualities necessary to their success. This fearful change must, in a great measure, be ascribed to the corruption of the publick press, which, as a whole, owes its existence to the schemes of interested political adventurers.

Those who are little acquainted with the world are apt to imagine that a fact, or an argument, that is stated publickly in print, is entitled to more credit and respect, than the same fact or argument presented orally, or in conversation. So far from this being true, however, in regard to the press of this country, it would be safer to infer the very reverse. Men who are accustomed daily to throw off their mistatements, become reckless of the consequences, and he who would hesitate about committing himself by an allegation made face to face, and as it were on his personal responsibility, would indite a paragraph, behind the impersonality of his editorial character, to be uttered to the world in the irresponsible columns of a journal. It is seldom, in cases which admit of doubt, that men are required to speak on the moment; but, with the compositor in waiting, the time pressing, and the moral certainty that a rival establishment will circulate the questionable statement if he decline, the editor too often throws himself into the breach. The contradiction of to-day, will make a paragraph, as well as the lie of yesterday, though he who sees the last and not the first, unless able to appreciate the character of his authority, carries away an untruth.

Instead of considering the editor of a newspaper, as an abstraction, with no motive in view but that of maintaining principles and disseminating facts, it is necessary to remember that he is a man, with all the interests and passions of one who has chosen this means to advance his fortunes, and of course, with all the accompanying temptations to abuse his opportunities, and this too, usually, with the additional drawback of being a partisan in politics, religion, or literature. If the possession of power, in ordinary cases, is a constant inducement to turn it to an unjust profit, it is peculiarly so in the extraordinary case of the control of a public press.

Editors praise their personal friends, and abuse their enemies in print, as private individuals praise their friends, and abuse their enemies with their tongues. Their position increases the number of each, and the consequence is, that the readers obtain inflated views of the first, and unjust notions of the last.

If newspapers are useful in overthrowing tyrants, it is only to establish a tyranny of their own. The press tyrannizes over publick men, letters, the arts, the stage, and even over private life. Under the pretence of protecting publick morals, it is corrupting them to the core, and under the semblance of maintaining liberty, it is gradually establishing a despotism as ruthless, as grasping, and one that is quite as vulgar as that of any christian state known. With loud professions of freedom of opinion, there is no tolerance; with a parade of patriotism, no sacrifice of interests; and with fulsome panegyrics on propriety, too frequently, no decency.

There is but one way of extricating the mind from the baneful influence of the press of this country, and that is by making a rigid analysis of its nature and motives. By remembering that all statements that involve disputed points are *ex parte;* that there is no impersonality, except in professions; that all the ordinary passions and interests act upon its statements with less than the ordinary responsibilities; and that there is the constant temptation to abuse, which ever accompanie: power, one may come, at last, to a just appreciation of its merits, and in a degree, learn to neutralize its malignant influence. But this is a freedom of mind that few attain, for few have the means of arriving at these truths!

The admixture of truth and falsehood in the intelligence circulated by the press, is one of the chief causes of its evils. A journal that gave utterance to nothing but untruths, would loose its influence with its character, but there are none so ignorant as not to see the necessity of occasionally issuing truths. It is only in cases in which the editor has a direct interest to the contrary, in which he has not the leisure or the means of ascertaining facts, or in which he is himself misled by the passions, cupidity and interests of others, that untruths find a place in his columns. Still these instances may, perhaps, include a majority of the cases.

In a country like this, it is indispensable to mental independence, that every man should have a clear perception of the quality of the political news, and of the political opinions circulated by the press, for, he who confides implicitly to its statements is yielding himself blindly to either the designed and exaggerated praises of friends, or to the calculated abuse of opponents. As no man is either as good, or as bad, as vulgar report makes him, we can, at once, see the value that ought to be given to such statements.

All representations that dwell wholly on merits, or on faults, are to be distrusted, since none are perfect, and it may, perhaps, be added, none utterly without some redeeming qualities.

Whenever the papers unite to commend, without qualification, it is safe to believe in either venality, or a disposition to defer to a preconceived notion of excellence, most men choosing to float with the current, rather than to resist it, when no active motive urges a contrary course, feeding falsehood, because it flatters a predilection; and whenever censure is general and sweeping, one may be almost certain it is exaggerated and false.

Puffs, political, literary, personal and national, can commonly be detected by their *ex parte* statements, as may be their counterpart, detraction. Dishonesty of intention is easily discovered by the man of the world, in both, by the tone; and he who blindly receives either eulogium or censure, because they stand audaciously in print, demonstrates that his judgment is still in its infancy.

Authors review themselves, or friends are employed to do it for them; political adventurers have their dependants, who build their fortunes on those of their patrons; artists, players, and even religionists, are not above having recourse to such expedients to advance their interests and reputations. The world would be surprised to learn the tyranny that the press has exercised, in our own times, over some of the greatest of modern names, few men possessing the manliness and moral courage that are necessary to resist its oppression.

The people that has overturned the throne of a monarch, and set up a government of opinion in its stead, and which blindly yields its interests to the designs of those who would rule through the instrumentality of newspapers, has only exchanged one form of despotism for another.

It is often made a matter of boasting, that the United States contain so many publick journals. It were wiser to make it a cause of mourning, since the quality, in this instance, diminishes in an inverse ratio to the quantity.

Another reason may be found for the deleterious influence of the American press, in the peculiar physical condition of the country. In all communities, the better opinion, whether as relates to moral or scientific truths, tastes, manners and facts, is necessarily in the keeping of a few; the great majority of mankind being precluded by their opportunities from reaching so high in the mental scale. The proportion between the intelligent and whole numbers, after making a proper allowance on account of the differences in civilization, is probably as great in this country, as in any other; possibly it is greater among the males; but the great extent of the territory prevents its concentration, and consequently, weakens its influence. Under such circumstances, the press has less to contend with than in other countries, where designing and ignorant men would stand rebuked before the collected opinion of those who, by their characters and information, are usually too powerful to be misled by vulgarity, sophistry and falsehood. Another reason is to be found in the popular character of the government, bodies of men requiring to be addressed in modes suited to the average qualities of masses.

In America, while the contest was for great principles, the press aided in elevating the common character, in improving the common mind, and in maintaining the common interests; but, since the contest has ceased, and the struggle has become one purely of selfishness and personal interests, it is employed, as a whole, in fast undermining its own work, and in preparing the nation for some terrible reverses, if not in calling down upon it, a just judgment of God.

As the press of this country now exists, it would seem to be expressly devised by the great agent of mischief, to depress and destroy all that is good, and to elevate and advance all that is evil in the nation. The little truth that is urged, is usually urged coarsely, weakened and rendered vicious, by personalities; while those who live by falsehoods, fallacies, enmities, partialities and the schemes of the designing, find the press the very instrument that the devils would invent to effect their designs.

A witty, but unprincipled statesman of our own times, has said that "speech was bestowed on man to conceal his thoughts;" judging from its present condition, he might have added, "and the press to pervert the truth."

Alexis de Tocqueville
OF THE RELATION BETWEEN
PUBLIC ASSOCIATIONS AND THE NEWSPAPERS

Alexis de Tocqueville (1805-1859) was a French historian whose visits to America resulted in his systematic study of American institutions, Democracy in America *from which this selection is taken.*

WHEN men are no longer united amongst themselves by firm and lasting ties, it is impossible to obtain the co-operation of any great number of them, unless you can persuade every man whose help you require that his private interest obliges him voluntarily to unite his exertions to the exertions of all the others. This can be habitually and conveniently effected only by means of a newspaper: nothing but a newspaper can drop the same thought into a thousand minds at the same moment. A newspaper is an adviser who does not require to be sought, but who comes of his own accord, and talks to you briefly every day of the common weal, without distracting you from your private affairs.

Newspapers therefore become more necessary in proportion as men become more equal, and individualism more to be feared. To suppose that they only serve to protect freedom would be to diminish their importance: they maintain civilization. I shall not deny that, in democratic countries, newspapers frequently lead the citizens to launch together into very ill-digested schemes; but if there were no newspapers, there would be no common activity. The evil which they produce is therefore much less than that which they cure.

The effect of a newspaper is not only to suggest the same purpose to a great number of persons, but to furnish means for executing in common the designs which they may have singly conceived. The principal citizens who inhabit an aristocratic country discern each other from afar; and if they wish to unite their forces, they move towards each other, drawing a multitude of men after them. It frequently happens, on the contrary, in democratic countries, that a great number of men who wish or want to combine cannot accomplish it, because, as they are very insignificant and lost amidst the crowd, they cannot see, and know not where to find, one another. A newspaper then takes up the notion or the feeling which had occurred simultaneously, but singly, to each of them. All are then immediately guided towards this beacon; and these wandering minds, which had long sought each other in darkness, at length meet and unite. The newspaper brought them together, and the newspaper is still necessary to keep them united.

In order that an association amongst a democratic people should have any power, it must be a numerous body. The persons of whom it is composed are therefore scattered over a wide extent, and each of them is detained in the place of his domicile by the narrowness of his income, or by the small unremitting exertions by which he earns it. Means must then be found to converse every day without seeing each other, and to take steps in common without having met. Thus, hardly any democratic association can do without newspapers.

There is, consequently, a necessary connection between public associations and newspapers: newspapers make associations, and associations make newspapers; and if it has been correctly advanced, that associations will increase in number as the conditions of men become more equal, it is not less certain that the number of newspapers increases in proportion to that of associations. Thus it is, in America, that we find at the same time the greatest number of associations and of newspapers.

This connection between the number of newspapers and that of associations leads us to the discovery of a further connection between the state of the periodical press and the form of the administration in a country, and shows that the number of newspapers must diminish or increase amongst a democratic people, in proportion as its administration is more or less centralized. For, amongst democratic nations, the exercise of local powers cannot be intrusted to the principal members of the community, as in aristocracies. Those powers must either be abolished, or placed in the hands of very large numbers of men, who then in fact constitute an association permanently established by law, for the purpose of administering the affairs of a certain extent of territory; and they require a journal, to bring to them every day, in the midst of their own minor concerns, some intelligence of the state of their public weal. The more numerous local powers are, the greater is the number of men in whom they are vested by law; and as this want is hourly felt, the more profusely do newspapers abound.

The extraordinary subdivision of administrative power has much more to do with the enormous number of American newspapers, than the great political freedom of the country and the absolute liberty of the press. If all the inhabitants of the Union had the suffrage,—but a suffrage which should extend only to the choice of their legislators in Congress,—they would require but few newspapers, because they would have to act together only on very important, but very rare, occasions. But within the great national association, lesser associations have been established by law in every county, every city, and indeed in every village, for the purposes of local administration. The laws of the country thus compel every American to co-operate every day of his life with some of his fellow-citizens for a common purpose, and each one of them requires a newspaper to inform him what all the others are doing.

I am of opinion that a democratic people, without any national representative assemblies, but with a great number of small local powers, would have in the end more newspapers than another people governed by a centralized administration and an elective legislature. What best explains to me the enormous circulation of the daily press in the United States is, that, amongst the Americans, I find the utmost national freedom combined with local freedom of every kind.

There is a prevailing opinion in France and England, that the circulation of newspapers would be indefinitely increased by removing the taxes which have been laid upon the press. This is a very exaggerated estimate of the effects of such a reform. Newspapers increase in numbers, not according to their cheapness, but according to the more or less frequent want which a great number of men may feel for intercommunication and combination.

In like manner, I should attribute the increasing influence of the daily press to causes more general than those by which it is commonly explained. A newspaper can only subsist on the condition of publishing sentiments or principles common to a large number of men. A newspaper, therefore, always represents an association which is composed of its habitual readers. This association may be more or less defined, more or less restricted, more or less numerous; but the fact that the newspaper keeps alive, is a proof that at least the germ of such an association exists in the minds of its readers.

This leads me to a last reflection, with which I shall conclude this chapter. The more equal the conditions of men become, and the less strong men individually are the more easily do they give way to the current of the multitude, and the more difficult it is for them to adhere by themselves to an opinion which the multitude discard. A newspaper represents an association; it may be said to address each of its readers in the name of all the others, and to exert its influence over them in proportion to their individual weakness. The power of the newspaper press must therefore increase as the social conditions of men become more equal.

SELECTED BIBLIOGRAPHY

Adler, Ruth, *The Working Press,* New York: G. P. Putnam's Sons, 1966.

Agee, Warren K., ed. *Mass Media in a Free Society.* Lawrence: University Press of Kansas, 1969.

Alsop, Joseph, and Stewart Alsop. *The Reporter's Trade.* New York: Reynal & Co., 1958.

Barnouw, Erik. *Mass Communication.* New York: Holt, Rinehart & Winston, 1956.

Barrett, James Wyman. *Joseph Pulitzer and His World.* New York, 1941.

Beard, Charles A. *American Foreign Policy in the Making.* New Haven: Yale University Press, 1946.

Berelson, Bernard, and Morris Janowitz. *Reader in Public Opinion and Communication.* New York: Free Press, 1953.

Bird, George, and Fred Merwin. *The Press and Society.* Englewood Cliffs, New Jersey: Prentice-Hall, 1957.

Blumberg, Nathaniel B. *One-Party Press.* Lincoln, Nebraska: University of Nebraska Press, 1954.

Bordon, Neil H. *The Economic Effects of Advertising.* Chicago: Richard D. Irwin, 1947.

Carlson, Oliver. *Brisbane.* New York: Stackpole Books, 1937.

———. *Handbook on Propaganda for the Alert Citizen.* Los Angeles: Studies of the Foundation for Social Research, 1953.

———, and Ernest Sutherland Bates. *Hearst, Lord of San Simeon.* New York: Viking Press, 1936.

Casey, Ralph D., ed. *The Press in Perspective.* Baton Rouge: Louisiana State University Press, 1965.

Casty, Alan. *Mass Media and Mass Man.* New York: Holt, Rinehart & Winston, 1968.

Chafee, Zechariah. *Government and Mass Communication.* Chicago: University of Chicago Press, 1947.

Cobb, Irwin. *Exit Laughing,* Indianapolis: Bobbs-Merrill, 1941.

Coblentz, Edmond D. *William Randolph Hearst, 1863–1951.* New York: Simon & Schuster, 1952.

Cochran, Negley D. *E.W. Scripps,* New York: Harcourt, Brace & World, 1933.

Cohen, Bernard. *The Press and Foreign Policy.* Princeton: Princeton University Press, 1963.

Commission on Freedom of the Press. *Toward a Free and Responsible Press.* Chicago: University of Chicago Press, 1947.

Cooper, Kent. *Kent Cooper and the Associated Press.* New York: Random House, 1959.

Cox, James M. *Journey Through My Years.* New York: Simon & Schuster, 1946.

Dale, Edgar. *How to Read a Newspaper.* Glenview, Illinois: Scott, Foresman & Co., 1941.

Davis, Elmer. *But We Were Born Free.* Indianapolis: Bobbs-Merrill, 1954.

Dexter, James A., and **David Manning White.** *People, Society and Mass Communication.* New York: Free Press, 1964.

Emery, Edwin; Philip Ault; and **Warren Agee.** *Introduction to Mass Communication.* New York: Dodd, Mead & Co. 1960.

Ernst, Morris. *The First Freedom.* New York: Macmillan, 1946.

Ford, Edwin H. *A Bibliography of Literary Journalism in America.* Minneapolis: Burgess, 1937.

——, and **Edwin Emery.** *Highlights in the History of the American Press.* Minneapolis: University of Minnesota Press, 1954.

Gerald, J. Edward. *The Press and the Constitution.* Minneapolis: University of Minnesota Press, 1948.

——. *The Social Responsibility of the Press.* Minneapolis: University of Minnesota, Press, 1963.

Golden, Harry. *For 2¢ Plain.* New York: Harcourt, Brace & World, 1959.

Gramling, Oliver. *AP: The Story of News.* New York: Farrar, Straus & Giroux, 1940.

Gross, Gerald, ed. *The Responsibility of the Press.* New York: Simon & Schuster, 1969.

Hiebert, Ray Eldon. *The Press in Washington.* New York: Dodd, Mead & Co., 1966.

Hocking, William. *Freedom of the Press.* Chicago: University of Chicago Press, 1947.

Hohenberg, John. *Foreign Correspondence: The Great Reporters and Their Times.* New York: Columbia University Press, 1964.

Howe, Quincy. *The News and How to Understand It.* New York: Simon & Schuster, 1940.

Irwin, William H. *The Making of a Reporter.* New York: G. P. Putnam's Sons, 1942.

——. *Propaganda and the News; or What Makes You Think So?* New York: McGraw-Hill, 1936.

Johnson, Gerald W. *Peril and Promise: An Inquiry into Freedom of the Press.* New York: Harper & Row, 1958.

Klapper, Joseph T. *The Effects of Mass Communication.* New York: Free Press, 1960.

Larsen, Otto, ed. *Violence and the Mass Media.* New York: Harper & Row, 1968.

Lasswell, Harold, and **Ralph D. Casey.** *Propaganda, Communication and Public Opinion.* Princeton: Princeton University Press, 1946.

Lavine, Harold, and **James Wechsler.** *War Propoganda and the United States.* New Haven: Yale University Press, 1940.

Lederer, William J. *A Nation of Sheep.* New York: W. W. Norton & Co., 1961.

Lee, James Melvin. *A History of American Journalism.* Boston: Houghton Mifflin, 1917.

Lee, Richard W. *Politics and the Press.* Washington: Acropolis Books, 1970.

Lewis, Jerry D. *The Great Columnists.* New York: Macmillan, 1965.

Liebling, A. J. *The Press.* New York: Ballantine Books, 1961.

————. *The Wayward Pressman.* New York: Doubleday & Co., 1948.

————. *The Wayward Pressman's Casebook.* New York: Doubleday & Co., 1949.

Lindstrom, Carl E. *The Fading American Newspaper.* New York: Doubleday & Co., 1960.

Lippmann, Walter. *Public Opinion.* New York: Crowell Collier & Macmillan, 1922.

Lyons, Louis M. *Reporting the News.* Cambridge: Harvard University Press, 1965.

Macdonald, Dwight. *Against the American Grain.* New York: Random House, 1962.

Mannes, Marya. *But Will It Sell.* New York: Lippincott, 1964.

Mayer, Martin. *Madison Avenue, U.S.A.* New York: Harper & Row, 1958.

McLuhan, Marshall. *The Gutenberg Galaxy.* Toronto: University of Toronto Press, 1962.

————. *Understanding Media.* New York: McGraw-Hill, 1964.

————, and Quentin Fiore. *The Medium Is the Massage.* New York: Bantam, 1967.

Merton, Robert. *Mass Persuasion.* New York: Harper & Row, 1946.

Mott, Frank Luther. *American Journalism.* New York: Crowell Collier & Macmillan, 1947.

————. *The News in America.* Cambridge: Harvard University Press, 1952.

Parton, James. *Life of Horace Greeley.* Boston: Houghton Mifflin, 1889.

Pollard, James. *The Presidents and the Press.* New York: Crowell Collier & Macmillan, 1947.

Pool, Ithiel de Sola. *The Prestige Papers: A Survey of their Editorials.* Palo Alto: Hoover Institute Studies, 1952.

Regier, C. C. *The Era of the Muckrakers.* Chapel Hill: University of North Carolina Press, 1932.

Reston, James. *The Artillery of the Press.* New York: Harper & Row, 1966.

————. *Sketches in the Sand.* New York: Alfred A. Knopf, 1967.

Rivers, William. *The Opinion Makers.* Boston: Beacon Press, 1965.

————, and Wilbur Schramm. *Responsibility in Mass Communication.* New York: Harper & Row, 1969.

Rowse, Arthur. *Slanted News.* Boston: Beacon Press, 1957.

Rutherfurd, Livingston. *John Peter Zenger.* New York: Dodd, Mead & Co., 1904.

Schramm, Wilbur. *Communication in Modern Society.* Urbana: University of Illinois Press, 1948.

————. *Mass Communication.* Urbana: University of Illinois Press, 1960.

————. *Responsibility in Mass Communication.* New York: Harper & Row, 1957.

Seldes, George. *Lords of the Press.* New York: Messner, 1938.

Siebert, Frederick; Theodore Peterson; and Wilbur Schramm. *Four Theories of the Press.* Urbana: University of Illinois Press, 1956.

Seitz, Don C. *Joseph Pulitzer: His Life and Letters.* New York: Simon & Schuster, 1924.

Smith, Henry Justin. *Deadlines.* New York: Harcourt, Brace & World, 1922.

Smith, Henry L., and Edwin Emery. *The Press and America.* New York: Prentice-Hall, 1954.

Steffens, Lincoln. *Autobiography.* New York: Harcourt, Brace & World, 1931.

Steinberg, Charles S. *Mass Media and Communication.* New York: Hastings House, 1966.

Stone, I. F. *In a Time of Torment.* New York: Random House, 1964.

Swanberg, W. A. *Citizen Hearst.* New York: Charles Scribner's Sons, 1961.

326
SELECTED
BIBLIOGRAPHY

Talese, Gay. *The Kingdom and the Power.* New York: Harcourt, Brace & World, 1969.

Tebbel, John. *The Life and Good Times of William Randolph Hearst.* New York: E. P. Dutton, 1952.

Villard, Oswald Garrison. *Fighting Years.* New York: Harcourt, Brace & World, 1939.

———. *Some Newspapers and Newspapermen.* New York: Alfred Knopf, 1926.

Wolseley, Roland F. *Understanding Magazines.* Ames, Iowa: Iowa State University Press, 1965.

Wood, James P. *Newspapers in the United States.* New York: Ronald Press, 1949.

AS PN 4857 .K55

Kirschner, Allen, 1930–
  Journalism; readings in
the mass media
  #161227   3/82

LANSING COMMUNITY COLLEGE LIBRARY
419 N. Capitol Ave.   Box 40010
Lansing, Michigan   48901   DEMCO